Planets in Aspect

Robert Pelletier

Planets in Aspect

*Understanding
Your Inner Dynamics*

Para Research
Distributed by Schiffer Publishing, Ltd.
West Chester, Pennsylvania 19380

Planets in Aspect: Understanding Your Inner Dynamics
by Robert Pelletier

Copyright © 1974 by Para Research, Inc.

Library of Congress Catalog Card Number: 74—82711
International Standard Book Number: 0-914918-20-6

Designed by Bob Boeberitz
Edited by Margaret E. Anderson
Typeset in 10 pt. Palatino on a Compugraphic II
Printed by R. R. Donnelley & Sons Company
on 55-pound SRT II Paper
384 pages

Published by Para Research, Inc.
A division of Schiffer Publishing, Ltd.

This book may be purchased from the publisher.
Please include $2.00 postage.
Try your bookstore first.
Please send for free catalog to:
Para Books
Schiffer Publishing, Ltd.
1469 Morstein Road
West Chester, Pennsylvania 19380

Manufactured in the United States of America.
Fifteenth printing, May 1987, 6,500 copies
Total copies in print, 76,500

*This book is dedicated
to my parents,
Fred and Aline Pelletier*

Acknowledgments

I wish to extend my appreciation for the
encouragement I received from my friends
and students, which gave me the incentive to
write *Planets in Aspect*. I am deeply grateful
to the following individuals for their support:

Doris Boucher
Gilbert Ferreira
Geri Giannandrea
Natalie Hanratty
Magdelyn Hayes
Claudette Olson
Marilyn Revelli

A special debt of gratitude is due to Frank
Molinski for his courage and daring in publishing
Planets in Aspect, the first book by this writer.
I cannot overestimate the enormous amount of
effort and support Mr. Molinski provided during
the preparation of the book, in addition to his
duties as president of Para Research, Inc.

Contents

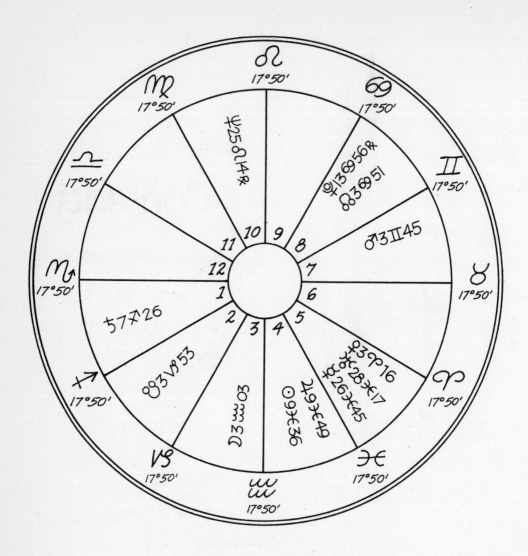

Natal chart of Robert Pelletier

Birthdate: Birthplace:
February 28, 1927   Dover, New Hampshire
        Longitude 070W53
Birthtime: Latitude 43N12
11:20 P.M. Standard Time
3:20 Greenwich Mean Time   Ascendant calculated for
10:08:25 Sidereal Time   Geocentric Latitude

Calculations by Para Research

Foreword

It is a real blessing to encounter a well-seasoned work by a mature thinker who can draw upon more than a quarter century of experience as an astrology teacher and counselor. It is indeed a pleasure to tell the world that Robert Pelletier has produced a work that every knowledgeable astrologer and student will surely find indispensable. I think he has tackled a formidable job with remarkable insight, fleshing out a solid skeleton of traditional astrological precepts with descriptions of human character and circumstances that can only accrue from long experience. I will gladly predict that *Planets in Aspect* will come to be accepted as a standard reference work and that it will enhance the rapidly growing reputation of astrology as a combined psychological, scientific, and metaphysical discipline.

As one who has studied the subject of planetary combinations, I am particularly sensitive to the difficulty of integrating individual applications of the various planetary aspects with the theories of how these aspects *ought* to operate. Moreover, the same horoscopic energy pattern can manifest itself at so many different levels that it is often hard to know which of many possibilities to emphasize. I am glad that the author refrained from setting up an artificial dichotomy of "good" versus "bad" aspects, choosing instead to show how potential assets and liabilities fit into a larger, nonjudgmental picture.

An astrological guidebook such as this one is extremely difficult to produce, because the author must deal with people on many different rungs of the ladder of human development. We all know that on any given day thousands of babies throughout the world are born with basically similar horoscopes, at least as to the planetary aspects. Yet each one will utilize his allotment of stellar energies in a unique fashion. Who is to say whether the Mars force will hit above the belt as the desire to initiate a new spiritual endeavor, or below the belt as the desire to make a sexual conquest—or both at once? Will an upcoming Saturn transit bestow a disciplined effort to eliminate nonessentials or will it result in a jail sentence?

The main job of the astrologer is to know where the subject of the horoscope stands on the path of evolution, and this knowledge can come about only by cultivating the God-given faculty of intuition. Hence, astro-diagnosis will always be as much an art as a science, and a sacred art at that. To one who takes the broad view of life, as the astrologer necessarily must, the art and science of horoscopy are no more in conflict than the art and science of medical diagnosis. They are complementary halves of an essentially therapeutic system.

To what extent, then, are we destined to react to impinging planetary energies, according to the astrological traditions expounded in this and other textbooks? Most knowledgeable astrologers maintain that an individual is born at a certain moment because his soul, or immortal essence, deliberately decides to align itself with the current of life-energy flowing into the physical world through a particular outlet of time and space. However, this assumption may require some modification. One of the most persistent problems of astro-metaphysics is this: to what extent does an individual select his own horoscope, and to what extent does the horoscope act to make him the kind of person he is?

Does the soul really choose every astrological factor, which it then personifies, or is the personality largely an outcome of the vortex of forces set in motion at the time of birth? Or can both of these be true? For instance, a woman may buy a dress because it impresses her as being rich and tasteful. Then, when she wears it, the costume itself inspires her to play the role of an aristocrat.

In order to resolve this question it is necessary to compare the horoscope to a complete outfit of clothing rather than to an assortment of fabrics. If a piece of cloth is cut like a shirt, it will also have sleeves, pockets, and a collar. If it has the cut of an evening gown, then the neckline, waist, and hem will have to be appropriate. There may be wide variations in style, but the general pattern is determined by the function of the garment.

Astrologically, every moment in time contains the potential for a particular set of defining characteristics. In order to obtain a pattern with the Sun in Aries and the Moon in Aquarius squaring Mars, it may be necessary to accept everything else that accompanies this configuration. Yet an astrologer who observes the behavior of this Arian individual will probably find that most of the hundreds of subsidiary factors involving aspects, nodes, midpoints, transits, and progressions do work out to some extent in the complexity of day-to-day living.

Every student of astrology should practice the exercise of pretending to be a soul in search of a suitable time of birth. He should assume that an appropriate set of parents has been located and that he must acquire the new body within the next three years in order to keep pace with a spiritual group that is incarnating to accomplish a designated task. The student should scan the ephemeris for the coming years until he finds the particular horoscope with which he feels he can identify. He will thereby discover that adopting a natal chart is like moving into a house. If a few essential specifications are met, then a multitude of minor details must be accepted as they are, simply because that is how the house was constructed. There is freedom of choice in initiating the endeavor, but the final results are largely conditioned by what is available.

To obtain a desired Sun sign, it is necessary to be born within a given thirty-day period. The further selection of a Moon sign limits the possibilities to less than two and a half days out of the year, even without considering the placement of the remaining planets.

The same is true of the planetary configurations. If an individual must take on a square from Mercury to Neptune to accomplish his purpose, a multitude of other aspects will be operating simultaneously. One factor entails another, and these contingencies apparently outweigh the deliberately selected preferences.

The problem of whether the self makes the horoscope or the horoscope makes the self is like asking which came first, the chicken or the egg. Any rational explanation requires one to recognize that spirit and matter are not totally comparable—and man is born of both. In a general sense the soul selects its own horoscope, but by means of the mundane details of existence, the horoscope shapes the personality. Yet it may be these personal characteristics that determine what type of horoscope is chosen in the next incarnation.

A natal chart may not express the soul's intent in every minuscule detail, but even its gratuitous aspects have their uses. We must always use whatever is available, and this fact may help us see how the everyday fabric of events in the universe is woven into a total design from a multitude of seemingly random happenings. It is the nature of the system that all possible horoscopes taken together add up to one complete whole. That is, every general horoscopic pattern is shared by a group of people scattered throughout the planet. Within this group some individuals will actualize the higher, more positive possibilities of the aspects involved, while others will actualize the lower, more negative possibilities. Still others may have so little individuality that they respond mainly to the superordinate horoscope of their nation or tribe.

Thus each of us must perform his designated task in carrying out the cosmic purpose whose formula is written in the heavens, even while following the dictates of his own soul. For instance, I have often felt that I could have done without that crashing square from Mars and Uranus to the Moon and Pluto, yet in the larger scheme a channel of release for these energies had to be provided. We must all fill not only our own needs but also the need of the universe which brought us into being. Wisdom lies in learning to reconcile these two sets of requirements.

A material form can never entirely express the fullness of its spiritual essence. Similarly, no horoscope is ever quite consonant with the soul's karmic assets and liabilities. But presumably the residue can be adjusted by that "big computer in the sky" in which the akashic records are filed and which is continually being reprogrammed to account for everything that happens in the universe.

Normally there is more than enough good karma stored up in any individual's reservoir of deserved benefits to flow through the horoscopic energy pattern during a particular lifetime. However, if a person has been unremittingly selfish, his supply of accumulated blessings may run low. Then, even though the stressful aspects that precipitate an interlude of suffering and purgation happen to go hand in hand with a configuration of trines and sextiles, these harmonious aspects will fail to produce salutary results.

It may also be that toward the end of the round of earthly existences, an evolved soul will have worked off so much negative karma that there is none left to activate the so-called malefic aspects. His well of potential troubles has run dry, and even if the faucet has been left open by some distasteful aspect such as a Mars-Neptune square, nothing untoward can happen. In this, as in all else, the universe plays fair.

It seems to me, therefore, that the way in which the natal chart discharges its potential varies according to the age of the soul that has elected to accommodate itself to a particular pattern. Each horoscopic factor is like a pipeline through which flows a particular quality of the universal life-force. It is a *conductor*. Thus all conduct or behavior is a function of the kind of channels we have been able to construct.

Because the manner in which the inpouring energies of the planets and signs are expressed is largely determined by the age of the soul, the accuracy of any given astrological delineation must ultimately depend upon the intuition of the interpreter. First he must analyze, then he must synthesize a variety of disparate factors, all the while taking account of the caliber of the individual for whom he is reading. He must, however, begin with a sound grasp of the meanings of the basic planetary interactions that are described in this book. *Planets in Aspect* should enable its readers to comprehend both the subjective rationale and the objective rules of astrology and allow them to apply these rules in individual cases. Its approach is dignified, in contrast to the flippancy of much popular astrological literature now flooding the market. The information will be invaluable to the practitioner who must deal with a variety of human problems in a concrete, common-sense manner, as well as to the novice who simply wants to understand himself. Many who peruse these pages will feel as though they are having a heart-to-heart talk with a wise and compassionate friend.

This book will be of help to those who aspire to broaden their appreciation of how man and the universe combine to manifest the glory of the divine unfolding. May it strengthen all of us who seek to work together in the fellowship of the stars!

Marcia Moore

Directions

An accurately cast horoscope is the first requirement one must have before applying any of the material presented in this book. The primary object of this volume is to provide you with a detailed synthesis of all the combinations of angular relationships between the planets and between the planets and the Ascendant of your chart. These combinations are called "aspects," and we have presented the six different aspects that we consider the most significant in chart analysis. There are many others, but we do not feel that their effects are strong enough to be included here.

In addition to the table of contents, you may find it convenient to use the thumb index in the margin. Although these are astrological symbols, you should acquaint yourself with them so that reference to aspects can be made easily. If you are unable to locate a specific aspect in this manner, the index in the back of the book will refer you to the exact page. Aspects which are astronomically impossible or not occurring in this century are so noted in the index.

What is an Aspect?

An aspect is the angular relationship between two points in the 360° of the zodiac. All the planets in a horoscope are located in the zodiac, and the angle between any two planets, given in degrees, is called an aspect. The number of degrees is significant, and each angle has a particular meaning. Although there is no angular relationship between two or more planets that occupy the same degree, this condition is still an extremely sensitive one and is referred to as a conjunction. When two planets are separated by 60° in their zodiacal positions, the sextile aspect is formed. When 90° separate them, the square aspect is formed, and so on. The angular distance from a planet to other sensitive points in the horoscope, such as the Ascendant, is also called an aspect. The Ascendant is the degree that was rising or ascending in the east at the moment you were born.

The aspects used in this book, their names, their degrees, and their symbols are as follows:

Aspect		Degrees Apart	Symbol
Conjunction	*CJN*	0°	
Sextile	*SXT*	60°	
Square	*SQR*	90°	
Trine	*TRT*	120°	
Inconjunct		150°	
Opposition	*OPP*	180°	

Always use the shortest distance between the two planets to determine their aspect. Because we are dealing with the circle of the zodiac, no aspect can be more than 180°, which is the greatest distance between two points in a circle. Take, for instance, one planet at 0° Aries and another at 0° Scorpio. The distance between them along the zodiacal belt is 210°, seven signs away at 30° per sign. But the shortest distance is 150°, five signs away at 30° per sign, which would indicate that the aspect separating these two planets is the inconjunct.

Although it sometimes happens that two planets are separated by the exact number of degrees denoting the aspect, most often this will not be the case. The deviation from the exact angle is called the "orb." When planetary positions deviate by plus or minus 6° from the exact angle of an aspect, they are still considered as being "in aspect." When the Sun, Moon, or Ascendant is involved, this orb of deviation is extended an additional 2°, giving an orb of plus or minus 8°. For the inconjunct aspect, a 3° orb is used.

All aspects are measured by the angle as viewed from the Earth. Because Mercury and Venus are closer to the Sun than the Earth is, they cannot form all angular relationships to the Sun. Mercury cannot form any aspect to the Sun except the conjunction, because the two bodies are never more than 28° apart. Venus, which is never more than 48° from the Sun, can form only the conjunction, semi-sextile, and semi-square aspects to the Sun. The last two aspects are not considered in this book.

Once you have determined the angular relationships between all the planets and between the planets and the Ascendant, make a list of all the aspects you have found. Arrange them in groups according to the type of aspect. That is, conjunctions together, then sextiles, squares, trines, inconjuncts, and oppositions. Within these groups list each aspect in the following order: Sun, Moon, Mercury, Venus, Mars, Jupiter, Saturn, Uranus, Neptune, Pluto, Ascendant. For example, if you have a sextile between Jupiter and Mercury, Mercury is the faster of the two and is therefore the planet "making" the aspect. It will be found in the Sextiles section under Mercury sextile Jupiter. You will not find it as Jupiter sextile Mercury, because in the order presented above, Jupiter can make aspect only to Saturn, Uranus, Neptune, Pluto, and the Ascendant. This will be apparent when you refer to the cross-indexed aspects in the back of the book. The index will refer you to the proper heading of the aspect you are looking for.

If you do not have calculations for a chart available, you have the option of having a computer do the work for you. Para Research offers a 30-page computer printout complete with all planetary calculations accurate to a minute of arc. These calculations are more accurate than any that could be calculated by hand.

The Para Research report, called the *Astral Portrait*, includes all the aspects from this book that pertain to a person's horoscope. Also included are a Sun-Moon polarity analysis, discussion of the Ascendant and the house position of its ruler, and interpretations of each planet in the houses they occupy.

Although the computer allows an eight-degree orb for Sun-Moon, a three-degree orb for inconjunct, and a six-degree orb for all other aspects, you can use this book to read about other aspects that may be beyond these orbs.

To get your *Astral Portrait*, fill in one of the coupons in the back of this book or send to Para Research your name, address, place of birth (town, city, and state), month, day, year, and local clock time (AM or PM) of your birth.

Introduction

The Planets: Dynamics of Behavior

Before one can apply the information put forth in the main body of this text, it is essential to examine and understand the nature of each planet and how it corresponds to the psychology of man. It may be that the planets have a direct influence on man's behavior and everything that happens on this Earth; however, whether they do or not, astrology is still an effective tool for understanding man, his potentials, and his destiny. It is not the purpose of this book to indulge in the controversy of planetary effects versus the "influence" suggested by C. G. Jung in his *Synchronicity: An Acausal Connecting Principle*, a theory we prefer.

Although the Sun and Moon are correctly termed the Luminaries, or Lights, in this book they will be regarded as planets along with the true planets for the sake of simplicity. Each planet represents a special and unique dynamic of behavior that functions at all levels of being—physical, spiritual, mental, and emotional. In combination, the planets' individual roles produce an enormously complex being. Therefore, they must be clearly understood individually before any attempt is made to synthesize the variables they represent in the spatial configurations called "aspects." It would be futile to attempt synthesis without this understanding. When joined by aspect, the planetary concepts produce effects and create complexes that have their own integrity. The natures and influences of the planets are the building blocks on which an accurate analysis begins and on which the final synthesis depends.

The signs occupied by the planets also have an influence that must be appraised, but this will be examined in another presentation. In this text, only the planets' influences and the significance of the various aspects are considered. The different aspects have specific meanings, which are imparted to the planetary natures they join.

The Sun represents the ego, individuality, will, striving for significance, and the conscious side of the personality. It is the primary indicator of what an individual is trying to achieve in his being. It is the active life-force aggressively trying to use all potentials and develop all available resources. The Sun, the creative urge sustained by the will to live, indicates the future, in which the whole idea of self can be fulfilled. In this sense it has much to do with destiny. Planets in aspect to the Sun are greatly energized and infused with creative force. The Sun imparts initiative to the planet it configurates.

The Moon is the unconscious side of the personality, the set of habits and instincts. It is the constantly changing personality that responds and reacts to external stimuli. The individual's feelings and emotions interfere with the development of creative self-expression because of accustomed patterns of behavior, and the person shows vulnerability to aggressive forces by withdrawing for protection. The Moon is the herd instinct that finds safety in numbers. It rules the past and the nostalgia associated with the past, and therefore it inclines to follow tradition. It is the need to feel wanted; hence it represents emotional security. It attracts the individual to matters that require attention and to people who require protection. The Moon is maternal love rather than romantic love and demands ownership of affection to satisfy emotional insecurity.

Mercury, which represents the intellectual faculties, indicates curiosity and wanting to know all there is to know. It is the ability to sort out and categorize all the information the Moon has ingested. It is the reasoning faculty that assigns meaning to every experience and stores experience as memory. Mercury interprets and solves problems with deductive logic. Although it is the gateway to understanding, it is not profound in itself. It indicates thought, but not thoughtfulness; eagerness for knowledge, but not the application of knowledge. It is the awareness of external matters and the recognition of being separate from them. Mercury represents the lens through which all experiences must be focused in order to assimilate their meanings and catalogue them for future reference. It is the communication that usually precedes a relationship, which this planet also rules in part.

Venus shows adjustments made to encourage a relationship. It is the hand extended in the hope that it will be warmly received. Through the influence of this planet, the individual's best behavior is shown, if only to provoke a similar response from others. Venus is tenderness and affection, understanding and compromise, refinement and beauty. It is the desire for companionship, which can be satisfied either through personal relationships or through social contacts. It seeks a life of comfort and ease, with much emphasis on financial security. It is the appreciation of fine works of art, good music, a comfortable home with fine furnishings and good food in abundance. Venus indicates active participation in social affairs, because this satisfies the need to be among people.

Mars is the fuel that operates the ego, as ruled by the Sun. It represents the residual traces of man's animal nature, which enables him to assert his aggressive nature and prey on those who are weaker. It is the dominant male characteristic, although it occurs in both sexes. Mars is the assertion of self rather than will and is constantly in search of challenging competitors.

It is the force in nature that establishes the survival of the fittest and therefore directs evolution toward perfection, even though this is not intended. It indicates the desire nature so essential to the survival of the species. In the animal kingdom this role is extremely important. When this urge becomes distorted by self-seeking, it can seem coarse and vulgar. It is especially resistant to reason and logic, preferring to act first and think later, if at all. Mars, the divisive force, reduces harmony to conflict so that it can then proceed to restore unity. In this way it compensates for the indulgent apathy that limits development and growth. It brings about disorder, which induces its polar opposite, Venus, to restore order; thus an endless dynamic action-reaction is established.

Jupiter is the high expectation that the future will reward one's best hopes. It is the higher mental faculty that seeks meaning in the affairs of life beyond what is provided by their physical labels. Every process that urges growth and expansion of consciousness is given a spiritual value, and a distinction between right and wrong is established. Jupiter is the eagerness to replace the harshness of physical survival with the immortality promised in Shangri-La. Religious fervor is thus induced, and there is pronounced enthusiasm for a rich and fulfilling life. It promotes interest in philosophy and education, and a sense of propriety in social behavior. It increases aspirations, but there is a tendency to take on more than one can handle. A negative expression of this planet is the expectation of reward without making any contribution, which allows some to indulge in gambling or scheming in order to satisfy their desires. It is the belief that failure is unlikely, and that any restraint is intolerable.

Saturn is the development of personal worth. It is the realization that reward is a direct result of personal effort and responsibility. It is facing reality and accepting the burdens of duty. It is judgment refined by experience. Saturn defines the fear of the unknown that too often inhibits progress because of lack of confidence. Once confidence is regained, the individual is assured of growth and can realize objectives that were always available as potentials. One earns the freedom that was denied by fear of inadequacy. Saturn establishes priorities to allow efficient management of personal resources in planning goals. When functioning negatively, it denotes pessimism and defeat. When hope is dimmed by the overwhelming burden of responsibility, even the slightest effort is laborious. Self-discipline is essential to assure that one's efforts are always productive. It is absolutely necessary to adhere to the laws of nature to gain the advantage over those who do not, as demonstrated by the evolutionary process of the survival of the fittest. Saturn is the wisdom that results from the thoughtful application of knowledge.

Uranus is the individual need to be free from the bonds of responsibility. It is the identification with mass consciousness and the insistence that everyone without exception must have the opportunity to fulfill his own destiny. It is the refusal to submit to any master except the one personally selected. It shows development beyond physical boundaries to new dimensions and realities where the inner spirit can find comfort. Conventionality and tradition are rejected as being too binding to allow the full expression of individuality. Uranus functions best in amoral situations in which the detached intellect can be used fairly and honestly. Ingenuity and originality are shown in dealing with the public, which is treated with aloofness, although the concern is sincere. The concern is for the mind of man and for expansion of prevailing social attitudes to bring about true freedom and progress. In the personal life Uranus represents an interest in novelty and originality. Pure materialism is offensive because it restricts development. When negatively applied, Uranus indicates anarchy, fanaticism, eccentricity, and the imperious display of power and authority. In this case, it deals with revolution against any authority—in the home, in youth groups, at the academic or career level, against society and its customs, or against government and elected officials. When positively applied, it expresses great spiritual concern that society enjoy freedom from the shackles of ignorance.

Neptune is the dynamic by which social obligations are fulfilled in response to an obscure feeling of guilt and spiritual duty. The need to serve society is difficult to determine precisely, so one wanders aimlessly in search of some relief from the anxiety it produces. Neptune is extreme sensitivity to the injustice of whole segments of society being caught in an inextricable web of negative circumstances. It is the unconscious, sympathy, empathy, aesthetic appreciation, utopia, rhythm, illusion, and poetry. It is music, imagination, and psychism but also fantasy, eroticism, and slavery. When Neptune is positively expressed there is exquisite appreciation for the highest and most sublime creative manifestations. It shows motivation to compensate for the decaying human conditions that afflict society. Personal satisfaction comes from restoring order to the chaos in environmental circumstances. It shows interest in the activities of institutions such as those for criminal, mentally afflicted, emotionally disturbed, or genetically impoverished people. The interest is also directed toward religious establishments and ministerial work. In any case, the individual is motivated to pursue this kind of life by social concerns, and hopes to be rid of personal guilt about the existence of these conditions.

Pluto is the urge to sacrifice oneself to the demands of an evolving social structure or to use every available resource to determine the form of that evolution. Pluto refers to subtle individualized sources of energy coalesced into a massive reservoir of power. It is the power that is available to large organizations, which have the economic leverage to control the destiny of man. It describes the awesome political, religious, and sociological upheavals that periodically bring about a reexamination of the values that had previously sustained man. When this dynamic is used positively, it eliminates the parasitic growths that would otherwise destroy its host, man. When used negatively, it is the festering malignancy that reduces man to little more than his former animal nature. Pluto can thus represent either the advancement of each member of society or the destruction of the creative force by individuals who prey on society to satisfy their personal lust for power.

Orb of Aspect

The matter of orbs has always been a confusing one. No other factor has produced such differences of opinion, except the method for determining the intermediate houses of the horoscope. It is obvious that there must be some regulatory process to establish a degree of reliability. The customary method has been to use an orb of 8° for the conjunction, square, trine, and opposition, 4° for the sextile, and 2° for the inconjunct. An additional 2° is allowed when the Sun or Moon is involved in the aspect.

However, we do not adhere to this use of orbs nor to the doctrine that there exists a point at which an effect begins or ends with some degree of certainty. We prefer to compare the effect of aspects to the sound of an approaching aircraft; the sound grows steadily from the moment it is initially perceived, is loudest when directly overhead, and fades as the plane vanishes in the distance. This effect can be overpowered by the sound of a locomotive passing at close range, but this does not deny the sound or the presence of the passing aircraft. It simply makes the reception more confusing and difficult to isolate. We have come to use a 6° orb for all aspects except the inconjunct, for which we use an orb of 3°. We extend the orb to 8° when the Sun, Moon, or Ascendant is involved, except with the inconjunct, for which we maintain the 3° orb. Even in this orb assignment, we remain flexible to the "fading" effect of a planetary configuration. We abhor the extreme application of this theory, however, which allows anything to be "read" into an aspect. We have observed astrologers who use orbs so wide that the aspect could have been equally a square or a trine! This we regard as irresponsible and completely indefensible. The astrologer must exercise good judgment based on the available variables.

Every factor in a chart is inextricably tied to every other factor, and this intimacy must be dealt with. On rare occasions complexes are found that seem to bear no relationship to other configurations in the chart. Even in such cases, however, there is usually a thread linking them to the rest of the chart. The integrity of the whole chart is preserved in spite of the fact that the parts are separate.

We suggest that an aspect begins to operate when the aspecting planet is within six degrees before the point at which the aspect is exact. However, we also admit that in some cases an aspect may be operating when the planets are separated by more than the orb usually allowed. We leave it to your discretion to determine whether there is a perceptible effect when the planets exceed the allowable orb. However, the "tighter" the aspect (that is, the greater the degree of exactitude), the more significant is the effect of the planets. You alone can decide how flexible you will be in determining the degree of influence.

Pay particular attention to the planets making the most exact aspects. They will be extremely important and will overpower the influence of the planets that make less exact aspects. Try to establish a proportional decrease in effect as the planets are increasingly distant from the point of exactitude. It is sometimes necessary to allow wider orbs when no planet is making an aspect within a narrow orb of perfection. In your own chart check to see if an aspect that exceeds the orb allowed does in fact have meaning for you when you read the text. Don't restrict yourself only to those within the suggested six-degree orb. This experience will help you to know how flexible you can be in applying the aspects in other people's charts.

The closest aspect in a chart is the most important one and will usually be characteristic of the individual who has it. We suggest you obtain a copy of *The Circle Book of Charts*, compiled by Stephen Erlewine, and a good biographical dictionary such as *Brief Lives: A Biographical Companion to the Arts*, published by Atlantic-Little, Brown. With these two sources, check the horoscopes of the persons listed. It is comparatively simple to accumulate a sizable record of the closest aspects and the planets making them from the information given. You will then have a valuable tool to assist you in judging the effects of aspects according to the extent of the orb of the planets. Learning astrology is far simpler when you use the proper tools.

Planetary Protocol

An aspect is always made by the faster moving planet, except in the case of transits, when the current planets make aspects to the static position of planets in the natal chart.

Planetary protocol depends upon the relative speed of the planets in their revolution around the Sun. In natal horoscopy the order is as follows: Moon, Mercury, Venus, Sun, Mars, Jupiter, Saturn, Uranus, Neptune, and Pluto. This means that the Moon makes the aspect to all the planets, Mercury aspects all the planets except the Moon, Venus aspects all the planets except the Moon and Mercury, and so on. When an aspect involves Mars and Neptune, the active force making the aspect is Mars. The description of the aspect will be found in the text under the heading of the type of aspect. For example, Mars square Neptune is found under the heading of *Squares* and in the section dealing with the square formed by Mars. You will not find it under the squares made by Neptune.

Although the planet making the aspect is the active force, the slower planet it aspects impresses its influence on that of the faster planet. This writer's experience has shown that the slower planet, the one having greater rank, gains compliance and submission from the faster planet with less rank. Although a process resembling dilution takes place, it will be observed that the faster planet does little to alter the influence of the slower planet it aspects. The personal planets — Sun, Moon, Mercury, Venus, and Mars — are especially vulnerable to the effects of the remaining five planets — Jupiter, Saturn, Uranus, Neptune, and Pluto. It was Dane Rudhyar, I believe, who once referred to this process as "the tide rushing in and the tide rushing out," that is, Man rushing out to exploit his potentials and being forced to submit to the rigorous discipline of the unknown factors of his external world. Thus he is continually refined to ever higher levels of perfection.

Guidelines For Applying the Aspects

It would be convenient if we could apply the aspects just as they are given in the text that follows. Unfortunately, this is not possible, because man is complex, and applying the aspects in a horoscope is a complex procedure. It is the astrologer who complicates these matters, but they can be made simpler by using guidelines. This will become apparent as you use the information in the text.

The synthesis must include, in addition to the natures of the individual planets, the nature of the aspect that brings them together. The aspect establishes the behavioral conditions through which the planets will be manifested, along with the conditions determined by the planets themselves.

It is simplest to view aspects according to the zodiacal correspondences with which they are identified. The planets that rule the signs related to the zodiac, beginning in Aries, impart their natures to the aspects as follows. Starting with Aries, a point 60° forward is Gemini and a point 60° in reverse is Aquarius. This means that the sextile aspect has the nature of Gemini and Aquarius. The sextile also deals with the circumstances of their corresponding third and eleventh houses, plus the planets Mercury and Uranus as rulers of those signs and houses. The square has the quality of Cancer and Capricorn, which are both 90° from Aries. It has the nature of the Moon and Saturn, which rule these signs, and it relates to the circumstances of the fourth and tenth houses because of their sympathetic ties with the corresponding signs. The other aspects are worked out in the same way. This technique, while it seems complicated, simply reveals the complex nature of man and gives the astrologer a vast amount of information with which to make a detailed and comprehensive analysis of planets in action.

It is necessary to observe planetary protocol when determining aspects. The faster-moving planet always aspects the slower-moving planet. Consider the slower planet as being on the Ascendant, regardless of its sign position, and the faster-moving planet as occupying the house placement that its sign position requires. In the case of a trine (120°), the aspecting planet will be in either the fifth or the ninth house. This aspect obviously shares the natures of Mars (first house), the Sun (fifth house), and Jupiter (ninth house). The planets in this configuration maintain their individual integrity, but their combined effect will also result from the natures of Mars, Sun, and Jupiter and the circumstances usually assigned to the first, fifth, and ninth houses.

We have included the inconjunct with the other significant aspects, sharing the same importance as the conjunction, sextile, square, trine, and opposition. Our experience has demonstrated that the planetary natures brought together by this aspect never fail to make the individual overreact to the presumed expectations of others and to the sacrifices this entails. This aspect also shows how an individual rises to excellence by developing his skills so that he commands the highest premium for his services.

In writing these aspects, we have tried to synthesize the variables that are possible when two distinct planetary influences are brought together by specific angles of relationship. A proper synthesis of two planets in aspect excludes any other consideration and does not make allowances for the same or other aspects to other planets. It is the task of the astrologer to exercise judgment and make adjustments for the intrusion and infusion of one or more additional factors. It is in this area that matters become complex, for skill and experience are required to apply the proper amount of adjustment to an aspect. There is no easy solution to this problem except practice. We have tried to simplify the task by providing a reasonably firm foundation on which to build your analyses.

Let us take an example to demonstrate this procedure. Assume that the chart before you has the Sun conjunct Mars and Sun square Saturn. Referring to the text on Sun conjunct Mars, we learn that the individual assumes he can exercise his will when he chooses and never feels he should have to compromise with anyone. He seeks recognition for what he is, not for his achievements. Now refer to the text of Sun square Saturn, and we learn that the individual is serious and sometimes even profound. He matured early and is no stranger to discipline. He is willing to work for what he wants and to accept responsibility. He achieves his ambitions because he invests heavily of himself for that purpose. He is recognized for his achievements and admired for his self-assurance.

From the texts of these two aspects it is obvious that a new synthesis is required. Assuming that the orb of both aspects is the same, the Sun conjunct Mars is an extremely powerful aspect, and in the early part of his life the person will be inclined to behave as though it were the only aspect. But the Sun square Saturn is also a strong aspect, and as the person matures, planetary protocol will prevail and the Saturn influence will be increasingly felt. The synthesis will then be as follows:

"You exercise your will to advantage in seeking your goals because you know from past experience exactly how much you can assert yourself and still get the results you want. Realizing that aggressiveness is not enough, you plan your moves efficiently to avoid wasting time and energy in nonproductive effort. You will not compromise unless you are proven wrong in your position. You want recognition only if you know you've done your job well. You are not afraid to take responsibility for what you do, because you only take on tasks you can be worthy of."

Special Complex Patterns and Stelliums

Planetary patterns involving three or more planets in a tight aspectual complex are particularly important. Noteworthy among these complex configurations are the Grand Trine, the Grand Cross, and the T-Cross.

The Grand Trine occurs when three or more planets are at the same degree in signs of the same element and are thus separated by angles of one hundred twenty degrees. It indicates vast resources of creative ability that can be exploited. Close aspects to any of the planets involved by a planet outside the Grand Trine will be especially important in stimulating creative expression.

The Grand Cross occurs when four or more planets are at the same degree in signs of the same quality and are separated by angles of ninety degrees. It shows a major struggle to keep from spilling energy in diverse and unrelated directions. Many obstacles will interfere with the realization of goals. Close aspects to any of the planets involved by a planet outside the Grand Cross will significantly reduce the pressure and provide an easier channel through which to apply the energies of the planets.

The T-Cross is exactly the same as the Grand Cross except that one of the four arms of the cross is missing, so the formation looks like the letter T. It shows much dynamic force that is often frustrated unless the qualities of the open end are adopted. Close aspects to any planets involved by a planet outside the T-Cross will alleviate the tension and make it possible to express the dynamic potential satisfactorily.

A stellium is a group of planets in one area of the zodiac, usually in the same sign and containing multiple conjunctions. The planets so configured are extremely important, because an aspect from another planet elsewhere in the chart to any one planet in the group involves all of the planets. Sometimes four or five planets are spread out the length of the sign, so that a planet in an early degree is technically "out of orb" of aspect to a planet in a late degree. But if the early-degree planet is in orb of aspect to a planet in a later degree, and this second planet is in orb of aspect with still another planet in a later degree, and so on, a "domino" effect is produced that unites all the planets in a massive configuration much like a conjunction. In this case, a planet aspecting any one planet of the stellium must be considered as aspecting all the planets. This is an extremely complex situation requiring considerable analysis to arrive at a proper synthesis. It generally indicates a person who is enormously complex.

Chapter One
Conjunctions

The conjunction, the most powerful aspect possible, indicates two planets in the same degree of the same sign. It also indicates the joining of two planets when one planet is in the later degree of one sign and the other planet is in the early degree of the following sign. In this case the effect is slightly weaker because the adjacent signs create a greater complexity. This is usually referred to as a *dissociate* conjunction.

This aspect produces an intense concentration of the planets involved and some condensation of their individual natures. It acquires the energizing effect of Mars, which it resembles. A conjunction produces a more concentrated energy and force so that the planets involved are more easily expressed. It inclines the person to assert the blended qualities of the two planets with little regard for the effect this has on other people. The person seems unable to compromise or to make any concessions for the sake of greater harmony. There is usually an inability to face reality and a tendency to be indifferent to the concerns of others.

A conjunction indicates considerable creative expression of the planetary dynamics involved and an eagerness not found with any other aspect. The person with this aspect is positive and enthusiastic and enjoys a tremendous reserve of energy to persist in spite of any obstacles encountered. It stimulates competition and a willingness to take up challenges, which are always seen as exciting. This person is self-indulgent, self-motivating, and fearless when personal desires meet resistance. He or she is righteously indignant when freedom is curtailed and believes in the doctrines of "might makes right," and "he who hesitates is lost."

This aspect indicates a painful reaction to criticism as well as discomfort when a vulnerable characteristic is revealed in competition. The person functions best when his energy is directed toward useful endeavors in which his resources can be used to advantage.

Let us take an example to demonstrate this process, say the Sun conjunct Uranus. The Sun is the will, the striving for significance, and the creative force. Uranus is the urge for independence, originality, and freedom from the confinement of a material existence. When these bodies are combined by conjunction, there is a powerful self-awareness that never concedes to domination by earthly matters. The will to live is matched by ingenuity in seeking complete fulfillment. Though there is ambition to achieve, the responsibility that goes along with accomplishment and prominence is fully understood. Care must be taken that the self-seeking drives do not overwhelm common sense or betray those who have given support in the climb to positions of authority. Failure to compromise is the hallmark of tyranny.

Sun Conjunct Moon

The conjunction of the Sun and Moon shows that your temperament is unilateral, or almost unaffected by conflicts with the will of others. Your personality is basically integrated, but this does not mean you will have a trouble-free life. It merely indicates that you are reasonably satisfied with yourself and with the goals you hope to realize. You do not adapt to circumstances unless doing so will serve your best interests. Because you are highly motivated to achieve your objectives, success is more than likely. You waste very little effort in activities unless they will benefit you in some way. You know how to coordinate your available resources with your life pursuits and always have the skills required to carry out any special task you choose.

No one is allowed to interfere in your affairs, nor do you concern yourself with the affairs of others. You establish a barrier between yourself and others and do not permit anyone to intrude. You allow yourself the privilege of going beyond that barrier, but you rarely do. Generally, a person who wants to meet with you will have to make the first gesture. You would rather not have to extend yourself if it can be avoided. Because you prefer to be independent of close involvement with people, you have to rely on your own ingenuity when the going gets rough. In this way, you are self-sustaining and self-defeating at the same time.

You can become enormously successful in your own estimation, even if others can't judge your success. You don't measure your level of accomplishments by the same devices most people use when making comparisons. You can best succeed when you work alone or at least can determine for yourself how or when you do your work. You are qualified for positions of authority, although you may be resented by those under you because you are so sure of yourself. You have the power to help others become integrated, although you may decide it isn't worth the effort.

In spite of your seeming self-assurance, you are not too successful in relating to people except at the social level. You are so afraid to have your emotions trampled that you keep personal contacts at arm's length. Your sensitive nature is your Achilles tendon, which you try to protect.

You depend heavily on small quiet moments to give you the spiritual nourishment that your outer life feeds on. Irritated by the constant distractions and the hustle and bustle of competitive society, you must periodically rejuvenate your forces privately, perhaps in meditation.

Sun Conjunct Mercury

The Sun conjunct Mercury shows that you are extremely subjective in your opinions, which you express forcefully. You tend to irritate people by refusing to listen attentively to their opinions or by dismissing them as unimportant. You are ego-centered, and your interests generally relate to matters involving yourself. Other people's concerns are only of casual interest to you. Usually the first to start a conversation, you also insist on having the final word because you want to leave a lasting impression. In your haste to be first in everything, you make decisions quickly and sometimes prematurely. You aren't always careful to get all the facts before making a judgment, so you may frequently have to retract your opinion at a later date. But it isn't easy for you to say you're sorry, since this is an admission of having made a mistake.

All the same, you are an "idea" person with great skill in commanding attention when you present your thoughts. Communication is easy for you, and you express yourself articulately. But because you lack objectivity, it is difficult to gain supporters for the programs you inaugurate. The people who seem to support you probably have been intimidated to yield to your demands. You are especially gifted at stimulating people who lack enthusiasm and will function best in positions that require this skill. Any profession in which you must deal with the public would interest you. You speak with authority and love to give orders that won't be challenged. But you may meet resistance because you fail to show that you are serious. You have a youthful quality that makes you less convincing, especially to older or more mature individuals. Also, your audacity and arrogant know-it-all attitude may be resented by these people.

You are creative and sometimes even inspired. But you would be a much more effective leader if you took the time to be better informed before asserting yourself and if you were less indifferent to people's feelings. Try not to take yourself too seriously, and cultivate humility.

You function with a lot of nervous energy, but your compulsion to be constantly on the go can cause you to become extremely fatigued. You need to slow down and give all of your faculties a chance to rest.

Sun Conjunct Venus

The Sun conjunct Venus represents a strongly developed love nature. Although it may not be apparent to a casual observer, you are extremely eager for people to like you. In fact, you make subtle adjustments in your urge for recognition so that they will be warmly disposed toward you. But you may not always compromise, simply because you don't want to give an impression of being weak in character. In more intimate contacts with persons you know well, you are not afraid they will misjudge you this way, so you behave more naturally.

You especially want people to recognize you as a substantial individual who offers many important values to those who are willing to share them. You are open to communication with others and will listen enthusiastically in conversation with them. You enjoy people and are generally cheerful and sociable in large or small gatherings. On the chance of meeting someone who can be useful at another time, you take care to circulate freely and "touch base" with everyone. You know how to make lasting impressions by dramatizing yourself, for you don't want to be overlooked merely because you didn't take the time to make your presence known.

Your greatest problem is that you assume people will think well of you even if you do nothing to deserve it. You can become pompously presumptuous that your presence alone is enough to merit everyone's attention. You are a romanticist at heart and can be swayed by a display of affection. Appreciative of the finer things in life, you get a sense of fulfillment when you indulge in them, in addition to the comfort and pleasure they give you.

Sun Conjunct Mars

The Sun conjunct Mars gives you a sense of power in asserting your will. You don't feel that you have to compromise in your dealings with anyone. Since you project your will so forcefully and with undeniable intensity, your presence may unintentionally threaten less hardy individuals. You are ambitious to be recognized, not so much for your achievements, but simply for yourself. But this may antagonize others, who will resent your assumption of superiority without having any achievements to justify it. It is difficult to determine whether you are driven by egocentricity or merely by having energy to spare. In any case, you respond quickly to competition and use every skill at your command to win. Because you find status quo conditions intolerable and apathy unforgivable, you stimulate people to take action when they might have indolently failed to do anything. Your considerable physical strength sustains you in expressing your boundless enthusiasm.

You have enormous creative ability and can excel in any leadership capacity. The kind of work you do isn't as important as the manner in which you accomplish your objectives. Intolerant of insubordination, you react violently to criticism. You tend to be uncompromising with people whose opinions differ from yours, and you are blunt in reprimanding them for it. You feel that anyone who expresses a different opinion is making a direct, personal attack on your credibility.

Your temperament is suitable for competitive occupations in which hazard and danger are commonplace. Sports, racing, exploration, military service, working with machinery, or hunting would provide good means for creative expression, as would more intellectual pursuits, such as medicine, surgery, law, or police work.

Your insistence on asserting your own desires with no consideration for others is a distinct liability. In evaluating the facts before taking action, you often disregard common sense, which makes it necessary to repeat the work later. You are inefficient in managing your energies and waste a lot of effort in unrewarding enterprises. A trusted adviser could help you plan your tactical moves, serve as your spokesman in disputes, and restrain you from destructive impulsive action.

Your powerful libido urges you to violence when your desires are not satisfied. Not only that, but you are insensitive to the feelings of others; you must learn to make adjustments for those whose feelings are not as intense as your own.

Because you react impulsively when you are angered the chance of physically hurting yourself is increased. You waste large amounts of energy in fruitless effort that could be utilized constructively. Being hyperactive, you need sufficient rest to preserve your health.

Sun Conjunct Jupiter

The conjunction of the Sun and Jupiter indicates that you almost never act in moderation. In everything you do you show boundless enthusiasm, and you never really believe you will fail. Because of this faith in your ability to do anything you set your mind on, you may overestimate your capabilities and suffer disappointment on occasion. But even then, you can pick up the pieces and start in on another venture. If you learn to plan your actions more carefully, your successes would be more consistent. Lacking the ability to efficiently manage your talents, you tend to wander aimlessly from endeavor to endeavor, trusting that everything will eventually work out satisfactorily. While you don't necessarily rely on it, luck seems to attend you when you need it most.

Although you want recognition for your efforts, you are not driven by ambition. For you it is more important to live a full life, rich in experiences and with abundant possibilities for using all your potentials. You are generous to a fault, and no one who brings you a tale of woe will go away empty-handed. This is one of the many reasons why you have some difficulty saving money. Even when thrift is essential, you are self-indulgent.

Your occupational interests are varied, but you are generally inclined toward a profession, such as medicine, law, education, philosophy, philanthropic endeavors, travel, or any other field that offers opportunities for growth. You quickly tire of routine jobs that have few chances for progress and development or jobs that don't use your imagination. You work best when you are permitted to use your creativity and work to the

full measure of your enthusiasm. You are well informed on many subjects and always eager to learn more.

You tend to be liberal in your religious views and somewhat indifferent to religious organizations, a matter that you feel rather apologetic about. An avid reader, you feel you must develop your own philosophy to guide you in life. You have high hopes for the future and never allow yourself to get into a rut that limits your progress. Subtle spiritual urgings tell you that everything that occurs in the outer world has a purpose in the inner world of consciousness. You have enormous faith, although it does not follow any structured ideology, and it sustains you by enabling you to fulfill your destined role.

Your emotional contacts are primarily with individuals who share your enthusiasm about life, who are eager to share their experiences with you and are not exclusively preoccupied with material concerns. You appreciate the sanctity of all life — vegetable, animal, and human — and you are warmly disposed toward anyone with a similar feeling. You are an emotional glutton, though, and may have some difficulty finding a partner who will satisfy your physical, emotional, and spiritual needs in a totally satisfying relationship.

Your physical problems come about through lack of moderation. Doing too much for prolonged periods of time without sufficient rest can easily produce physical weariness; also, your blood pressure could become troublesome. Cultivate healthful living habits.

Sun Conjunct Saturn

The conjunction of your Sun and Saturn shows that you are serious and perhaps profoundly moved by everything that gains your attention. Every experience teaches you a lesson. You are more capable of handling responsibility than most people, but you may resent it if others always expect you to be the one to take the burden. You may feel that your struggle to gain mastery over material circumstances seems more harsh than what others must face.

You matured rather early and probably were disciplined more strictly than other children. You may have encountered restriction from either or both parents in your formative years. No one ever gave you anything, and now you don't expect anyone to, in your driving ambition to realize your goals. Austerity is a familiar way of life to you, which probably helped you learn to stand on your own feet as you developed. You have depended for success on your ability to effectively mobilize your personal resources.

You don't generally express your opinion unless there is a reason for doing so. Although you are not quick to assert your will, when you do, you expect others to listen. You don't indulge in idle conversation, and you don't put up with it from others, unless they have something worthwhile to discuss.

You must be careful not to feel sorry for yourself if achieving your goals seems to be a laborious and painful process. Self-denial is easier for you, since it is consistent with your early training. Once you realize your objectives, they will be permanently secure because you have made such a tremendous investment in them. You will tenaciously hold on to the benefits brought by reaching your goals. It is not easy for you to be generous; you've worked too hard to get what you want, and you can't forget the lean years.

Your success results from your ability to efficiently consolidate your resources in order to exploit them to full advantage. Many fields need talent such as yours, including industrial management, teaching, politics, science and research, mathematics, and law. Each is a very demanding occupation; the only ones who survive are those who can discipline themselves and who are not afraid of responsibility.

You will choose a partner who has self-respect, for you consider this an important quality. Your mate must be willing to share your determination to rise above past or present circumstances. He or she must have humility and sincerity and be able to accept temporary limitations in anticipation of future growth and success.

Your greatest problem is that you react negatively to setbacks and become bitter. Some physical problems can develop, such as digestive ailments and ulcers, unless you maintain an attitude of hope and high expectation for the future. Try to establish goals that can be realized in the near future. It is also very important that you occasionally get away from familiar routines and indulge yourself a little. Wasting time once in a while will allow you to return to your responsibilities with renewed vigor and enthusiasm. Don't get into a rut—this limits you, so that challenges no longer seem exciting.

Sun Conjunct Uranus *Kathryn*

With the Sun conjunct Uranus, you are highly aware of yourself. You move freely in your environment, expressing yourself in your own unique fashion, unmindful that some people regard you as an eccentric. A very willful person, you are shocked if anyone dares to restrain you in any way. You jealously guard your rights to be yourself and speak your mind without compromise. When your freedom is curtailed or denied, you have the courage to fight to regain it. You are intolerant of tradition and the social limitations resulting from it. Your permissive attitude could hinder success, because even people who are impressed by you may misinterpret you as being essentially unstable.

Your arrogant nature developed early in life, in keeping with your accelerated individuality. In childhood you were as difficult to control as you are now. You took much less time than most to reach maturity, for you were too impatient to endure the restraints imposed by your elders. Because you grew up so quickly and had such a short childhood, you were maligned by some and admired by others.

You love being free, and your profession must provide you with freedom to perform your assigned tasks in your own way. The possibilities for a career are almost unlimited. Politics, science, education, or some technical aspect of industry would allow you to exploit your creative potentials.

Your philosophy is progressive, and these fields would benefit from your intuition and forethought. Progress is your most important product; you accept the lessons of the past only as a basis for continued development.

You enjoy the company of others who share your excitement and expectations for the future. Your free-wheeling temperament, however, needs to be balanced by having a more down-to-earth mate. Otherwise it is too easy for you to lose contact with reality and meaningful social contact, which can enrich your life.

Sun Conjunct Neptune *Tow Kris.*

With the Sun conjunct Neptune it is difficult for you to express yourself with confidence. You are very uncertain and doubtful about your capabilities. However, at times you do express yourself as though you were

25

in complete command, but then you suffer disappointment. Your veiled outlook on life allows you to avoid unpleasantness and ignore personal responsibilities. In your mind you tend to create the kind of reality you can accept, even though it bears little resemblance to the facts as others understand them.

When your attention is focused on art, poetry, music, or drama, you are exteremely creative and inspired. There is a mystical quality to your artistic expression that sets it apart from that of the average person. You have special gifts, but you must have training in order to use them constructively and gain social recognition from them.

You should choose a profession that will provide you with sufficient freedom to use your creative abilities. A nine-to-five routine hardly captures your imagination, unless it involves using your talent and inspiration. Group enterprises related to the arts in general would be rewarding and fulfilling for you. Craft activities would also enable you to express your creative potential constructively. The most important thing is to work at a job that does not inhibit your desire to make a significant contribution. In such professions as education, medicine, welfare activities, and church and social programs for the public benefit, you would derive as much benefit as those you serve.

It is important to remember that you must face life's realities, which are unusually abrasive to your sensitive nature. Seek an advisor whom you trust and who can make an honest appraisal of what you must face in the professional activities that interest you. Do not project unrealistic expectations, or you will be unnecessarily disappointed.

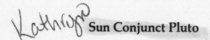 **Sun Conjunct Pluto**

The conjunction between your Sun and Pluto indicates that you are an extremist. Your likes and dislikes are intense, and acting in moderation is difficult. You have a powerful ego, which you assert whenever you can. At times you act courageously, but at other times you show a surprising lack of common sense.

Driven by a lust to gain important positions of authority, you may resort to pressure tactics against people who stand in your way. You meet competition directly, even at the risk of financial loss, just to prove to others that you are a power to reckon with.

Because you are especially sensitive to social conditions, you make a great effort to bring about improved conditions in your environment for everyone's benefit. When defending those in need or working to correct social injustices, you can truly achieve greatness. You are not tolerant of weaknesses, either in individuals or in political systems, that allow unfair or intolerable human conditions.

You have strong physical desires and are likely to throw a tantrum if your advances are rejected. Figuratively, you are a hunter or predator in constant search of prey. It is part of your nature that you aren't content unless you achieve victory in every pursuit. Your magnetic charm has a hypnotic effect on people. However, unless you are willing to serve others when they are unable to help themselves, even those who are charmed by you will respond with anger.

Avoid driving yourself beyond safe physical levels of tolerance. If you will use your energy constructively, success is guaranteed.

Sun Conjunct Ascendant

The Sun conjunct the Ascendant shows that you have a great desire for recognition and are creative in finding ways to gain attention. You may be so satisfied with your own ego and identity that you fail to recognize how much these same elements mean to those you deal with. In general you are uncompromising, because you fear that otherwise you may be required to submit to another's authority. But you have great faith in your ability to rise above any of life's negative circumstances. You know how to use your vast creative resources in a direct assault against any adversary, and you believe that eventually you will succeed. Most often you do, but when challenged by stiff competition and unsure of the outcome, you will resort to brute force to demonstrate that you don't give in without a fight. You know how to win friends and influence people, and you use this talent effectively. In spite of this gift, however, you are surprised to find that some people are not won over, and this bothers you. To be truly comfortable in your profession, you need to have a position of some authority over others.

Moon Conjunct Mercury

The Moon conjunct Mercury means that you are sympathetic and understanding. A person of strong emotions, you are never without ways to show how much you care for those close to you. You have a rich imagination and the intellectual know-how to express it in a variety of ways. It is comparatively easy for you to enjoy people and to relate to them. You are prepared to accept whatever happens to you as an opportunity for enlarging your total worth. You learn more from experience than from deliberate study, although your capacity to absorb information through traditional learning is greater than for most people. Probably your early training stimulated your interest in acquiring knowledge, and because of this you will never suffer from boredom. You adapt easily to changing conditions and look forward to the new opportunities they provide for growth.

You may have some difficulty in keeping your feelings and intellect from contaminating each other. Sometimes your emotions alter the clarity of your understanding, and at other times your intellectual evaluation interferes with what should be a simple emotional reaction. You don't want to be thought of either as an insensitive intellectual or as an unreasoning emotional person. This should not cause you any serious problems, though, because most people will simply regard you as being human. You are sensitive to criticism and sometimes read more into someone's reaction to you than is actually there.

Because you are friendly and easy to get along with, it is easy for you to work with people, even those who are in competition with you. You rarely feel threatened by challenges because you are sure of what you know. You don't take on a challenge unless you feel certain you can succeed. People feel comfortable in conversation with you. The may even tell you their innermost secrets, because you are a good listener and gain their trust. With this planetary combination, you will have to be careful that you don't accidentally violate that trust.

You will be a good parent and will impart to your children the same advantages you acquired from your parents. Young people feel comfortable with you, for you can identify with them. Neighbors' children might form closer ties with you than with their own parents, because they feel they can talk freely with you.

Moon Conjunct Venus

The Moon conjunct Venus shows that you relate to people easily and without pretense. You don't necessarily wait for the other person to make the first gesture to meet you, for you know that this is difficult for some. When you meet someone, you are willing to make adjustments if it will relieve any tension that seems likely to develop. A very sensitive person, you feel hurt whenever anyone deals harshly with you. You respond to tenderness and abhor rudeness. You are fond of people and try to be on friendly terms with everyone you have to deal with. For the most part, people appreciate that attitude, as you are aware.

Your early years probably were fairly pleasant, which enables you to look forward with anticipation to having a home and family of your own. You learned the value of money and how to manage your affairs in order to have some degree of security. You enjoy the comforts of a good home, fine furniture, plentiful food well prepared, and the joy of pleasant guests. You are warm toward your friends and always civil to everyone, regardless of their attitude toward you. Your tact and diplomacy serve your purposes, it is true, but you act that way mainly because you feel it is the right thing to do.

Unless you are careful, you can become too "nice," which may arouse suspicion as to your motives. Don't fawn over people so that it becomes sickening. Try to remain courteous, of course, but don't overextend yourself to them. If you give them the opportunity to show their interest in you, they will feel more comfortable.

You can succeed in any occupation that requires you to come before the public. You gain people's confidence because you demonstrate a genuine interest in their affairs. Sympathetic to their problems, you usually try to use your resources as best you can to help solve them. You are generous with your offers to help those who are less fortunate than you.

You will enjoy pleasant emotional relationships with those you care for. Love and romance are important to you, but you will carry lingering family ties to your love partnership, which can cause some problems. You may prematurely enter a binding contract before you are really ready to make your partner the exclusive person in your life. You tend to be more concerned with gratifying your desires than with accepting the discipline required to share a total life endeavor with your mate. On the whole, though, you should not have too much difficulty in making the transition from self-seeking to mutual sharing.

Moon Conjunct Mars

The Moon conjunct Mars indicates emotional anxiety and impatience. Your feelings are strong and always in turmoil, because you are extremely sensitive to what people say or do to you. Your imagination works overtime inferring slights against you that were never made. You defend yourself against these imagined insults by abusing the people you deal with, even though they don't deserve such treatment. In your self-preoccupation you are sometimes unsympathetic toward people who are trying to compromise with you. In time, they will start to avoid you. When you feel threatened by persons who relate to you aggressively, you retaliate by putting them in their place. You want desperately to establish close relationships, but you don't know how to cope with them when you do. This proabably started in childhood, when your parents erroneously accused you of wrongdoing.

This planetary combination does not of itself incline you toward specific professional interests. It does indicate problems in relating to co-workers, no matter what your occupation is. When you lose you are not especially gracious and may even imply that your competitor had an unfair advantage. In other words, you're a sore loser. You are so thin-skinned that even a minor criticism is enough to set off a temper tantrum. On the other hand, you can easily launch an almost sadistic verbal attack against another person, and then you are appalled at the response you get. There is a large inconsistency between your overly sensitive response to criticism and your indifference to other people's sensitivity. If you wish to achieve in occupations that involve close contact with the public and/or co-workers, you will have to solve these problems.

You assert yourself in extreme ways to satisfy your emotional needs. When you are rejected, you can be incredibly unkind, even vicious and vindictive. The people you care for need a variety of human companionship, but you are blind to their needs, and your jealousy distorts your reason. You complain bitterly of being "abandoned" by them. Compromise is something you expect from others, but you fail to see any reason to make compromises yourself.

You have a lot of homework to do before you can expect to attain peace of mind. Start by postponing any decision pertaining to a relationship until you have *all* the facts. Try to put yourself in the other person's shoes, to imagine what it's like to be on the receiving end of your cruel outbursts. If you are honest with yourself, you will realize that you often behave immaturely and unjustly. You have only yourself to blame if you can't get along with people. Try to assume they are *not* out to get you; the chances are that you have been imagining it.

Moon Conjunct Jupiter

The conjunction of the Moon to Jupiter denotes that you are deeply sensitive to your environment, which you truly want to understand as fully as possible. Your reactions to outer stimuli are largely emotional; nevertheless, you feel you can make an important contribution to society because you have an intellectual understanding of the solutions to many social problems. Your concern for others is sincere, and you insist on being given the opportunity to show that you care. Always present when there is an important job to be done, you are ever willing to offer your sevices, demonstrating your broadly sympathetic nature. You are ingenious in finding ways to care for those who are unable to care for themselves. In your ambition to help people in need, you courageously seek the support of political and religious organizations. You are generous in giving asylum to anyone who really needs it. Although you don't seek the limelight, you gain recognition for your efforts just the same.

Your early training taught you that it *is* more blessed to give than to receive, and this true generosity makes you appreciated and admired by everyone who knows you. As a parent, you will encourage your children to devote themselves unselfishly to others. Yours is the kind of faith that can move mountains, and you realize this as you turn the first spadeful of earth. You are always hopeful that no matter how dismal a situation may be, there can be a change for the better. You are strongly convinced that you can always do something to elevate a person's spiritual consciousness. In fact, you regard it as a moral obligation if you are aware of the need.

Your restless nature can find comfort in welfare programs, public relations, acting as public defender, working with the underprivileged, or in managing homes for foster children, halfway houses for parolees, or rehabilitation centers for former drug users. You might travel on behalf of organizations such as CARE, UNICEF, the Peace Corps, or VISTA. Medicine, law, and the ministry may also prove rewarding avenues for expressing your abundant sympathy for others. In any of these endeavors, your spiritual insight strengthens you to be daring when the odds against your succeeding seem overwhelming.

Your family and associates hold you in high esteem, while your friends and the faceless numbers you serve regard you with admiration and sincere appreciation. You will accumulate a rich heritage to leave to those who will carry on your tasks.

Your single most important physical problem is getting sufficient rest and relaxation. No one needs rest more than you do. Physical exhaustion is almost a certainty unless you exercise moderation in your schedule and get some assistance with your burdensome responsibilities.

Moon Conjunct Saturn

The conjunction between the Moon and Saturn shows that you are emotionally defensive, cautious, reserved, and extremely apprehensive about your experiences. Perhaps during your childhood your parents or guardians disciplined you so much that you assumed they did not love you. Because of your extreme sensitivity, you tend to overemphasize negative effects anyway. Almost certainly you did have traumatic experiences with your parents during the early conditioning years, and there is still a residual negative effect, probably caused by the parent who had the most authority in the home. Your early conditioning did not prepare you to deal successfully with the circumstances of everyday living, and you have learned to expect the worst.

Perhaps the guilt projected onto you during the formative years is the cause of the difficulty you sometimes have in forming close, emotional ties in your adult years. It often happens that you are unsuccessful in developing a partnership. Even so, you must deliberately stop thinking that happiness will always elude you. You must recognize your self-worth in order to project yourself optimistically toward others.

You are very likely to succeed professionally because you focus your efforts in worldly areas where your feelings don't have to function. Because you protect yourself by insulating your emotions, you could achieve success in business. In your professional dealings you are basically honest (sometimes painfully so), and you demand the same honesty from others. Management is your particular strong point, and you should rise to prominence in that area. Women will find you stern but will respect you for your fairness. You demand competence from those under you, and you demonstrate it by your own efficiency. If you have a position of authority you will not hesitate to fire someone who doesn't measure up to your expectations; you regard each person under you as an extension of yourself.

You could work well as an employee of professional people such as judges, lawyers, doctors, industrialists, educators, or politicians. You would gain the trust that is necessary in order to function effectively, and you would also serve their interests capably. It is also possible that you could undertake such a profession yourself. Your emotional detachment would allow you to provide unbiased opinions, which would serve the interests of your clients.

Emotional fulfillment will come about through contact with mature and serious individuals. A permanent relationship is possible only if your partner regards you as a mate in all areas — socially, spiritually, and professionally. It is essential for you to share your life with another, but that sharing must be total. Most important, you must always respect each other.

In the area of health, you may have problems involving your back, which may restrict you on occasion. The reproductive system could also cause you difficulty at some time in your life. Above all, try to look at the brighter side of life. Certain negative experiences may seem dismal at the time, but the lessons learned from them should enable you to become more optimistic as you grow.

Moon Conjunct Uranus

With your Moon conjunct Uranus, you are somewhat of a character, and your personality is exciting. You are very expressive, especially when emotionally aroused. You prefer to have few secrets and thus remain free of the anxieties often brought on by them. Although you may become involved in emotional situations, you always try to examine them intellectually and as realistically as possible. You believe that this is the only way to solve such problems.

In your circle of friends, you are popular because of your tolerance and understanding. You rarely take sides on an issue because you can always find something worthwhile with both sides, and you know that there is common ground for mutual accord. Your basic honesty is what endears you to others. You are so hopeful and optimistic that others feel better in your presence, even when they are experiencing personal difficulties. But you can't always solve your own problems as easily as you solve those of others. When this happens, you may suffer from intense strain and nervous irritability.

Your romantic life is filled with unusual types who run the gamut from saint to sinner. You enjoy the thrill of forming relationships with "impossible" individuals; an average person never seems to turn you on. Although you are often the matchmaker for others, you may remain unmatched yourself. When you do fall in love, you fall hard, and if the love is not returned, you may become distraught.

Being such a free individual, you are impatient with any restraints. You insist on the right to determine your own way of life, and consequently your life style bears little resemblance to that of your parents. You consider your success or failure to be an exclusive personal matter and will not permit yourself to be the product of someone else's conditioning.

☽ Moon Conjunct Neptune

The Moon conjunct Neptune shows that you are imaginative, emotional, sensitive, and sometimes given to daydreaming. Your psychic ability enables you to respond to outside stimuli that others are unaware of. You are inclined to offer assistance to anyone who seems to need help. However, this may get you into difficulty, for some people will blame you if their problems aren't solved. Disappointments are common in your life for even though you suffer with others in their grief, you may be left alone when they experience joy.

Your professional life must have sufficient challenge to keep you alert and reasonably "on the go." Avoid any occupation that involves long periods of time spent in repetitious and boring tasks. In such a job you would find escape in daydreaming and dawdling, and would accomplish little. You would probably be fired as lazy, incompetent, and indifferent, which would be accurate only in those circumstances. Your latent ability should find an outlet through public-oriented endeavors, such as service and welfare programs, nursing, working with the mentally retarded, or rehabilitation of the handicapped. Working closely with others who depend on you would serve as a catalyst for your energies, and you would participate with attentiveness and vigor.

Your love nature is extremely romantic, and it is truly difficult for anyone to measure up to your expectations. You've mesmerized yourself to escape from the abrasions of reality. Most individuals you meet disorient you, so you categorize them according to your own way of thinking. In time, when their human nature becomes painfully apparent, you are shocked in disbelief. Learn to accept people at their level of development and don't give them attributes they haven't earned or deserved. You will be admired by others for your sympathetic understanding of their "highs" and "lows." You can express your imagination in artistic pursuits — designing, painting, music, or poetry. Help others by painting joy in their lives, by designing activities for them, by letting a song ring out to relieve their stresses, or by sharing tender moments in poetic escape.

Moon Conjunct Pluto

Moon conjunct Pluto shows that you love deeply and tenaciously. Rather than waste your time in casual relationships, you continually look for someone who can respond to you with feelings as deep as your own. You will wait for this rare and elusive person rather than fall in love impulsively. Once in love, you can be very possessive and extremely demanding. If you are rejected, you can be vindictive and callous, even toward the one you love.

Domestically you can be a tyrant and therefore difficult to live with. Unless you are careful and observant you may permanently alienate your loved ones, thereby creating your own loneliness.

Sex is very important to you, and you will sometimes involve yourself in a physical relationship in order to satisfy your deep cravings for fulfillment. Even with a totally satisfying physical relationship, however, you will feel frustrated. You want more; you demand the heart and soul as well.

Your drive to find a complete relationship will force you to continually re-evaluate your partners and yourself. In time your personality may undergo drastic changes, and old acquaintances may find it difficult to recognize you as the person you once were.

This aspect is a powerful one and indicates that you will not appear to be in control of your emotions. A very idealistic person, you want the very best relationship or none at all. You prefer to continue looking rather than settle for second best.

If you don't find that perfect someone, you will wait and suffer, punishing yourself for craving the depth of human companionship that only an intimate relationship can give you.

Even in friendship you choose only close, select companions, for any kind of superficial relationship rubs you the wrong way. In time you will learn to detach yourself from those who want just a casual relationship.

The Moon here shows emotions, love, and fluctuating moods, and Pluto shows a deep sense of regeneration. The conjunction of the two tells that you have a drive for new relationships, new loves, new romances.

You may live half your life before you discover that a love you had years ago was the one most important to you. But this realization comes too late, for you discarded that love for a new one.

Your vulnerability to love allows others to take advantage of you, and your fear of this leads you to be defensive. However, with your drive, you can also take advantage of others. In time, you will need to sort out your various experiences in order of their importance to you.

This may sound difficult and hard to live with, but it can be a blessing when you find and enjoy your true love. If this is the love of your life, it will be deep, emotionally satisfying, and a means for your spiritual growth.

Moon Conjunct Ascendant

The Moon conjunct the Ascendant shows that you have some emotional hang-ups. You want close, intimate contacts with people, but you tend to keep people at arm's length because you are afraid you will become obligated to them. This fear forces you to deny yourself many rewarding friendships in order to be safe from anything that might develop into an intimate contact. You are a mass of contradictions: making demands on people but complaining when they do the same to you; expecting others to make overtures to you and withdrawing when they do; hoping for warm social contacts, but severing ties before they can be established. When you do succeed in forming a close relationship, you rarely make any commitment of your affection until you have been assured that the feeling is mutual. Although you are highly imaginative, you react to stimulating people in a generally negative and critical way. You are so emotional that it is nearly impossible for you to make a fair evaluation of people's motives toward you. On the surface you are independent, but you yearn for a quieter role in which you can enjoy the comfort of knowing that someone really cares for you. This can only happen when you lower your defensive barriers and learn to compromise by meeting people halfway.

Mercury Conjunct Venus

The conjunction of Mercury and Venus shows that you have an affable manner and social grace. You get along well with most people because you know when you should make compromises in order to maintain harmony. But this doesn't mean that you give in when you know the other person is in error. You generally try to be fair in making judgments so that you do not offend people without just cause. You know how to express your opinions skillfully so that no one feels threatened or intimidated by you, and you are resourceful in gathering information to document what you say. Not usually hostile or argumentative, you prefer to give everyone you deal with the benefit of the doubt when a difference of opinion arises. It is part of your refined nature that you let people have the opportunity to convince you of their point of view before you take any action.

Your gentle and easy-going personality is an asset in most professions, but you might find it difficult to cope with the abrasive elements of close and direct competition. This possibility should be taken into consideration when choosing a profession. It is better to work alone or with a small group of people so you won't have to worry about troublesome competitors.

You could find enjoyment in public speaking or the dramatic arts. Writing could also prove satisfying because you have a natural talent for expressing yourself well. Your imaginative style is fresh and charming and appeals to people who want to be entertained as well as informed. You are most comfortable with subjects that are not too dense and cumbersome.

You are fairly clever in devising schemes for improving your financial condition. You use your talents effectively and can usually translate your ideas into cash. Your associates will support you in your enterprises, because your balanced judgment reassures them that you can't be too far off base. You convince them you will succeed and generally win the cooperation you need. But you don't ask others to take risks you aren't willing to take. Because you are careful to adequately prepare yourself in advance of any action, the element of risk is greatly reduced anyway. And you shy away from complex projects that require prolonged effort before any benefits can be obtained.

Mercury Conjunct Mars

Your Mercury conjunct Mars indicates that your mind is restless and eager to gain new information, but you always feel that the answers you get are somehow not final. Your creative ideas are imaginative, and you exploit them energetically. However, you lack the patience to stay focused on any one interest for very long. No matter what position you take, you are positive in your opinions and very insistent about voicing them. You are argumentative and enjoy locking into debate with anyone who challenges you. But unless other factors in the chart provide it, you don't bother to get all the facts before you express yourself. Always sure that you are right, you are generally premature in your judgment. It isn't easy for you to say you're sorry when you are wrong, but you may do so when it is expedient. You tend to interrupt others who are already in conversation and to arouse their antagonism by volunteering information before being asked. Almost nothing escapes your attention, and you may have overheard someone say, "Here comes the know-it-all," as you approached.

With your sharp mind, creative ideas, and aggressive disposition, there are many professions in which you will be comfortable and free to express yourself. These include teaching, public relations, law, vocal coaching, acting, and writing. These occupations would give you unlimited opportunities to display your talents. Because you have plenty of energy to apply yourself to your goals, you can establish your own degree of progress. It would probably be best for you to work by yourself. Few people have enough nervous energy to maintain your pace, and you would be brutally frank in reprimanding them if you thought they were "dragging their feet." You might be wrong, but no one could convince you of that.

You do not like to be rejected by someone you are emotionally interested in, but you do not dwell on it for very long. You feel that you can always find someone else, for you are progressive and rarely look back. But this actually causes you to make the same mistakes again and again; you don't take the time to reflect on past experiences and learn from them. Your defense is that you are too busy to concern yourself with unimportant matters. It would be wise to spend a little time examining this so-called trivia, because it might reveal why you are not developing as well as you could.

Try to slow down. Your mind races at breakneck speed, and your nervous system suffers. Your mentality may be healthy and energetic, but your physical frame won't stand the abuse you expect it to take.

Mercury Conjunct Jupiter

The conjunction of Mercury and Jupiter shows that you have excellent reasoning ability and the enthusiasm to remain interested in whatever gains your attention. You have an insatiable appetite for knowledge, and your mind is a treasure chest of information. Communication is your greatest talent, and you express your opinions persuasively. Because you insist on always finding out the truth, you are sure of yourself and of what you know. You develop your creative ideas cleverly and with extraordinary ingenuity. You have much inspiration to draw on as you exploit your creative potentials.

Early in life, you began asking questions and would not be silenced until you had the answers. This curiosity has continued and will be active as long as you live. Each answer you get opens broad vistas of still more unanswered questions. Suffice it to say that your whole life is a process of learning about everything, old and new. You are flexible enough to revise your thinking when new evidence suggests that you should. Although you study the past for whatever knowledge can be gained from it, your primary interest lies in the future.

Your incredible mental capacity can be applied to such fields as education, philosophy, history (modern and ancient), public relations requiring direct communication with people, writing (journalistic and independent), and travel. Eventually, you will be recognized as an authority in your field and respected for your contributions to society. The explorer Sir Richard Burton, Emily Dickinson, and O. Henry all had this planetary combination, so you are in good company.

You must understand the necessity of getting a higher education, if you don't already have it. Education will enable you to make a real contribution; the world will be poorer if deprived of your enormous creative potential.

You may experience some difficulty in focusing on one subject to the exclusion of all others, but don't be too alarmed at this. Like Erle Stanley Gardner, with self-discipline you can take up several interests at once and pay exclusive attention to any one of them when you choose. Such unique abilities give you the potential for greatness.

In a debate or argument you are a formidable opponent because of your vast resources of information. Your only problem is deciding on a life objective and defining the goals you wish to reach.

You may have some nervous ailment that will require you to detach yourself from your ambitions while you recuperate. Rest is extremely important to you, and this cannot be overemphasized.

Mercury Conjunct Saturn

The conjunction of Mercury to Saturn shows that you are responsible, contemplative, and serious, partly because of your early training. You solve problems logically and waste little time with superficial matters. A veritable storehouse of information, you extract something meaningful from every experience. You are a good listener and cautious about voicing your own opinions in conversation. Rather than indulge in fanciful dreams, you prefer to apply yourself to goals that are well within your reach. You are sometimes pessimistic and may become severely depressed by reversals.

Your professional interests could be in mathematics, drafting, engineering, architecture, conservation, teaching, or politics. In fact, there is a wide range of occupations in which you could be successful. However, you will lose interest in your job if it doesn't make demands on your talents. But if you know your efforts are appreciated, you will make enormous contributions. As you tend to be a loner, you will work better if you can set your own pace. Generally you would rather work alone because you are irritated by distractions from associates. Your employer will always get his money's worth because you are honest and sincere and insist on fulfilling your part of the contract. You don't expect to get something for nothing.

Though you are intellectually capable and reasonably ambitious, recognition of your abilities may be delayed or overshadowed by your gregarious competitors. Be especially careful not to let your co-workers pick your brains; you are so eager to demonstrate how things should be done that you unwittingly divulge information that you should keep in reserve. However, don't be afraid to speak up when you have a good idea. If you are shy, get someone you trust to present it for you.

Because of your air of indifference people may think that you are not interested in social contacts. Actually, you are usually engrossed in deep thought triggered by something said earlier. You may be absent-minded at times. Even in a large gathering you may become so dissociated that others do not realize you are there, nor do you.

You need to be able to confide in someone close to you whom you can trust. Your romantic interests are stimulated by a person who is mature, honest, sincere, and responsible. Tradition and custom represent security to you, and you respect them. Your religious beliefs are probably the same as your parents' and reflect your childhood training. You resist change unless it can be proven to be an improvement over the past.

Unless you take time to unwind often, you will invite tension. Take frequent "little vacations" and just waste time doing nothing productive. Try to look at the bright side and learn to laugh at your own mistakes. It is essential to avoid bocoming morbidly obsessed with the big important issues.

Mercury Conjunct Uranus

With Mercury conjunct Uranus, you are bright, articulate, curious, intuitive, and mentally courageous. You are excited by everything you observe and fascinated by anything different or unusual. Your mind races eagerly as you seek answers to your questions, because you cannot tolerate the darkness of ignorance.

As a child, you were interested in what made your moving toys operate, and your parents probably never had to worry about keeping you occupied. Your creativity developed early, and you even devised new subjects to explore that further captured your interest in all things.

Truth is an important factor in your life. Consequently, science, philosophy, psychology, and human behavior are fields in which you could succeed, since they deal with seeking answers to problems. In industrial research and development your inventive ability could be applied with a reasonable guarantee of success. Technical writing might also serve as an avenue of expression for you.

To hold your continued interest, the partner you select must have a similar temperament, or you will be bored. You tend to form platonic relationships with your associates, based on mutual interests. You will quickly sever a relationship with someone who violates the truth in dealing with you.

Futuristic in attitude, you rarely look back at what might have been. You prefer to look forward to what will be, if you have any say in it. The possibilities for your self-expression are limitless, except for the lack of continuity that this combination often creates. If you can learn to isolate yourself and resolve one problem at a time, you will overcome the only liability of this conjunction.

Mercury Conjunct Neptune

With Mercury conjunct Neptune your imagination often works overtime. When you state an opinion, your interpretation is likely to be as faulty as the "facts" on which you base your judgment. Because you are uncomfortable with reality, you often bend the truth into a shape that you can accept. You are extremely sensitive to your environment and intolerant of painful experiences, which you try to escape or withdraw from. It is essential that you find a constructive means for expressing your highly developed and sensitive mentality.

Your profession must give you the opportunity to use your artistic talents. Your appreciation for art in all its forms may enable you to succeed in a field such as writing, acting, or dancing. In these professions your imagination and rhythmic sense can be applied to advantage. Any occupation you choose will gain your complete devotion.

You must have training in order to fully capitalize on your creative potentials. An education is absolutely necessary for you to clearly understand the best use of your talents. Mystery, romance, and illusion fascinate you, but be careful that you are not overwhelmed by the desire to use them to escape from reality and responsibility.

Be especially cautious in your romantic relationships in order to avoid unnecessary disappointments. You idealize beyond attainable levels, overdramatizing other people's qualities and underestimating your own. You tend to be influenced by the illusion and glamour of famous or even notorious people. You often imitate the people you admire and may romantically "cast" yourself in a personal role with them to vicariously enjoy a relationship you've created. You are quite responsive to suggestion and should therefore avoid artificial stimulants.

Mercury Conjunct Pluto

The conjunction of Mercury and Pluto shows that your mind is deep, penetrating, and inclined to extremes. You interpret your experiences like a detective reconstructing a crime, looking for hidden meaning in obscure details. You evaluate matters subjectively, and your psychic sense often reveals clues that are hidden from less sensitive observers. Curious almost to a fault, you go to extremes in gathering the information you need to solve your problems.

You have a genius for asserting yourself persuasively whenever it seems the only way to accomplish something. You are fearless in pursuing your objectives, and others admire your determination and perisistance. Once your mind is made up, you don't change it unless the evidence is overwhelming. But because you defend your views so vehemently, people may find your attitude offensive.

You are fascinated by the mysterious and the occult. With your quick observation of details and understanding of their value, you could succeed as an analyst or investigator. Such fields as crime detection, chemistry, research, pathology, or surgery would enable you to apply your skills and potentials constructively. You could become an explorer or a financial analyst and advisor.

You should moderate your anarchistic inclinations. Even when you are not actively vindictive toward those who defy you, you nevertheless think revenge. Social injustices are a particular irritant to you, and you could vent your hidden anger by directing your talents toward correcting them. You know how to dramatize situations to gain the attention of people in power so that changes can be made. You could easily become the spokesman for those who lack the courage to speak for themselves. Perhaps politics would give you the leverage to accomplish many worthwhile objectives for yourself and others.

In personal relationships you are demanding and sometimes extremely intolerant of weakness. Although you seek out those who will submit to you, then you are contemptuous of them for doing so. This is the paradox of this planetary combination and accounts for the difficulty others have in relating to you. The fact is, you admire strength and respect authority, so you challenge others to demonstrate these qualities. Ideally, your mate should be strong and be able to take a position with you so that you could contribute to each other's development and objectives. Sharing goals and motivation would produce a permanent bond between you.

Mercury Conjunct Ascendant

Mercury conjunct the Ascendant shows that you are intensely preoccupied with yourself. You probably start your conversation with "I" more often than most people do, and the word "me" crops up regularly in your dialogue. This is not such a terrible thing, but it is boring to others. Your mental faculties are well developed, and for the most part you are bright and witty, so your incessant use of the personal pronoun may be tolerated. Intellectually enthusiastic about every bit of information you receive, you are inclined to burst out with rash statements of opinion when provoked. You pride yourself on how easy it is for you to learn and may show disdain for anyone who has to concentrate harder. You are mentally impulsive and rarely give anyone the chance to answer your questions. In a crowd, you can dominate the conversation by asking questions that you answer yourself or by posing problems that you immediately solve. An original and creative speaker, you often dramatize what you have to say with a display of acting ability. People are fascinated by your command of language and effective delivery. You are not afraid to speak up when you know you are right, but the fact is, you aren't always right. When your views are criticized, you become indignant and argumentative. You are no shrinking violet and would rather put up than shut up.

Venus Conjunct Mars

Venus conjunct Mars shows that you have a strong desire nature which you need to express at all times. You may prefer to satisfy your desire through relationships, but you are willing to satisfy them through other alternatives, so that you don't have to endure frustration. These alternatives include artistic endeavors or social functions that can prove very rewarding to you in themselves and may additionally provide you with opportunities to meet persons with whom you can identify and relate. Your emotional warmth and generous nature attract people to you, but you may not be aware that you communicate physical suggestions both to groups and to individuals. Your intentions may be easily misunderstood because of this, and you will experience some difficulties, which will force you to bring your defenses into play.

In your eagerness to make social contact, you tend to be indiscriminate about the kinds of people with whom you associate. Generally the aggressor in relationships with the opposite sex, you may be resented for being "pushy." But your aggressiveness increases your chances of success in meeting competition, because you don't give up without making every attempt to demonstrate your abilities. This planetary pairing does not of itself signify a specific professional interest, but you will gain attention for your determination to be given the same opportunities as others. You would probably work best in a job that requires you to meet and deal with the public. Working alone or without contact with the public and co-workers would deprive you of the fulfillment you need and would probably lead to boredom. You are too much of a "live wire" to be happy away from the busyness and crises of close human encounter.

You are attracted to individuals who are active, aggressive, and amorous, but they must not try to exercise control over you. You consider yourself a free person and will not tolerate anyone who tries to restrict you. You don't make concessions without a lot of thought, although you expect the other person to compromise. You demand a great deal from the person you love and may make demands that are difficult to comply with. Because of your "love 'em and leave 'em" attitude, many potential mates will look elsewhere when seeking a binding relationship.

Kathryn

Venus Conjunct Jupiter

The conjunction of Venus to Jupiter indicates that you are benevolent, kind, sympathetic, and generous. But you go to extremes in expressing these qualities and are indulgent with people even when they don't deserve it. Brutality and vulgarity are intolerable to you. You have a good sense of humor, although you have your contemplative moments, and you usually conduct yourself with decorum. In the presence of adversity you are especially optimistic and always hopeful that the situation will turn out for the best. Self-indulgent in acquiring material comforts, you prefer a life of ease that allows you to participate in all the pleasurable social activities that you love.

Domestic conditions in your childhood may not have been abundant in material comforts, but probably you were not deprived of anything truly essential. Love, kindness, and understanding between you and your parents established the foundation for your continued growth and development.

You are suited to occupations in which your effusive manner can be expressed, such as public relations, travel, working with young people as a teacher or guidance counselor, or directing social activities. Through your work in a welfare organization or foundation you could bring joy and hope to people who are disadvantaged by social, economic, or physical problems. Your talents might also be applied in rehabilitative therapy through crafts and other avocational pursuits.

Your breezy disposition and warm nature make you popular with almost everybody. You are too easy-going, though, and some individuals may try to take advantage of you. However, you are rarely embittered by such negative encounters. You seek and are sought after by people who are also self-assured and who expect to succeed. You respond to honesty and gravitate toward persons with that quality. But you react negatively to those who make sincere gestures toward others only if they have some ulterior motive. You don't waste time on people who waste their time. Any accomplishment, either material or personal, makes you glow with happiness. Difficult stress contact from Saturn to this planetary pair may make it burdensome to gain this happiness, but you would still be inclined to it.

Venus Conjunct Saturn

The conjunction of Venus to Saturn indicates that you feel you must make concessions to others to get what you want. You are always the one who is expected to adjust to the demands of others in order to have a satisfactory relationship. As a result, you are often dissatisfied with the contacts you make, either because they are not fulfilling enough, or because you feel you are being used. You may become resigned to making the best of a relationship in which you give more than the other person does. On the positive side, however, this shows that you take the relationship seriously. You are loyal and sincere in your affections but tend to be inhibited in demonstrating them, because you are afraid that others will take advantage of you.

You have reasonably good judgment, which is reflected in your material affairs. You are self-disciplined in handling money and prudent enough to always save something regardless of your income. Such prudence is a way to compensate for the disappointments you may have in personal relationships, and you consider it a reasonable substitute. Saving money also gives you security and allows you some material comforts.

You are temperamentally suited to occupations in which success depends on adhering to rules and regulations. Finance, banking, building trades, insurance, law, real estate, sales, and designing are some endeavors in which you can successfully apply yourself. Ideally, you should have a position that allows you to function independently. You are dutiful and responsible and would accomplish more without a supervisor breathing down your neck. You are certainly able to work with others, but you prefer working in privacy.

Your romantic interests are stimulated by individuals who are serious, sincere, and honest. You need a person you can respect and who will respect you too. A mature individual represents security to you, in addition to providing social status. Your lover must be tactful, polished, and have a strong and admirable character. You are repulsed by vulgarity and disturbed by disorder. Your objectives are well-defined, and you will expect your mate to cooperate in reaching mutual goals. Because of your deep concern for the integrity of the family, you will unhesitatingly withdraw from any external situation that threatens your family.

It is important that you look at the bright and positive side of life; negative attitudes can bring about negative effects. Problems in the throat glands may have a similar origin. You can improve your general well-being by adopting a more cheerful outlook, but the optimism must be genuine.

Venus Conjunct Uranus

With Venus conjunct Uranus you have a sparkling, effervescent personality. Popular and sociable almost to an extreme, you have a dynamic zest for living a full, unrestricted life. You seek every kind of human encounter in order to fully explore life in all its dimensions. You tend to disregard socially acceptable relationships unless they are exciting enough for you to feel uninhibited.

You are best suited to occupations that involve novelty and in which you can function in your own uniquely creative way. You don't take easily to routine, and a daily schedule of repetitious work would be unbearably boring. Professions dealing with the public are more in line with your sociable temperament. Public relations, party planning, social functions, fashion shows, investment counseling, and interior decorating are some of the fields that can give you the mobility and creative expression you need.

In your personal relationships you demand unlimited freedom so you can detach yourself without guilt when you lose interest. If a person continues to fascinate you, you form strong ties. But you may sever those ties suddenly if you meet someone whose unusual qualities gain your attention.

It may be difficult for you to establish a permanent relationship, since you are outgoing and probably career-oriented. It is better to defer marriage until you've had the opportunity to try making it on your own. Because your romantic responses are unpredictable, you would be well advised to be engaged for a reasonable time before marrying. If you marry on impulse, it probably won't be permanent. Only strong Saturn of earth qualities, determined elsewhere in your analysis, can reverse this trend. Your responsibility is somewhat lacking, indicating enduring ties are unlikely.

Venus Conjunct Neptune

With Venus conjunct Neptune you are a romantic idealist. Your trusting nature makes you vulnerable to deceptive individuals who may try to take advantage of you. You have a kind of delicacy and aesthetic refinement that finds comfort in art, music, and literature. You are artistically imaginative and thus find beauty where others cannot.

Your tender qualities are best suited to professions in which calm conditions are the rule. Avoid any occupation in which turmoil or aggressive behavior is expected, for you would find this intolerable. Any of the nonphysical arts, such as music, writing, fashion, or cultural functions, would be suitable expressions of your creativity.

The idealism of your romantic nature may cause some problems in your personal relationships. You seek relationships that are serene and trouble-free. But you are susceptible to and defenseless against attempts by others to exploit you negatively. It is difficult for you to see others realistically, so you can readily be victimized. This kind of behavior appals and emotionally crushes you. Since you are not a fighter by nature, you may simply withdraw. If such experiences recur, and very likely they will, you could resort to imaginary safe alliances. On the other hand, you may decide to protect yourself by employing similar deceptive tactics. Your rose-colored view of life can cause disorder in your affairs, unless you can understand that coarseness in some people and abrasive elements in the environment are natural aspects of reality.

Venus Conjunct Pluto

With Venus conjunct Pluto you will encounter recurring crises as your romantic nature seeks emotional fulfillment. You pursue the ultimate in physical and emotional release, and because of your ardent love needs, you will be attracted to a wide variety of partners. You are possessive of your current love interest, but you easily turn your attention to someone else who seems able to provide you with a deeper relationship.

You often demand tangible love tokens from those with whom you become emotionally involved. Since you are willing to make enormous commitments to the one you love, you feel it is only fair that your partner should make some material sacrifice to demonstrate genuine interest. In this way, you are reassured that the relationship is more than merely a physical attraction, and there is a possibility of a permanent bond between you. You are always hoping for that total partnership in which you enjoy all levels of companionship — physical, emotional, and spiritual.

You arouse deep responses in people, even those you contact casually. Your nature stimulates both positive and negative reactions; some individuals will find you irresistible and enticing, while others will be fearful of becoming trapped by your pervasive charm. In time, you will be freed from your physical preoccupation with sex, and you will be more able to enjoy all kinds of human contacts.

You attract others to you like a magnet. They may be interested in your dramatic sense or your artistic leanings, or they may be fascinated by your fearless involvement in deep and sometimes dangerous alliances.

Unable to accept social injustices, you feel strongly that something must be done about them. You are amazed at the indifference of public officials to such inhuman conditions. Once a program has been started to correct the situation, you may be willing to work for it, if it will serve those in greatest need. You may feel that no sacrifice is too great, if even a small improvement is made.

You will enjoy working in fund-raising campaigns, where your deep respect for human dignity could be constructively demonstrated. You know how to use pressure tactics, especially with your more well-to-do associates, to gain their support for your goals.

Venus Conjunct Ascendant

Venus conjunct the Ascendant indicates you have a personable manner and social charm, which win you the approval of everyone you deal with. This is exactly the sanction you seek, for above all, you want to be accepted. You find it easy to make whatever compromises are necessary to get what you desire. Fond of the finer things of life, you tend to associate with people who have similar tastes, in the hope of establishing a permanent relationship with such a person. However, you may not succeed in convincing everyone that you are only "acting the part" of the conniver. Regardless of the image you present to observers, underneath the veneer is a calculating machine on which you count the advantages and disadvantages of every association or friendship, every social contact and social function.

You are clever in exploiting your best qualities because you know how to win admirers with your charming ways. You are usually well behaved and refined, but when you can't get what you want, you become extremely aggressive and demanding. Everything has to stop until your wishes are satisfied. You provoke people to take advantage of you and then are annoyed at their presumptuous attitude. Learn to tone down your self-seeking and spend some time developing the more substantial talents that will make you worthy of the gifts you seek.

Mars Conjunct Jupiter

With the conjunction of Mars and Jupiter, you have an abundance of energy and enthusiasm to take on tasks that would frighten all but the most courageous. In order to get what you want you assert yourself fearlessly, even in the face of danger. You have a rather reckless faith in your ability to tempt fate and take chances, never doubting that you will succeed. What you lack in finesse you make up for in arrogance. You rise to a challenge at the slightest provocation, and your competitors have cause for alarm when you oppose them. You enjoy direct confrontation with your adversaries, and you revel in the accompanying glory and publicity. Fascinated by the entries found in the *Guinness Book of Records*, you would be pleased to find your name listed under some accomplishment there.

With your flair for the dramatic, you don't do anything in moderation. Not content to simply win over a competitor, you punctuate the victory with some kind of ritualistic, publicity-seeking display. You know how to achieve recognition by drawing the public's attention to your talents. Wayne Newton, Yoko Ono, Jim Nabors, Ray Charles, Lee Marvin, Roy Campanella, Hugh Hefner, and John F. Kennedy are some of the better-known personalities who had this aspect in their charts and who have distinguished themselves this way.

There are many ways you can use this very forceful dynamic aspect. You have an exciting combination of physical stamina and intellectual resources. Because you don't believe in failure, your chances for success are improved. If you express your creative abilities physically, you will apply your intellectual skill and common sense to obtain the best results from your efforts. Should you follow a more intellectually demanding life pursuit, it will be characterized by an incredible degree of physical endurance and competitiveness. Such fields as sports, exploration, law, government, acting, composing, or writing would provide you with vast opportunities to display your talents and demonstrate what you can do.

Your most persistent liability is your lack of moderation, which can cause physical exhaustion. Your driving ambition to rise above the challenges you set for yourself can cause deterioration of your physical resources. It is essential that you take periodic rest or vacations from the constant abrasion of close competition.

Mars Conjunct Saturn

Mars conjunct Saturn shows that you are fortunate in being able to use your energy constructively. The normal desire to assert yourself on impulse is balanced by realization of the consequences of such an action. This quality of restraint can mean great accomplishments for you because you don't waste energy on unproductive efforts. Your sense of economy and efficiency are characteristics of success; you know how to use your talents purposefully for specific objectives. You are realistic in applying good judgment before taking any action.

Your early training enabled you to take on major responsibilities without difficulty. Knowing your limitations, you rarely go beyond them. You are prudent and yet fearless, cautious and yet aggressive, hard-working and yet able to accomplish a great deal with economy of effort. Although you are a complex person, you use the most simplistic approach in solving problems. You represent the ideal in terms of a balance between aggression and self-control.

You are never indifferent to the feelings of others, but you can become angry when others try to interfere with you. Frustration brings out the most dangerous kind of energy in you. You are not accustomed to having your plans challenged and can launch vicious attacks against your adversaries, even resorting to physical violence. Other factors in your chart may indicate whether you would go to this extreme, but the potential for it exists in this planetary combination. Many professional pursuits are possible with this combination. Especially suitable are occupations requiring physical endurance and stamina, such as archeology, exploration, geographic surveys, and forestry service. In the industrial field, research and development seem appropriate. Military service would be another means of expression for your controlled energy.

In your romantic pursuits you easily play the roles of both prey and predator. You carefully evaluate the partner's line of least resistance in order to decide which technique you will use. The remark, ". . . pursued until you caught your pursuer," is descriptive of your method.

It is very important not to become chilled when indulging in physical activities. Cool off gradually and avoid cold liquids to prevent cramps. Use as little salt as possible when not doing strenuous physical work.

Mars Conjunct Uranus   Kris

With Mars conjunct Uranus you are unrestrained, forceful, and energetic in striving to achieve your goals. You establish your own rules and won't submit to anyone's restraints. As you work to get what you want out of life, you are completely uninhibited, guided by the belief that you must be free to do whatever is necessary to get what you want. There's never a dull moment when you're around, because you seek excitement, and when there isn't any, you create it.

This impulsiveness can cause you many problems. Society is stabilized by laws and rules of behavior, and the people who abide by them are irritated by your rebellious nature. If you truly want to accomplish your objectives, you will have to play by the rules.

Your courageous nature can best be used in occupations that require daring, such as sports, racing, mountain climbing, or exploration. Before contemplating any of these, however, be sure you understand that safeguards are necessary. Otherwise, the results will be tragic. Only a powerful Saturn in your chart can offer the protection you need.

You could easily become the champion for people who are too weak or perhaps too timid to demand social adjustment or change for themselves. You have the courage to instigate change by challenging powerful government officials. To dramatize your point, you may even threaten them, using the public support you've gained. Once you have all the evidence to confirm an allegation of wrongdoing, you won't be stopped from whatever action is needed to make sure that justice is served.

You have a powerful sex drive that cannot accept no for an answer. You would be refused mainly by those who expect an emotional response in addition to a biological one. You are primarily a "taker" and not much of a "giver."

Mars Conjunct Neptune

You have the planet Mars conjunct Neptune, indicating some conflict between your impulses to act and your willingness to accept responsibility for the results of your actions. You may not deliberately avoid the consequences, but it is often difficult for you to clearly see the burden of guilt. Your imagination is sometimes blocked because you are unable to plan ahead well enough, and you allow chance to determine the results. Almost everything you do on impulse will prove disappointing. Before you act, you must realistically weigh the energy you are investing against the probable effects. You are inclined to ignore reality and the feelings of others when you assert yourself.

People are drawn by your magnetic appeal. You easily take on characteristics that will please others and not appear threatening to them. The theater and related fields are especially suited to your active imagination and great creative potential. With your acting talent, you can also successfully "play the role" in many professional activities. To gain acceptance in your field of interest, you may have to resort to subterfuge. However, honestly developed skills must soon replace the act, if you expect to retain your position. If other factors of your chart indicate caution, reserve, and responsibility, medicine may be the best field for your sensitive nature.

Be extremely careful in your romantic relationships. What may seem to be true love could turn out to be merely an escapade for you or your partner. Such a disappointment would be very painful. It is easy for you to become entrapped in an alliance that would be embarrassing if it were revealed. Don't deceive others, or you risk being deceived by them too. Any contacts you make must be made honestly.

Be wary of medication unless a physician advises it. Good hygiene is essential, for you are more susceptible to infection than others.

Mars Conjunct Pluto

The conjunction of Mars and Pluto shows that you have a strong desire nature with the persistence and determination to get what you want. You may often find, when you get it, that you didn't really want what you were pursuing after all, that it was merely an exercise to prove to yourself you could. Satisfaction is the only motive for many of your pursuits. You may easily mistake willfulness for desire in your motivations.

In a crisis, you can contain yourself until the right moment occurs to act. Then you will use all your energy to cope with and resolve the crisis. You have enormous compulsions to assert yourself, especially if you suspect that anyone is trying to restrict you in any way. You don't tolerate domination, although you do respect authority if it is fairly administered.

In your personal relationships, you tend to be the aggressor, which may make others apprehensive about getting too close to you. You are possessive in love and demanding even of your friends. Your desire nature precedes you, stimulating others either to anticipate your physical charms or to feel threatened and avoid you. Your physical needs are strong, and your ambitions could induce you to use sex as a device for achieving your goals. You often justify your methods as being the only way to gain your objectives.

You are aware of the social problems in your environment and can be extremely useful in urging others to make the necessary changes to solve these problems. However, you are able to persuade others because your demands have a threatening quality. You have the courage to take on the most difficult tasks fearlessly and are resourceful in gaining financial support for your enterprises. You need to find a way to express yourself through constructive activities.

Mars Conjunct Ascendant   *Kathryn*

Mars conjunct the Ascendant gives you an inexhaustible supply of energy. You are constantly in motion, but sometimes it is motion without meaning. Lacking self-discipline, you take daring and unnecessary risks when challenged. Your supporters regard you as courageous, but your enemies consider you "pushy" and arrogant. However, you are not moved by either opinion, because you want most of all for people to recognize your superiority and give you the breathing room you need. You constantly have to see that people are in awe of your aggressive superiority, because inside you are not really that sure of yourself. The image you present hides a persistent inferiority complex. You probably win your arguments by making the most noise and wearing out your opponents with unceasing harassment. But you don't need to waste your energy this way, because you have enormous creative ability that merely needs to be harnessed to an objective. When you do this, no one can succeed as easily as you can, and with energy to spare.

A very physical person, you tend to brush aside any talk of compromise or concession as tactics fit only for the weak and spineless. It is almost impossible to have a simple friendly talk with you; when you think you are losing control and your position is weakening, you become angry and may resort to violence. You can be sure that people who converse with you in simple "yes's" and "no's" are aware of your short fuse. On the positive side, you are independent and self-confident. You know how to mobilize people and their resources to achieve your objectives. Although you can work as hard as the best of them, you prefer to play the role of instigator, sitting back and pulling the strings to make them do your bidding.

Jupiter Conjunct Saturn

The conjunction of Jupiter to Saturn shows that you have enormous potential for success, although it won't come without effort. In spite of overwhelming odds against success, you are eager to explore new means to make a massive assault and assert yourself in the world. You have the fortitude and staying power to mobilize all your resources for this task. Planning every step of the way is absolutely essential, along with knowing when to act and when not to. You have a vivid picture of your future already realized in your dreams, but you are realistic enough to accept the responsibility this entails. You know that even with driving ambition, striving for significance is not enough unless it satisfies a clearly pictured mental vision. You have the courage to be ostentatious about your belief in yourself, while remaining cautious enough to stay within your limits. Your capacity to achieve goals is in direct proportion to your willingness to accept self-discipline and hard work. The glow of success is so sweet that you can accept these facts.

You are hopeful yet realistic, eager yet serious, assertive yet deliberate. Generally you don't take chances, preferring to use proven methods to get what you want. You apply your talents in the most practical way so that little effort is wasted on nonproductive projects. You can find rewarding satisfaction and exploit your creative talents in law, education, medicine, accounting, or the ministry. To these fields you would bring a profound understanding of people and an ability to help solve their problems. You are patient with less gifted people and willing to be of assistance when they need you.

In your moments of relative leisure you enjoy reading informative books that are useful in your professional interests. In your constant striving to raise your level of competence, you might attend evening sessions at an educational institution. Never satisfied with the extent of your knowledge, you realize that competition requires you to keep abreast of current thought and developments in your field.

You respect the lessons of history, which stimulate your philosophical musings on destiny and the role of each individual in the destiny of man. Your retentive memory is a great help in crises that require an immediate solution; you may even be surprised that the necessary information comes to mind so readily at the right time.

Overdoing is your most persistent problem, for it can cause physical exhaustion. You especially need to get away from your daily concerns and truly unwind. Frequent "little vacations" are especially effective in restoring vitality and giving you a fresh approach to your goals.

Jupiter Conjunct Uranus

The conjunction between Jupiter and Uranus shows that you have high expectations for your future. You have much insight into ways to develop your talents to gain the most benefit from them. Your respect for knowledge is deep, and you admire the intellectual giants of the past and present. You have an insatiable desire to learn as much as you can, knowing that knowledge is freedom as well as power.

This reverence for education was probably fostered by your early conditioning, directly or indirectly. You are above average in your ability to absorb knowledge, and you can visualize its purpose — to open broad avenues for exploiting your potentials. You are eager for growth and never let an opportunity pass without taking advantage of it. In your pursuit of the truth, you are a kind of philosopher, finding significance in everything you do.

Although you might find politics fascinating, your best efforts will probably be in education. Your outlook is to the future, and you can easily stimulate others to become excited about their future. Although you are impatient with the past, you never fail to derive benefit from its lessons. If your interests are not in education, your next best contribution would be in law and government. You have the temperament and the skill to construct social guidelines and policies that will be studied by future historians.

Your social life is comfortable when you are with people whose attitudes are similar to yours. In your personal relationships you are exceedingly generous. You need to associate freely with progressive individuals so that your own enthusiasm for life is not dampened or restricted. Your romantic partner must also be fascinated with the new and exciting developments of each day. You need someone who will share your plans for the future and sustain your objectives. Remember to slow down occasionally in order to stay in sharp focus.

Jupiter Conjunct Neptune

With Jupiter conjunct Neptune you are inclined to do things to excess. You may talk about subjects you don't really understand or try to accomplish tasks beyond your capabilities. You trust others to maintain the confidences you share with them, carelessly assuming they deserve your trust. When you give others the benefit of the doubt, you may be sadly disillusioned, for they often seem to deceive you. Your faith in people is deep, but you assign it blindly.

You are philosophical about people and hopeful that you will find someone in whom you can confidently believe. From your experiences with others, you learn many lessons that help to refine your judgment. You have a spiritual understanding of your social obligations, which you fulfill by offering your talents, inspiration, and imagination whenever you can. You would work with particular effectiveness in the broad area of human welfare. Such professional activities as teaching or working in a Sunday school, orphanage, mental health program, medical relief agency, the Peace Corps, or VISTA are suited to your temperament and disposition. You can easily become totally immersed in providing sympathetic understanding to those who most desperately need it.

There is always a danger of abuse from people who may try to capitalize on your willingness to serve others. Unless you are alert, this can also happen in your personal relationships. You want to believe that your lover's feelings are those of true love, and you may encourage the relationship to develop, hoping it will lead to marriage. Unless you learn to question everyone's motives in relating to you, you will certainly be disappointed.

You must develop respect for the harsh realities of your surroundings. In your desire to experience the highest emotions and most exquisite sensations, you risk aligning yourself with escapist fanaticism. Avoid drugs, cults, and irresponsible charlatans.

Jupiter Conjunct Pluto

With Jupiter conjunct Pluto you seek to enjoy life at the fullest. You have enormous drive and ambition to achieve your goals as soon as possible and are impatient with anything that delays you. To others, your goals may be unrealistic but you strive for them with amazing determination. It rarely occurs to you that you may fail, for you do not accept defeat. You are driven by an insatiable appetite to get the most out of your potential. Your success at seemingly impossible tasks is almost inspired. Behind your ambition lies a powerful faith in your ability to rise above external limitations. Your accomplishments are acclaimed and envied by many.

Your professional interests are extremely varied and you can excel in many fields. Even though successful, however, you will be uncomfortable until you find a life work that offers unlimited growth potential. Essentially you are attracted to professions in which you must work closely with people, such as law, medicine, psychology, or religion. On the other hand, your preoccupation with self may lead you to seek recognition in fields such as sports, research and exploration, or even gambling, in which the risks are high and the dangers tantalizing. You will become involved in financial enterprises of vast scope which will generate significant returns for you.

In your personal affairs, your inclination for success will attract you to other successful persons. You will seek a mate whose strength of character, accomplishments, and recognition you admire. You will understand your partner's motives and enthusiastically stimulate your mate to achieve. Be careful, however, not to overemphasize your partner's earning ability and the resulting "good life," thus downgrading the fine personal attributes that make it possible.

Jupiter Conjunct Ascendant

With Jupiter conjunct the Ascendant, you are the epitome of optimism. You do nothing in moderation because you are always hopeful that some of your excesses will work out for the best in the long run. You have an endless source of ideas with which to plan your success, and you are sure that you will succeed. With boundless faith in your abilities and a certain measure of luck, you don't worry about tomorrow and you care even less about yesterday. You are ambitious, but in satisfying your ambitions, you bite off more than you can chew. You exaggerate your own importance, which can be a serious liability if you are seeking supporters in your endeavors. No one likes a braggart or a person who overestimates his worth. You are inspiring to those under you, but you should avoid making promises to them unless you are sure you can deliver.

You are generous, kind, sympathetic, benevolent, and the delight of anyone seeking a contribution in a fund-raising campaign, since you are a "soft touch." Generally you are well informed about subjects that have an important bearing on your professional goals as well as about matters of general interest. You have the highest regard for institutions of learning, and with your providential nature you will probably endow some school. You are too open with private or classified information, and if your competition beats you with a new product, the idea probably came originally from you. Try to be more conservative and serious. Your appetite needs curbing too, because you are inclined to put on weight, especially with advancing years.

Saturn Conjunct Uranus

The conjunction between Saturn and Uranus shows that you have the ability to give form to your many creative ideas. You are unusually mature in your attitudes, which enables you to derive some benefit from everything you do. Your desire for freedom is matched by your capacity to earn it by carefully and efficiently mobilizing your resources for particular objectives. This self-discipline will always sustain you. You have a healthy respect for authority and its lessons. You also have the drive and ambition to accomplish important, long-term tasks that can assure your future security.

Your professional potentials are almost unlimited because you are not afraid of responsibility and the demands of leadership. Almost certainly, you have much to offer the world in terms of understanding and experience. You comprehend the lessons of the past, and you act aggresively to help rid the future of ignorance. These contributions should be harnessed to group enterprises or sociopolitical endeavors. Fields such as science, mathematics, research, politics, the occult, and especially teaching are some of the areas in which your talents would be useful.

You are most comfortable in the company of rugged individuals who have high aims and ideals. You need to associate with adventurous types whose grip on the future is firm. People "on the move" and on their way up the ladder of achievement are those whom you can relate to meaningfully. You are impatient with trite, superficial people, since you doubt that they can serve the needs of the masses. Your life has purpose and direction, and your closest associates have similar goals.

You must relax periodically in order to recharge your energy center. You can easily drive yourself too hard, unmindful that your physical reserves are being depleted. When tired, you may become pessimistic about plans that would otherwise seem to be going well.

Saturn Conjunct Neptune

With your Saturn conjunct Neptune, it is very unlikely that you can be deceived for very long. You usually protect yourself by being distrustful of situations or people you are unfamiliar with. Even in spiritual or religious matters, you object to accepting dogma unless you can work it out logically. Perhaps in your early years you readily accepted those teachings, and later, as you began to question their validity, you felt guilty about them. In general, you have a mature attitude about religious matters and deep insight into your social obligations.

You are psychic in the most realistic sense, and your experiences guide you in the use of your developing intuition. You are suited to work in an executive capacity, for you can make important decisions with a high probability of success. Your professional affairs benefit from your ability to detect dishonesty or deception. In your pursuit of the facts, you insist that others prove what they say. You fear the unknown and are cautious about making a decision until you can examine all the facts. Your inspiration has practical value, and you can express it concretely.

In your romantic relationships you are similarly composed. You are an idealist, but a practical one. You do not generally make an emotional commitment unless there is solid evidence that the feeling is mutual. You don't offer yourself casually to anyone, friend or lover. Your temperament is not suited to superficial entanglements, but you are willing to make an enormous contribution to a relationship that obviously has substance.

Avoid taking medication that is not professionally prescribed. Artificial vitamins, stimulants, and depressive drugs are not for you, because they may cause unpleasant reactions.

Saturn Conjunct Pluto

The conjunction of Saturn and Pluto gives you a driving ambition to realize your goals. To do this, however, you must use all your resources and experience. An austerity program may be necessary, but you are willing to endure whatever is required so that your plans will succeed. The fear of an unfulfilled life drives you to accomplish as much as you can. You are certain that your determination and persistence will make success possible.

You may be forced into a particular profession before you realize which field will enable you to get the results you desire. Your inclination is to traditional occupations that can give you stability in the face of changing social values, which seem to financially threaten you. You may resist "getting in step" with changes and defiantly challenge anyone who suggests that you must, or you will make anxious adjustments to them. In any case, your approach to solving the problems you face is extreme. You either "join" and transform a liability into an asset, or you resist and suffer defeat from the relentless tide of progress.

Secretive about your plans and ambitions, you don't share your innermost thoughts with anyone. You work behind the scenes, patiently acquiring financial resources that you feel will protect you in later years. You are efficient in managing your financial affairs and resourceful in spending.

You are qualified to gain positions of power and authority. An effective organizer, you command the respect of those under you. You are almost faultless in observing the law, and although your judgment may be harsh, it is fair. You have an uncanny ability to understand people's motives, which serves you well in determining guilt or innocence.

Saturn Conjunct Ascendant

Saturn conjunct the Ascendant indicates that you are conservative and self-disciplined in your behavior. You tend to be shy about asserting yourself, so people may assume you are indifferent to them. You have strong doubts about your worth, which makes you cautious when meeting competition. This lack of self-confidence will eventually be replaced by self-assurance as you learn through experience to understand yourself. You do not have the kind of aggressive drive that impresses people on first meeting, but you show reliability, and they learn to depend on you. Others see your good qualities long before you realize them. Self-effacing by nature, you prefer the sidelines rather than the spotlight.

You are efficient in mobilizing your resources and are sure to realize your goals, but you underestimate your abilities. You are a "slow starter" who needs the reassurance of some successful endeavors before you define your objectives and make careful plans to achieve them. You are prepared to grow one step at a time in achieving the excellence you are capable of. When a decision is required, you tend to hesitate because you want to be sure first. You sometimes miss opportunities for fear you will be rediculed if you make the wrong decision. Responsible to a fault, you will never let anyone down who depends on you. Learn to love yourself more, so you can feel you deserve the good things in life that you work for so diligently. You can be victimized by people who take advantage of your unwillingness to fight for your rights, but you never forget such incidents. Although not a vindictive person, you bide your time until the moment comes when they need your assistance; then you repay them with cool indifference.

Uranus Conjunct Neptune

The conjunction of Uranus and Neptune shows that you are aware of your obligations to the social structure which you belong to and that you identify closely with its mass consciousness. You are keenly observant of the deception that the leaders often use to gain and maintain complete control of the people, and this disturbs you deeply. You recognize that this pattern can lead to loss of personal freedom unless steps are taken to eliminate the offenders. Since you belong to a generation that will not tolerate abuses of authority and power, you realize that freedom can be lost if not protected against political erosion.

No one living today has this planetary combination; it will appear next in 1992 and last through 1994. The last conjunction occurred in 1821 and lasted through 1824, but it might be interesting to examine some of the important achievements of those years. Among these were the invention of an ingenious process for waterproofing fabric and the development of cement, which later played a large role in the industrial revolution. These physical phenomena — cement and waterproof fabric — exactly parallel the strong foundations of the courageous individuals who have this aspect and the process they use to protect themselves and their rights.

You respond to people who need your understanding of their social predicament, whether it is a personal problem or one they share with others. Although you know that you can do little by yourself, the combined effort of those sharing your concern can be a powerful force against social injustice. Working together, you can restore order and freedom where there was chaos and privation.

Uranus Conjunct Pluto

The conjunction of Uranus and Pluto shows that if necessary you will go to extremes to preserve your freedom. Being free means many things to you. It means freedom from pollution, disease, unemployment, and economic control by the industrial establishment. You want the right to "do your thing," especially the right to make some important contribution to mankind along with others who are similarly motivated. You support local and national programs to improve the quality of life and may even become actively involved in seeing that this work is carried out. You realize that hard work by everyone concerned is the only way to reverse the continual plunder of natural resources, which leaves only a blighted landscape. You have a deep respect for all living things, including people, animals, and plants. When you observe how the earth is so freely desecrated by private interests, with little regard for those who will inherit it, you feel the need to dedicate yourself to preserving these elements.

This conjunction occurred from 1963 to 1968. Rachel Carson's book *Silent Spring* was a grim reminder of how seriously we were upsetting the balance in nature. The United States Government report on *Smoking and Health* pointed to the much higher incidence of cancer and heart disease among smokers than nonsmokers. Along with the disturbing reports of these publications, there was an increasing use of mind-altering drugs such as the hallucinogenic LSD, marijuana, and "hard" drugs such as heroin and cocaine. The use of the drug thalidomide by pregnant women in Europe produced deformed children, until the side-effects of this medication were understood.

You are offered two alternatives: either to turn your back on the decaying quality of life or to make some effort to restore order to the chaos that man's insensitivity has produced.

Uranus Conjunct Ascendant

Uranus conjunct the Ascendant shows that you are individuality personified. You have a personal chemistry that never fails to stimulate people to be friendly toward you. You are admired by most but feared by some, especially those who feel overpowered by your total self-awareness. You tend to make people feel insignificant in your presence, although you certainly don't try to give that impression. No one should feel any discomfort with you because you project yourself freely and honestly.

You relate easily to all types of people and are friendly to everyone, regardless of their social status. You don't measure anyone by the cut of their clothes, their school, or the social register, for you are intimately aware of the unfair limitations imposed by social custom and tradition. You view everyone you meet as a unique and individual person who cannot possibly be categorized except as a member of the human species. You are intuitively aware that the progress of man and of the society he conceives and constructs depend explicitly upon the individuality of its members. Therefore you aggressively defend every person's right to be an individual. In your view, the past and its traditions are important only for the lessons learned, and the future is possible only when our grip on the past is finally released.

Concerned primarily with the future, you are eager to participate in the development of a higher consciousness, which will be the nucleus for the greater awareness of man. You reject as inadequate a reality that is measured merely by its physical dimensions. Your greatest value to others is that you can give them access to explore the new freedom, a freedom that is denied them if they turn away from it.

Neptune Conjunct Ascendant

The conjunction of Neptune to the Ascendant shows that you are very sensitive and perhaps psychic. Your grip on the real world is loose; you need to grasp it more firmly. You are often away in a world of your own where you can escape the harshness of reality, which is especially painful to you. You are so physically sensitive to the injustices you observe in society that they can easily make you ill. Because your environment has such a powerful effect, you should try to make some contribution to relieve your anxieties about allowing these negative conditions to exist. You are particularly sensitive to the depressing social, economic, and inhuman conditions that plague much of the world's population. You are sympathetic toward the oppressed, understanding of the emotionally disturbed, and forgiving to those who seem guiltless in their transgressions against society.

When people fail in their dealings with you, you tend to give them the benefit of the doubt and silently bear your disappointment. You easily become distraught over conditions you are powerless to do anything about, and your feelings of guilt and failure can make you withdraw into a world that is safe from responsibility. If the abrasive effect of direct encounter is severe enough, you might resort to artificial means of inducing relief from painful reality. But it is especially important to avoid drugs and alcohol, since they increase your vulnerability. You attract strange characters and are especially vulnerable to powerful individuals who can gain control over you. You should associate with persons who have their feet on the ground to compensate for your aimless wandering temperament. You need to be stabilized in reality, where you can do a great deal of good. There is a great need for your sympathetic understanding, and you don't have the right to turn down anyone who extends a hand for help.

Pluto Conjunct Ascendant

The conjunction of Pluto to the Ascendant means that you have the power to determine the kind of world that can be constructed from its available resources. You know how difficult it is to function and develop under environmental conditions and economic pressures that frustrate you at every turn, but it is in your grasp to arouse the people to make public officials yield to their demands. You can play an important role in urging the public to eliminate the parasites who cause decaying social conditions and the depraved human qualities that lead to them. Because you speak and conduct yourself with authority, no one dares dismiss you as a troublesome critic. You are not easily aroused to taking action unless the situation is serious. If it is, you will use every trick you can devise to compel those responsible to take the actions that are necessary to restore order from chaos. You won't be satisfied until a system is working effectively.

You don't tolerate abuse in your personal affairs either. In general you know what you want out of life and are ready to make any investment in talent and effort to realize your goals. You defend those entrusted to your care, and the people you love know that you will protect their interests at all costs. You must guard against driving yourself or others to excess. Choose your adversaries with care, or you could antagonize someone who would deal violently with you. You tend to bring out the worst qualities in people.

Chapter Two

Sextiles

The sextile aspect combines the dynamics of planets that are separated by an angle of 60º. The signs occupied by the planets involved are congenial whether they are positive or negative, and this sympathetic relationahip is transmitted to the planets. The only exception to this is when the planets are related by more than 60º, as when one planet is in a late degree of one sign and the other is in an early degree of the other sign. This is referred to as a disassociate sextile, and the effect is weakened to some extent.

The sextile aspect compels the planets' influences to function mainly in the intellectual world of ideas. This aspect shows how a person thinks and what subjects are of great interest. The mentality is sharpened. The individual is bright, curious, inventive, clever, articulate, and communicative. There is considerable ease in gathering information and skill in using it effectively. The sextile has many of the qualities usually associated with the signs Gemini and Aquarius and with their ruling planets, Mercury and Uranus. It denotes the ability to understand complex subjects and to translate them intelligibly for others to understand. It shows eagerness for conversation that is sociable, creative and informative. The sextile is especially useful for creativity, since it provides a medium for expression, either in speaking or writing. It shows much flexibility of opinion, because the person having this aspect is able to continually adapt to new or additional information.

The sextile inclines the person to enjoy broad social contacts, which will enrich his life. It shows the person to be nonselective in choosing people to associate with and undemanding of those whose mental abilities are less developed.

Sun Sextile Moon

The Sun sextile the Moon indicates that, as a whole, your life will be reasonably happy and essentially tranquil. You relate easily to people in

71

general and will enjoy a lifelong pleasant relationship with your parents and other members of your family. You maintain a well-balanced attitude toward both the past and the present. Deriving much benefit from your experiences, you use the lessons effectively to become successful in future enterprises. You are sufficiently strong-willed to assert yourself when necessary, but you are careful not to offend people who may be sensitive. You try to treat people as you want to be treated, and your consideration makes you well liked. You understand people and make allowances for their negative qualities while enjoying them for their good points.

A very creative person, you have a wealth of ideas to draw on. Communication is relatively easy for you, and you strive for mutual understanding between you and the people you deal with. You are not afraid to make concessions to others if it will promote greater rapport between you. Because you are secure about your goals, you never really feel threatened when challenged. You feel that even though you may lose a few, you will win at least as many and probably more. Your ego is important, to be sure, but not so much that you would seek another person's submission in order to satisfy it. You prefer to relate to people as equals, regardless of their station in life.

There is every indication that you will succeed as a person. You can achieve fulfillment in whatever profession you choose and simply need the right opportunity to express your creative talents. You are on good terms with your superiors and co-workers, and you respect their trust in you. Because you are a good listener as well as a good talker, you learn well and can use what you learn.

You remember the lessons of the past, but you have no desire to return to it. You are content with the present, knowing it will provide you with what you need to courageously face the future, and you are grateful for it all.

You are equally comfortable with men and women. Your early relationship with your own parents has given you a healthy attitude about people and resulted in no important inner conflicts. You can probably always count on your parents to give you a helping hand when you need it. Your children will learn your uncomplicated outlook on life, and they will benefit from it as much as you have. If you can operate from your home, you will enjoy your career interests. Wherever you go in pursuit of your destiny, you will tend to establish residence, if only for a short time.

Sun Sextile Mars

The Sun sextile Mars provides you with such an incredible amount of energy that you can accomplish more work than two other people. You are gifted with many creative ideas, which you constantly strive to express. You use your intellectual abilities to find the best way to apply your special talents. Although firm in your opinions and forceful in projecting them, you are open to suggestions from others, realizing that their ideas are probably as valid as your own. You don't usually take action without thinking out the probable result, and anything you do has your stamp of approval. Although you may not enjoy doing so, you will admit any errors that you make.

Communicating is your greatest strength. You can find success in such areas as reporting, writing, teaching, the communications media, advising and speaking for persons in positions of leadership, or detective work. In such endeavors you could rise to a prominent position and gain recognition for your achievements and persistent striving for excellence.

Your avocational interests are varied; you could obtain great satisfaction from tutoring young people or from working with youth groups, preparing them for the future. You are an avid reader because you know that your competitive position depends upon maintaining an alert interest in contemporary affairs. You also want to be ready to accept an opportunity when it is presented. In your opinion a person who doesn't read has no advantage over one who can't. Though not particularly fond of reading, you want to improve your skills in your current or future employment. You'd rather stay in the mainstream, where the action is.

Although you can be pushy in expressing yourself, you generally relate to people in a polished way that doesn't threaten them. You are rarely on the defensive because you are secure in what you know. You seek the company of gentler persons who can compensate for your aggressiveness. You respect those who are less articulate and admire them for whatever talents they may possess.

Your physical desires are fairly strong, but you usually want to know a person quite well before you begin a romantic alliance.

Sun Sextile Jupiter

The Sun sextile Jupiter shows that you are philosophical, curious, and sympathetic, and you approach your goals with enthusiasm. You understand your capabilities and have great confidence in what you can accomplish. Your early conditioning has prepared you to strive for whatever goals you decide on. Only rarely do you indulge in pessimism. Even when you are the butt of the joke you can laugh at yourself, because you have a good sense of humor. You are serious about your life direction, but not ponderously so. You are quick to respond to opportunities, sometimes too quick for your own good. Although you have a fair appreciation of your limits, at times you push your luck.

Communication is the medium by which you put your best foot forward. For this reason, education, the news media, philosophy, law, theatrical enterprises, public relations, or the ministry would be excellent avenues for your creative expression. You are skillful in debate and can be devastating in an argument because you are so well armed with information. Because of your flair for theatrics, your delivery is dramatic and articulate. People will believe what you say, and you are subtly persuasive. Your role-playing is artful and convincing, and you fairly glow with the effects you produce. You are an avid conversationalist and never lack a subject for interesting discussion.

You are an "idea person" who needs constant opportunities to apply your creative thinking. The daily demands of routine obligations frustrate your intellectual enthusiasm and crush your creativity. You work best when you can decide for yourself how to use your talents for the best results. Rigid schedules are especially annoying to you, for they sometimes force you to submit work that does not meet your own standard of accomplishment.

Because you are an outgoing person, you probably have a wide circle of friends who enjoy your breezy manner. You usually cultivate the friendship of other individuals who are optimistic, courageous, and impatient with routine. You indulge yourself in acquiring the so-called "goodthings" in life, and you generously help others who have similar tastes. Pursuits that enable you to unwind from the demands of your career appeal to you, such as sporting events, travel, and other recreational activities. You generally get a lot out of life because you put a lot into it.

Sun Sextile Saturn

The sextile from the Sun to Saturn indicates that you have great depth of understanding and the capacity to help others understand what you have learned. You are modest in assessing your self-worth and are aware of your limitations, but you also know how to make the most of your potentials. You have a respect for authority and competence. Because you rarely voice your opinion unless asked, your views are considered authoritative and sincere. Usually you prefer to remain in the background and let others with greater needs gain the attention. You don't need anyone's approval for your actions because you generally observe the rules of good behavior.

Although you have a driving ambition to succeed, you methodically plan each step toward your goals, quietly and without fanfare. You have a distinct rapport with your professional superiors because you carefully avoid threatening them with your ambition. You always extract important lessons from your experiences.

You are suited for such occupations as teaching, research and development, industrial management, politics, or law. In any of these professions you would very probably rise to a management position. You take your work seriously and always strive to maintain your position by staying abreast of new developments in your field. It would be difficult for anyone to remove you from your position, because you have gained it by demonstrating competence, efficiency, integrity, and sincerity. In other words, you've earned everything you've gained.

You relate well to anyone who upholds the virtues mentioned above. Your mate probably shares your high regard for tradition and orderliness. Together you plan for a future made secure by your efforts.

Sun Sextile Uranus

With the Sun sextile Uranus, it is important for you to maintain communication with other people at all times. You are eager to share your experiences with others and impatient with those who are unwilling to include you in theirs. Your opinions are willful and outspoken, but you can usually justify them in such a way that they are accepted. Your attitudes are relatively uninhibited and not bound by tradition. You find life exciting, and you live every moment of every day. Boredom is something you never have to cope with because your mind is so active. In your philosophical view of life, everything has meaning. You take even negative incidents positively, so that you are rarely "down in the dumps."

Your original thinking and strong will are suited to the fields of politics, science, or education. You can adapt to any profession that clearly has the objective of improving the masses. You are able to project your ideas and opinions without demanding that others yield to them unquestioningly. But you are impatient with dawdlers who continually put off making decisions. Your development is accelerated, and your intuition is so finely honed that you can instantly evaluate facts and render a judgment.

Teaching others is probably your best avenue of expression. You can effectively dramatize knowledge to make learning easy for your students. Truth is something you insist on, and you deal harshly with those who distort it in their dealings with you.

Your restless mind and eager disposition contribute significantly to your romantic relationships. You are broad-minded and understanding of human nature. Although you will tolerate failure, you do not accept dishonesty from anyone with whom you are emotionally involved. You can easily detach yourself from an insincere or dishonest individual, as though you had never had any feelings for that person.

Sun Sextile Neptune

The Sun sextile Neptune shows that you are deeply aware of your creative potential. You understand your social responsibilities and know that you can be instrumental in relieving much of the suffering you observe. However, you prefer to leave the burden of changing adverse social conditions to those who have the strength and determination for it. Your task is to assist those who are affected by such conditions, to treat the symptoms. You are extremely sensitive, and any rejection of your attempts to render service hurts you deeply. This can cause some difficulty, since it is so important for you to relate to others in personal contact.

Your professional possibilities are quite varied. Like a chameleon, you can take on whatever characteristics are required in your occupation. In other words, you can "fit in" despite your personal preferences. Ideally, your work should involve public-related activities. Your imagination and creative talents could be exploited in writing or the communications media in general. Even working in a travel agency or on ships, planes, or resorts where people unwind would be an excellent outlet for you. If you are motivated to work alone, you must still relate to the public in some way. Arts and crafts, writing, or drama would draw out the best in you. Your sense of drama is an asset in bringing attention to your pursuits. Your inspiration and imagination become "alive" when you focus your energy on them.

Your personal associations are as varied as your professional interests. You freely relate to all kinds of people and are rarely shocked by the many characters you encounter. You admire the successful and sympathize with those who fail, but you are not demanding or intolerant of either. Generally you allow others to find their own level of accomplishment. You are particularly drawn to individuals who are sure of their own identity.

You accept the challenge of opportunities others would avoid, in order to prove to yourself that you can succeed in spite of complications. You are somewhat of a visionary and can "picture" the outcome of any situation you are involved in.

Sun Sextile Pluto

The sextile between your Sun and Pluto shows that you are fully aware of the intensity of your will. Deep within, you understand that you can accomplish almost anything you want without too much resistance from others. You realize that without knowledge, however, you can't fulfill your destiny.

Your ability to communicate your thoughts is so great that others are mesmerized by your words. This ease of communication is your greatest asset. You also have a flair for handling other people's resources, and you easily inspire their confidence in your abilities. Because your talents are so precious, you owe it to the world, as well as to yourself, to make them available to everyone.

You constantly pursue solutions to social conditions that seem to be unjust, disordered, or chaotic. You have the courage to attack environmental problems head on and the fortitude to see that they are corrected. You are tireless in your efforts to arouse the public to bring pressure on the proper authorities and force them to make necessary changes. Your dramatic qualities ideally suit you to be the spokesman for change or adjustment.

Even in more personal relationships, you strongly vitalize others when they fail, and you can restore their faith in themselves after reversals. You stimulate others to regain their self-confidence when they need a boost.

You are drawn to complex subjects such as mysticism, yoga, and the occult in general, which you understand easily. Your strong psychic abilities serve you even when you aren't aware of it. This is probably the key to your ability to sense immediately what is right or wrong about a situation. You don't have to make a logical appraisal or a deductive analysis to arrive at solutions to problems. Some people might even regard you as a mystic, since you always seem to have the right answer when posed with a problem.

Sun Sextile Ascendant

The Sun sextile the Ascendant shows that it is easy for you to express yourself. You project your ego with finesse and articulate skill, so that when you speak, people are usually attentive. You have an authoritative manner, and what you say adds to your credibility. Because you feel warmly disposed to people in general, you expect them to feel comfortable in your company. Your youthful outlook enables you to enjoy everyone, regardless of age, and it allows them to relate easily to you. Your magnetic charm encourages the people you know to do favors for you, because you have convinced them that you don't want anything from them. You have a breezy disposition and an infectious sense of humor. A good conversationalist, you always have topics to discuss that liven up a social gathering.

You are inclined to become restless in your career because you may think that you haven't been given the opportunity to demonstrate your creative potential. Without realizing it, you sometimes appear so sure of yourself that your superiors feel threatened about their own jobs. The fact that you have a wealth of ideas to draw on also makes them uncomfortable. You hate to think that you are being "used" by others for their exclusive benefit, but you should refrain from expressing this thought carelessly.

Your way with people is charming and delightful. You excel in making social contacts that can be helpful, but you rarely want anything from those you care for except sincere friendship. You insist on being honest and frank with everyone you deal with. Subterfuge and deceit are intolerable to you. If these tactics are used in a relationship, you sever further relations with those involved, and thereafter it is almost impossible for them to regain your lost confidence.

Moon Sextile Mercury

The Moon sextile Mercury gives you a sensitive and thoughtful disposition. You absorb information almost greedily, your level of comprehension is highly developed, and your ability to recall is above average. You have a strong desire to be useful to the people you deal with, which motivates you to continually broaden your knowledge. Because your emotions are rarely in conflict with your intellect, you can successfully deal with your problems without complicating them further. You enjoy the friendship of many kinds of people because you are flexible enough to make allowances for them. Fascinated by anything that arouses your curiosity, you aren't satisfied until you have explored it thoroughly. You are well read on many subjects. A delightful conversationalist, you inject charm and humor into any discussion and never fail to keep your listener's attention. You are so sensitive to the thoughts of those around you that you can "feel" it when they are dishonest or insincere. Your positive and happy disposition seems to spread to everyone around you.

Your talent for communication can be useful in many professional applications. Public relations would be ideal for you, but you could succeed in any endeavor that brings you before large or small groups of people. You make others feel comfortable with your genuine concern for them, as you imply that they are the most important people you ever dealt with. Your tact and diplomacy are so great that even your competitors have to admire you for these qualities. You are never too busy to take care of the endless details that most people find obnoxious.

Emotionally drawn to persons who are educated, bright, and cheerful, you can relate best to an individual who has defined a goal and has laid a plan for achieving it. You always insist on total communication and believe that silence is dull rather than golden. You want to share in your mate's plans for the future and participate in making the memories you will someday look back on together.

You can enrich your life with many interests. Although you seem attracted to hobbies you can pursue at home, you would enjoy the added social factor of outside interests. Perhaps you are a joiner and will find time for civic activities, or you might prefer functions that involve active participation by the whole family. In any case, you impart a broadening quality to those you love and to the environment you create for them.

Moon Sextile Venus

The sextile from the Moon to Venus indicates both the desire and the disposition for a happy and rewarding partnership. Knowing quite clearly what you want out of life, you freely communicate this to a prospective mate. You know you can offer many personal resources and can use your talents imaginatively to sustain a marriage. In order to add dimension to your relationship and maintain continuing interest in each other, you try to share every experience with your mate. You are creative, sympathetic, tender, and affectionate and will go to great lengths to introduce whatever is necessary to protect the relationship. You are prepared to compromise, and you expect the same from your mate. True sharing is the backbone supporting your mutual concern for each other. You can weather many stormy incidents that may otherwise threaten you, because you are secure in your feelings about the one you love, and this serves as a binding agent.

An extremely sociable person, you can always find something pleasant to say about everyone. You are optimistic that the most difficult situations will work out eventually, so you are not excessively preoccupied with them. There is no problem that cannot be made less burdensome if it is discussed sincerely.

You enrich your free time by involving yourself in social organizations, working with young people, or by teaching and learning new skills on your own. You are fairly clever in handling your financial resources and know how to stretch them imaginatively so that you always have enough money. You may resent it, however, if someone, say a relative of your partner, makes demands on your finances. You are conservative enough not to jeopardize your own family's security to satisfy another's needs. When you feel there is a genuine need, you are not indifferent to it, but you resent being told when and how much you should give.

In general, your affairs should not suffer from any tedious complications.

You have good reasoning ability, you make concessions when they seem advised, and you rarely fail to discuss a problem that develops between you and others through some misunderstanding. You consider silence indefensible if it alienates someone whose differences could otherwise be resolved.

Your own children will enjoy and benefit from having a parent who talks with them and shows understanding of their "overwhelming" problems and crises. There will be very little generation gap between you and your children, because you make it clear that you are genuinely concerned and always available for serious conversation.

Moon Sextile Mars

The sextile between the Moon and Mars shows that you tend to react emotionally when provoked. You are aware of this, however, so you try to keep your feelings in check in order to make a logical appraisal before reacting impulsively. You will still flare up on occasion, mainly when you are feeling argumentative and want to get something off your chest. But the results of such flare-ups should not be difficult to deal with. You don't generally hold grudges, preferring to clear the air between you and the other person by discussing your differences. You will be admired for not ending your outbursts with arrogant finality. Not wanting to close the door to any relationship, you try instead to leave it ajar so you will be able to communicate with that individual in the future. This is a sign of developing maturity.

You are a vital, energetic, and exciting person who can charm people with your infectious and personable manner. You respond to people eagerly, and your enthusiasm stimulates them to respond to you as well. You are a good companion to those close to you and on good terms with most, if not all, of your friends and associates. Knowing that you react to people in an emotionally biased way, you give them the benefit of the doubt in any confrontation. Your emotional vulnerability shows that you are human and not indifferent to the feelings of others. Because you learn from your experiences, your future is brighter with hope and anticipation of continued development.

Your ability to think twice before you act allows you to avoid many unnecessary complications in your dealings with people. You do this because you know that your first response is probably based only on emotion and therefore invalid. You can succeed in any occupation that brings you into close personal contact with the public or with fellow employees. You respond to challenges and are not terribly upset if you don't succeed with all of them.

Whatever your role in life, you will enjoy and appreciate it. You value your rights enough to fight for them when you feel they are threatened. Your domestic affairs are a source of pleasure and contentment, and your home is a refuge when your job puts you under the pressure of competition.

Avoid eating when you are angry and don't take your job home with you. Psychologically, you are a well-oriented individual without severe maladjustment between your emotions and your feelings of aggression. You should enjoy pleasing contacts with people at all times.

Moon Sextile Jupiter

The sextile from the Moon to Jupiter gives you considerable intellectual ability, modified by sensitivity of feeling. Therefore your personality is quite varied and exciting, since your emotional responses are accompanied by intellectual curiosity. You are quite effective in dealing with people because you have a well-developed understanding of their motivations in material affairs and relationships. Very little escapes your notice, and you are capable of absorbing enormous amounts of information. You can hold your own in a social gathering because you can discuss many subjects with better-than-average comprehension. Your friends and associates are kindly disposed toward you because you never forget those who have assisted you in the past.

You derive enormous benefit from every experience and can translate these beneficial responses into tools for future use. You can succeed in many occupations that require intellectual development and the ability to apply knowledge in solving daily problems. Medicine, education, public relations, legal endeavors, financial affairs, stock brokerage, training and rehabilitation of handicapped persons, and welfare programs are some of the fields in which your talents could be used successfully. Your excellent memory serves you well in earning a living. You are sympathetic toward less fortunate persons, and you help them face their problems with greater hope and optimism.

A journal of your life, including your relationships, your problems, and their solutions as well as the philosophy you have developed would make quite an impressive book. As a writer you could draw on your vast experience for material that would be both exciting and sincere.

You are warm in your personal contacts, sincere and honest in your efforts to stimulate the best responses in others. You have high hopes for acquiring a true companion in the person you choose to share your life. You want to share both the great and small issues with that person and to know that the relationship enhances each of you. The supreme optimist, you are proud and sometimes vain, but always humble in your genuine desire to be useful and helpful to anyone who seeks your protective guidance.

People are never in doubt about your intentions when you let them into your life. You guide them when you can or refer them to others when you can't, and you don't generally judge people for their frailties. You can always see the potential good in people, even those who may have gotten off to a bad start.

Moon Sextile Saturn

Your Moon sextile Saturn shows that you are serious, reserved, and cautious in your feelings toward others. As a result of early conditioning, you always try to understand the people who mean something to you. Perhaps you were expected to listen and help your brothers and sisters when they brought their problems to you. Now you are always ready to discuss any problem that develops between you and another person. You realize that emotions must be understood before any conflict can be resolved. This realistic approach to emotional difficulties can generally produce a constructive effect.

Your native intelligence, integrity, and common sense should enable you to achieve success in your occupation. Fields such as law, medicine, industrial management, politics, education, or public relations are especially fitting for your talents. You are patient and practical in coping with everyday problems because you are well aware that you achieve the best results that way. You are orderly in your thinking and don't allow yourself to indulge in fanciful, emotional daydreams. You are modestly ambitious and willing to learn as you progress in whatever you choose. However, you would not sacrifice integrity for the sake of ambition.

What you lack in enthusiasm, you make up for in determination. You communicate well, and teaching could be a useful means of expression for you. You are self-disciplined and impatient with "dawdlers" who waste your time and theirs. Students would certainly learn from you, because you project your knowledge with clarity and authority.

You enjoy the company of selected friends whom you can confide in and trust. Very probably you will find comfort and emotional satisfaction among persons who are similarly dedicated to truth. Your mate will have to be serious and thoughtful. Even if your partner has not achieved success, you will accept someone who has established plans for achieving goals and whose intentions are sincere. You will want to help your mate become successful and would not feel left out if professional demands required absence from you. By itself, a sexual relationship is totally inadequate for you. You respond to persons with substantial resources of mind and spirit and stable emotions.

In your free time you often read or study, recognizing that growth is possible only if one continues to expand in knowledge. You always want to be prepared to take advantage of an opportunity that could prove beneficial in the long run.

Moon Sextile Uranus

With the Moon sextile Uranus, you realized early in life that you were different from other people. You were unique in that you understood the significance of your experiences much more than others ever could. You learned something from every situation or event that involved you in any way. Perhaps your parents asked why you weren't like all the other kids. Your emotional and intellectual development was accelerated, mainly because you are not blindly loyal to the past. You respect the lessons of the past, but you set your sights toward the challenging future.

Your best expression is in teaching, because your feeling of excitement in discovery is instantly communicated to others. History, particularly comes alive as you discuss, examine, and derive meaning from it. You effectively dramatize the importance of history, which can benefit others. You especially want people to enjoy the freedom from ignorance that serves progress. You encourage them to put aside emotional loyalties that hinder individual development.

Regardless of the particular profession you follow, you have enormous opportunities to stimulate others. You would be capable as a writer, reporter, politician, or a researcher in medicine. In science you would be certain to make distinct progress. However, you are impatient with the laborious effort often required in research and development, and you would probably work best if you could determine your own pace. Your highly developed intuition allows you to solve many problems with amazing ease. For this reason you might have found the usual pace in school too slow for your accelerated learning ability.

You are drawn to relationships that involve your logical nature, realizing that a strictly emotional rapport is not enough to bind you permanently to anyone.

Moon Sextile Neptune

The Moon sextile Neptune indicates that you have a vivid imagination. You are psychically sensitive and have the intellectual skill for expressing yourself creatively. Your deep feelings urge you to respond to your social obligations in some way. Decayed or otherwise unacceptable social conditions arouse sympathetic anxieties within you. You are reasonably explicit in voicing your objections, and you can stimulate public anger to remedy conditions among the socially or economically disadvantaged.

Your involvement with the outside world provides you with several excellent career outlets. Writing is particularly recommended as a profession, as well as any other work associated with the gathering of facts and dissemination of truth. The essential factor is for you to serve as intermediary for the public welfare. Another possibility would be to work on a newspaper "task force" investigating the activities of public officials who are alleged to be serving themselves rather than the public. You have a capacity for alleviating people's burdens. As a doctor you could skillfully diagnose complaints, as an artist you could easily convey any message or sentiment, as a nutritionist you could serve the masses by advocating better eating habits.

You are sensible about personal relationships and are rarely upset when people demonstrate their failings. Your understanding and tolerance enable you to fully experience all levels of human expression. Be careful, however, not to overcompensate for those who may deliberately exploit your natural desire to be helpful.

You should enjoy a rich and rewarding life. You are able to fulfill all your domestic obligations in addition to serving your community when required. Save some precious solitary moments for yourself in order to regain physical energy and recharge your psychic batteries.

Moon Sextile Pluto

With Moon sextile Pluto, you have an intellectual understanding of love. You always try to understand the motives of others, especially those with whom you are emotionally involved. Love is important to you, and your emotions are powerful. You are demonstrative of your feelings and expect others to be, as well. Hearing someone express their love for you is very important.

Your emotional priorities are reasonably well established. You can provide the warmth and tenderness your children or close friends need, while reserving the ardent side of your nature for intimate moments with the one you love.

You are responsive to the suffering of others and will offer your services to provide relief. Imaginative and resourceful in handling your daily affairs, you readily adopt new ideas to make life easier and less complicated. You are concerned about the environment and about your civic responsibilities.

Your special talent is your ability to communicate with young people in order to better understand them. They confide in you because your sincere concern makes them feel secure. With you they are not threatened by authority, but accept and respect it. You communicate warmth and tenderness, which helps young people become stabilized in their independence as they mature.

You have good business sense and are efficient in management. These characteristics will help you gain financial security. You are orderly and know how to unclutter your life by letting go of nonessential elements that interfere with progress. With your capacity to respond to others, you are suited to any occupation that involves meeting the public, such as public relations, insurance, finance, rehabilitation, or physical therapy.

Moon Sextile Ascendant

The Moon sextile the Ascendant shows that you try to understand why you react so sensitively to what people say to you. You also try to understand the various circumstances in your life, so there is harmony in these areas of your life. It wasn't always this way; until you matured, you felt apprehensive that people were criticizing you, or that you were handling situations less skillfully than you should. Even now, there are times when you have some difficulty in separating fact from fiction, but you are learning all the time. You are not becoming less sensitive, just more understanding. You tend to become overly emotional in your dealings with people and to underestimate your competence in successfully handling the situations that develop. The truth is, most people consider you quite competent, so stop worrying about it.

You have a wealth of ideas, which you should capitalize on. Perhaps in your work you can make meaningful suggestions that could be used constructively by your superiors. Your work is very important to you. You accept your tasks eagerly and want to prove your competence by performing them well. In reaching the goals you set for yourself, you continually strive for excellence. Once you get over your feeling of inferiority, you can succeed in meeting any challenge from competitors.

In a personal relationship you hope to be appreciated for the contributions you make to sustain it. You are more than able to share mutual interests without shirking your responsibilities. Most people realize this, and some may try to take advantage of your compliant nature. You have a wide circle of friends with whom you enjoy many pleasant social gatherings. You love to be included in social affairs where you can converse with people on a variety of subjects. You are fairly well read and can make a substantial contribution to discussions on many topics.

Mercury Sextile Venus

The sextile of Mercury and Venus shows that you have an affable manner and social grace. You get along well with most people because you know when you should make compromises in order to maintain harmony. But this doesn't mean that you give in when you know the other person is in error. You generally try to be fair in making judgments so that you do not offend people without just cause. You know how to express your opinions skillfully so that no one feels threatened or intimidated by you, and you are resourceful in gathering information to document what you say. Not usually hostile or argumentative, you prefer to give everyone you deal with the benefit of the doubt when a difference of opinion arises. It is part of your refined nature that you let people have the opportunity to convince you of their point of view before you take any action.

Your gentle and easy-going personality is an asset in most professions, but you might find it difficult to cope with the abrasive elements of close and direct competition. This possibility should be taken into consideration when choosing a profession. It is better to work alone or with a small group of people so you won't have to worry about troublesome competitors.

You could find enjoyment in public speaking or the dramatic arts. Writing could also prove satisfying because you have a natural talent for expressing yourself well. Your imaginative style is fresh and charming and appeals to people who want to be entertained as well as informed. You are most comfortable with subjects that are not too dense and cumbersome.

You are fairly clever in devising schemes for improving your financial condition. You use your talents effectively and can usually translate your ideas into cash. Your associates will support you in your enterprises, because your balanced judgment reassures them that you can't be too far off base. You convince them you will succeed and generally win the cooperation you need. But you don't ask others to take risks you aren't willing to take. Because you are careful to adequately prepare yourself in advance of any action, the element of risk is greatly reduced anyway. And you shy away from complex projects that require prolonged effort before any benefits can be obtained.

Mercury Sextile Mars

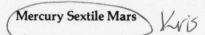 *Kris*

With Mercury sextile Mars, your mentality is sharpened by an insatiable curiosity that will not rest until you have acquired all the knowledge you desire. But obviously that point will never be reached, and you will never stop learning. You make sure that you are reasonably well informed before making any statements, because you want the approval of the people you are talking to. You express yourself imaginatively, and your delivery sparkles with drama. Even people whose opinions differ from yours are convinced by your arguments and won over to your position. You know how far you can extend your ideas to people before reaching a point of diminishing returns. Usually they will concede to you long before this happens. You don't jump to conclusions without being sure of the facts on which you base them.

You are a genuinely friendly person and don't wait to be introduced to others, for you see no reason to waste time waiting for a formal introduction. You enjoy meeting people and conversing with them. Although you are a persuasive talker, you are also a good listener. That is one way you've learned so much; when you need information you are never afraid to ask someone who knows.

Your friendly attitude and mental agility can bring you success in many endeavors. You may be inclined toward such fields as law, teaching, writing, public relations, or any occupation that requires trigger-fast mental responses. You have the mental chemistry to succeed as a reporter, and the mobility of the profession would especially appeal to you. Your eager interest in anything new would never lack stimulation in this work, and you could write interestingly and breathe life into even the most somber subjects. Communication is your strong talent, and you should always strive to exploit this ability. Politics would also stimulate your talents. You enjoy a good fight, and there would be excellent opportunities to present your opinions to those who want to be informed.

You are friendly to everyone, but heaven help the person who tries to deceive you. Your response is as sharp and incisive as a surgeon's scalpel, and that person will know better than to provoke you again. You are truthful even when it hurts, but you are also able to admit it and laugh at yourself when you make a stupid mistake.

Mercury Sextile Jupiter

Your Mercury sextile to Jupiter indicates that your mind is never at rest. You have a limitless thirst for knowledge and an awesome capacity to accumulate information. But you aren't satisfied with simply being informed; applying your knowledge constructively is as important to you as acquiring it in the first place. You have excellent reasoning ability and keen judgment. Because of your masterful command of language, you can speak and write convincingly. Truth is very important to you, and you will challenge anyone who makes a suspicious-sounding statement. Leaving nothing to chance, you will persist until you discover whether the statement is correct. It truly bothers you when public speakers make irresponsible remarks on a subject about which they are totally misinformed.

Knowledge can be a weapon in the wrong hands, and you are quick to respond when you observe it being used to gain control of people's minds. Adolf Hitler had this planetary combination, and history documents his use of rhetoric. Temperamentally unable to stand such abuse, you will challenge the right of anyone to take such liberties with the public.

Education, public speaking, public relations, journalism, and writing novels with historical and timely themes—these are some ways you could use your creative resources and inspiration. Even in fields not mentioned above, you could succeed if the essential function were communication of classical knowledge or current information for practical application.

Your desire for knowledge and search for truth will never end. As a teacher, you would inspire your students to seek the heights of their own development.

Travel would be especially broadening for you, for it would help you to understand the differences among national and ethnic origins. You could translate your reactions into a thoughtful essay that would be illuminating to the reader.

While you may not be a fervent member of any organized religious organization, you recognize the importance of believing in something. You allow everyone the liberty of his own beliefs, and you certainly would not try to force your ideology on others.

Mercury Sextile Saturn

Your Mercury sextile to Saturn shows that your intellect is well developed and that you are resourceful, thoughtful, and organized. You believe in yourself and are willing to demonstrate your capabilities. You are courageous in stating your opinions about subjects that interest you because you know you are well informed. You can usually document what you say by giving statistics or citing the evidence on which your opinion is based. You seek the truth so that you will always be secure in your dealings with people.

Early in life you learned that you owed it to yourself to capitalize on your talents. You disciplined yourself to be as fully informed as possible, knowing this would sustain you when competing with others. You always have the answers that enable you to progress in your field of endeavor. There are literally hundreds of occupations open to you because you can learn to do whatever you want. Some suitable fields would be education, politics, science, research, industrial management, mining, conservation of natural resources, government, or architecture. You know how to plan for what you want and persist with great determination until you get it. Success comes through no accident or stroke of luck.

Your youth might have been lonely because you were uncomfortable with others of your own age. Perhaps you were precocious in your development and preferred the company of older persons with whom you could enjoy more mature conversations. Your memory is good and your comprehension better than average. You are probably one of those who became bored with school because you were required to endure the classroom pace of the average student.

You are an eternal student, one who will always continue to accumulate knowledge, whether formally or otherwise. You have an insatiable desire to know as much as you can. This is one reason for your polished social behavior. Your deportment reflects good taste, and you are admired by your superiors as well as your inferiors.

Once successful in your particular field, you may turn to writing about your exploits as an avocation to enrich your private life. If you choose writing as a profession, your work will probably have historical settings or will record current information for posterity. You would bring great depth of comprehension to your writing, and the documentation would probably be monumental.

Persons who are mature, honest, and sincere appeal to you particularly, and your partnership would be securely based on mutual understanding and respect. Your marriage could be platonic and yet be as solid as one that is more sexually oriented. A merely physical relationship would not be enough for you. In later life it is possible that you will have a May-December partnership, if there is sufficient intellectual rapport.

Mercury Sextile Uranus

The sextile between Mercury and Uranus indicates that your intellectual ability is above average. You are impatient with ignorance, but reasonably tolerant of those who cannot learn at your pace. You are extremely alert, curious, and well-read on many subjects. Your easy way with words never ceases to fascinate your audience. You are not selfish with your knowledge, being willing to share it with anyone who shows a genuine interest. Your parents were probably amazed at your mental development, which was more advanced than the average child's. As you grew you continued to astound them by your discussions with adults, which showed genuine comprehension of difficult subjects.

Your professional goals should be in education or any other field in which you would not be mentally confined. Freedom is necessary for you to exploit your knowledge in your own unique, dramatic way and achieve the most effective results. You don't accept traditional methods unless they have been proven. Progressive in your thinking, you respect the past only for the lessons learned from it. You are inventive in finding ways to light the spark of enthusiasm in others so they can recognize their own potentials.

To be successful you do need the self-discipline of persistence. Establish definite objectives and construct a positive plan for realizing them. Don't postpone your self-expression until you have all the answers, because you never will. It is your obligation to share what you know when you discover it. New truths will be revealed to you all the years of your life.

It is not easy for you to slow down because your mind is in constant motion. Learn to unwind and relax; there's always tomorrow. Your impatience and excitability can lead to nervous exhaustion.

Mercury Sextile Neptune

The sextile from Mercury to Neptune shows you have a fertile imagination, which you use constantly in your daily life. Your intuitive insight enables you to cope quite easily with difficult problems. In your personal encounters you are thoughtful and contemplative about your varied experiences. You are eager for knowledge and for the chance to use it to benefit yourself and others. Being aware of the dangers of accepting anything at face value, you generally seek out as many details as possible in order to get at the truth. You have an insatiable curiosity, and because of your ability to interpret events, you gain more from experience than others do.

Your creative potentials permit you to choose from a variety of professions. Journalism, education, medicine, art, music, designing, and social welfare programs are some of the fields in which you could succeed. Others appreciate your skills because of your sympathetic understanding and warmth. Communication in some form should be an integral part of your professional interests. Because you communicate well, people are comfortable in your presence and relate to you freely.

In order to take advantage of your imagination and inspiration, however, you should get a higher education. You are extremely perceptive of the world around you, and with training, your possibilities are unlimited. It is essential to establish your goals early in life and realistically plan a course of action to gain them. You must avoid letting others distract you, for once you digress, it isn't easy to start over with the same enthusiasm.

Your personal relationships are usually warm and meaningful. You relate especially to philosophical people who are not preoccupied with material or physical things. Although you are an idealist, you don't really expect anyone to fulfill your image of perfection. You accept those who at least strive for perfection. You are spiritually hopeful and are guided by the realization of your moral and social responsibilities.

Kris

Mercury Sextile Pluto

The sextile between Mercury and Pluto shows that you have an analytical intellect and can understand the most elusive and obscure subjects. Your comprehension is deep, your perception keen, and you derive more meaning from your experiences than others do. Your pronounced psychic ability is used more often than you are aware. You will gradually become conscious of this faculty and learn to take advantage of it. It is easy for you to find logical explanations for most seemingly mysterious events.

There are many professions in which you could use your abilities. Criminal detection, research, psychological analysis, medicine, chemistry, and teaching are some of the fields suitable to your mental chemistry. In teaching, you would help others to seek the truth and to develop their own perception. As a researcher, you would solve problems readily because you perceive the solution psychically long before you deduce it mechanically. You have an important contribution to make in guiding people, both individually and collectively, as they search for answers.

Courageous in explorng new ideas, you assemble a wealth of information about any subject that interests you. You are reasonably self-disciplined in using your resources effectively. You can easily gain financial assistance for developing your ideas because you present them sincerely and honestly.

Your fertile imagination is expecially useful to those in your immediate environment. Social problems that seem to defy solution are suddenly easy to resolve when you examine them and offer your suggestions.

In personal relationships, you expect others to be as sincere as you are. If you find that someone is deceiving you or misrepresenting the facts, you quickly bring it to their attention. You never forget such incidents. Though you are eager to form relationships with others, when your trust is violated you can break it off forever without a single backward glance.

You will look for a partner who can provide mutual trust, sincerity, and open discussion of any problem that develops. The partner must have self-confidence and the ambition to succeed. Handling joint finances is not difficult for you, because you understand the value of money and how to get by on a modest income.

Mercury Sextile Ascendant

Mercury sextile the Ascendant shows that you are bright, witty, expressive, and extremely curious. You know exactly who you are, and you understand your capabilities and shortcomings. In dealing with people you try to accentuate your positive qualities to put others at ease. You express yourself clearly and precisely so that no one has to guess what you mean. You aren't afraid to express your views because you always examine the facts in detail before giving an opinion. Because you are so eager to be well-informed on as many subjects as possible, you are never at a loss for something to talk about. Communication is one of your skills, which you probably use extensively in your career. You are adept at writing and can certainly hold your own in a debate. Although you enjoy the mental exercise of a good argument, you are not generally argumentative. You prefer to regard it as an exciting discussion.

You work at developing your creative ideas in hopes that they may prove financially rewarding to you at some later date. Your friends encourage you to believe that your ideas are worthy, and they may even flatter you for your ingenuity and cleverness. You bring these qualities to your career, where you are so highly regarded for your worthwhile suggestions that you often work out the details required to implement them. But you must be wary of having your ideas stolen by superiors who feel threatened by the recognition you receive for your competence.

You understand what motivates people to act the way they do even when they claim a different motivation. Analytical by nature, you instinctively know what people expect from you. You function best when your job requires you to deal with the public, for you like people. You know how to relate to them harmoniously, and they feel comfortable with you. There are few individuals you can't successfully deal with.

Venus Sextile Mars

Venus sextile Mars gives you a warm, affectionate nature. Your physical needs are considerable, but you know how to contain them until you meet a person with whom you can enjoy a comfortable relationship. You don't display your feelings until you know the person fairly well and can determine whether the attraction is social and intellectual as well as physical. You realize it is necessary to compromise with people to win their continued friendship. Others are inclined to make concessions to you because your attitude encourages them to. You don't threaten other people's opinion of themselves by calling attention to their failings. Although you allow for human frailties, you expect to see the better qualities manifested.

You prefer to enjoy the more beautiful elements of life rather than preoccupy yourself with the seamy side of it. Your artistic nature inclines you to enjoy good music, fine works of art, good literature, interesting social contacts, and congenial friendships. Professional interests are not specified by this combination of planets, but you would be suited to any occupation requiring human contact in a reasonably intimate way. With people you don't know, you like to strike up a conversation over some trifling matter just so you can introduce yourself and eliminate the strain of unfamiliarity. You have an optimistic outlook and generally wear a smile that shows the world that you are a congenial person. Public relations work would be enormously satisfying to you, and people would enjoy doing business with you, since you immediately put them at ease.

You probably still have the friends you made years ago, even though you may no longer be directly in touch with them. You retain good memories of the times you enjoyed with them and tend to forget any painful incidents that may have occurred.

You may marry someone who will cooperate with you in achieving the good things in life. But whether you marry for security or for purely emotional reasons, the relationship will prove enriching.

You are inclined to be a little careless about financial matters and may spend more than you earn. In your preoccupation with the refinements of life and the fine things money can buy, you are unconcerned with economy. When you indulge in a whim, one would think you had an endless supply of cash available. Conservation is a quality you need to develop.

Venus Sextile Jupiter

The sextile from Venus to Jupiter shows that you have an outgoing personality. Your ease in expressing yourself endears you to everyone whom you deal with. You know how to say the right thing at the right time for the results you want. You are generous with praise when it is deserved, and sometimes even when it isn't. Others think of you as a kind, sympathetic, and understanding person who can always find the time for someone who needs assistance. Even people who are inclined to pessimism come away with hope because you can always visualize a solution to their problems. You don't generally interfere in the affairs of others, but you will make yourself available if necessary. Your attitude is, "If they need me, I'm as close as the telephone." You are popular because you don't make excessive demands on people, being tolerant of their frailties.

You can apply your talents in many diverse directions, for this planetary combination does not of itself give a specific talent. It does give a personable quality that is a distinct asset in certain professions and fields. Any occupation involving public contact is far easier with this kind of temperament. It would be especially beneficial, both to you and to others, to work with the public in some capacity, perhaps as social director of some large organization, as a teacher, or as a travelers' guide. Writing would be another avenue of expression for your creative ability. You are not patient enough to submit to the rigorous discipline required for writing lengthy stories, but essays or magazine articles would certainly be suitable.

The "good life," with comfortable surroundings, a lavishly furnished home, good friends, and plenty of social activity, is what you desire. You would find it difficult to accept a life of austerity that allowed only the barest essentials.

You round out your daily living with a variety of avocational interests. Reading, travel, social activities, music, art, and theater are some of the many interests that enrich you and give you pleasure. You not only enjoy these interests as a spectator, but you also participate in them when you can.

You expect honesty and sincerity from anyone with whom you have more than a casual relationship. Even among your casual acquaintances, you are "turned off" if you discover them to be deceptive, indifferent, insensitive, or coarse. You identify with people who are not content to stand still in their development and are always eager to improve themselves.

Venus Sextile Saturn

The sextile between Venus and Saturn shows that you know what you want and are willing to endure privation to get it. No sacrifice is too great if you know you can obtain your wishes thereby. Realizing that little is ever gained by wishing on a star, you accept your responsibilities as an investment in the future. You quietly go about your business, knowing that the benefits you gain will be worth the adjustments or concessions made earlier.

Your early conditioning prepared you to accept public and private responsibilities. Even among your friends, you can be depended upon to fill any obligation you've taken on. Reliable, sincere, honest, and fair, you have the respect of casual acquaintances as well as those closest to you. You are willing to earn your way and you refuse to become obligated to others by allowing them to do favors for you. Knowing you can succeed on your own merits, you pursue your goals independently and without assistance, if necessary. You are willing to meet people halfway, but no more. You like everything to be in order and plan your affairs very carefully, trusting nothing to chance.

You have exceptionally good judgment and understanding. When you communicate your ideas, other people know precisely what you mean. You are also a good listener who is willing to learn from those who have greater experience. These qualities lend themselves well to occupations in the fields of finance and banking, building trades, insurance, law, real estate, sales, or design. You are reasonably easy to get along with because of your patience and ability to meet others halfway.

You don't volunteer your feelings about a person until you are quite sure the feeling is mutual. You may even be considered shy and withdrawn, but the truth is that you make overtures only to those who mean something to you. You have social grace and polish and unfailingly conduct yourself with refinement and good taste. You dislike vulgarity, preferring to direct your attention to more cultural interests.

Your brother and/or sisters probably look to you for help in their problems because of your mature outlook on life and dependable judgment.

You are reasonably optimistic about the future, knowing you will meet the "right" person with whom you can share a rich and fulfilling life. The many good qualities you bring to a relationship can help assure its permanence.

Venus Sextile Uranus

The sextile between Venus and Uranus indicates that you are clever in social dealings, reasonably competent in facing challenges, and charming in your romantic affairs. You are sufficiently aware of others to compromise in deference to their desires. In this way you enjoy exciting and satisfying contacts with others. You project sympathy and understanding by becoming familiar with people's hopes and wishes, their goals and problems.

You have strong hopes for yourself too, but in achieving them you refuse to deprive others of their desires. You have the intellectual ability to communicate your genuine concern for others, and people regard you as basically honest and sincere. You don't threaten people or put them on the defensive. You enjoy being free, but you value freedom for others, too. Of course, you have a wide circle of friends, most of whom will remain close to you for a long time.

You are highly creative and may find expression either in socially oriented activities or in artistic pursuits. Occupations involving children and teaching would be especially beneficial, both to them and to you. Your sense of drama infuses learning with excitement.

You can relate to large groups as well as to individuals. You are detached enough to be objective and at the same time emotional enough to be sensitive. Because of these qualities you could succeed in politics. You would strive to merit the trust others have given you.

You should enjoy warm, meaningful romantic ties with your beloved. You are generally willing to make a substantial contribution to ensure that the relationship will always be exciting.

You are not overly preoccupied with money for its own sake, but consider it merely a means to satisfy your most sincere goals and objectives.

Venus Sextile Neptune

The sextile between Venus and Neptune shows that you have an active imagination and the capacity to use it effectively. You have a talent for translating your sense impressions into patterns that are easily recognized by others. You can always find a means for expressing your creativity, and this enriches your life. You are compassionate and try to understand others as they strive to solve their problems.

You can be effective in many diverse occupations. Solving problems is easy for you, especially those involving people. You have a soothing quality that calms others when they are distressed, and thus you could succeed in activities related to medicine or physical therapy. As a mediator in conflicts, you would be able to restore some semblance of order in spite of strained conditions. Social organizations are especially suited to your temperament and disposition. If you choose to function in a personal or largely private way, you are well qualified to pursue music, art, or writing.

You are a romanticist and emotionally vulnerable to people who have similar ideals. You are especially drawn to refined individuals who are as impatient as you with the ugly facts of life. In your eagerness to experience the most sublime kind of love, you are spiritually prepared to invest yourself. However, you must keep your expectations within reasonable bounds, or you will suffer disappointment.

You are generally willing to make the necessary adjustments in order to establish a relationship with someone, and you recognize that you may have to make additional compromises to sustain and secure that relationship.

There may be times when you will feel oppressed by temporary difficulties. When this happens, be alert to the negative tendency to become indolent or perhaps apathetic. Because of your sensitive nature, you respond more deeply than others might under similar circumstances.

Venus Sextile Pluto

The sextile of Venus to Pluto gives you an understanding of the power of love. You recognize that an emotional contact always requires both parties to adjust somewhat if the relationship is to be meaningful. You consider harmony an important factor, for it allows intense physical expression to endure. Consequently, you try to establish a good level of communication with your lover before making any commitment. You may find that you are attracted to certain people because of their appearance; however, when you get to know them, you are completely turned off by their superficial attitudes.

Generally, you are able to accurately perceive and evaluate people's motives in their dealings with you. You still adhere to the strong opinions about love that you formed early in life. Perhaps you feel that superficial relationships are such a waste of time and effort that you will defer any permanent tie. You intend to make sure that this relationship is broadly based on mutual interests. In other words, you don't want and will not accept just anybody.

You respond to individuals who want to develop their potentials and themselves to ever higher levels of accomplishment. You relate best to those who have more than mere physical assets to offer and who are willing to compromise and make adjustments to other people's desires.

In the broad spectrum of society, you are impatient with insensitive public servants who fail to respond to the most basic human needs. In fact, you are temperamentally capable of going to extremes in exposing those who are guilty. Singlehandedly, you may launch a campaign to uncover the most damaging evidence and then enlist the support of the media to publicize it. You are especially keen on exposing the misuse of public funds. To you, this is just as bad as being personally robbed, and you refuse to look the other way.

You would be suited to such positions as company treasurer, financial advisor, insurance agent, or lawyer in the field of wills and trusts. Any of these can bring you rewarding creative expression and the opportunity to enrich others.

Venus Sextile Ascendant

The sextile from Venus to the Ascendant shows that you strive to maintain harmonious relations with everyone you contact. You are inclined to make substantial concessions if it seems to be the only way to resolve a situation. A peacemaker by nature, you often try to smooth out the difficulties people have in reaching an amicable relationship. When you have a difference of opinion with someone, you tend to give that person the benefit of the doubt. You feel that if that person is wrong, he will eventually realize it. You don't push your views on others, preferring to find some basis for compromise.

You know what you want out of life, and you express that conviction freely. Not being a deceitful person, you consider it best to disclose that you intend to do whatever is necessary to realize your goals. Because you are somewhat timid, however, people don't really expect that you will go to great lengths to satisfy your desires. Above all, you want security in your later years, and your plans are geared to that objective.

In your career, you try to do everything that is expected of you, but you should refrain from becoming too familiar with co-workers or superiors. You are too easy-going and indulgent for your own good, and this encourages others to try to take advantage of you.

Basically an honorable person, you prefer to operate within the law at all times. You dread the thought of becoming involved in an uncomfortable legal situation that would disturb the general harmony of your life. But be alert to the danger of becoming implicated in the legal problems of close associates, which could prove costly to you. There are times when giving others the benefit of the doubt can be a liability. On the whole, however, your relations with people are compatible, and any problems that develop can be settled to your mutual satisfaction through compromise.

Mars Sextile Jupiter

Mars sextile Jupiter indicates that you can effectively use your considerable resources of mind and body to gain your objectives. You tend to establish ambitious and demanding goals, but you are prepared to take any steps necessary to see that your ideas are constructively implemented. Early in life you exploited your intellectual abilities whenever you could. Perhaps you applied your creative skills to devise games or indoor activities in which you could test your ability to meet challenging competition. You were giving your mental-physical muscle workouts that prepared you for later confrontations with serious opponents.

You know how to assert yourself under pressure and have developed your talent for effective communication through dramatic delivery and clever use of words. Never one to withdraw from a debate, you always document what you say with convincing evidence. You are quick to defend anyone who cannot defend himself because he lacks information or is not trained in the art of persuasive argument.

Your abilities can be easily applied to many professions or occupations. You will probably lean to the more intellectual pursuits, in which you shine, such as law, teaching, writing, drama, government, or the communications media. Any of these would be an excellent field in which to distinguish yourself and gain recognition. Still, recognition is not really as important to you as having the opportunity to fully utilize your talents.

You project yourself amazingly well and gain many admirers for your effusiveness. Young people are especially impressed with you and may even regard you as an example to aspire to. You can be blunt in saying what is on your mind, and it is rare that you will alter the truth as you know it.

You are drawn to persons who have a reasonably clear idea of where they are going and what they expect to achieve. You have great respect for anyone who has the courage of his convictions, even if they differ from yours. But you insist that honesty and integrity accompany one in seeking goals.

Your feelings are intense, and you need a loving companion with whom to share your experiences. Your sexual desires are strong, but probably they are best satisfied with someone whom you have an intellectual rapport with. This planetary combination unites spiritual and physical properties in an intellectual combination.

Mars Sextile Saturn

The sextile between Mars and Saturn indicates a blending of brain and brawn. You always try to assert yourself intelligently so you won't have to do something over again. You think before you act, which pays dividends in the results you achieve. Others can appeal to you through your logic and understanding, and you are appreciative when their proposals are reasonably acceptable. Your self-discipline and patience enable you to accomplish more than your competitors because you take the time to understand every detail of a problem before attempting to solve it.

Although your interests may be in generally physical areas, you prefer occupations that also require mental skills. Because of this you may show an inclination for fields in which both physical and mental skills are essential, such as archeology, exploration, forestry service, wildlife management, research and development in industry, or perhaps physical education.

Your avocational pursuits can follow many interesting avenues; ecology projects, Big Brother or Sister organizations, working with groups such as the aged or the shut-in, fund-raising campaigns for the physically handicapped, and other such enterprises could enrich your private life. You may be fascinated by all kinds of crafts, and eventually a craft could become your primary source of income.

You enjoy discussion groups, and you hold forth with clever use of language. You don't have to retreat from your position in a debate, because you rarely make a statement that you can't back up with very impressive evidence. Debate is one of your accomplishments and could lead to a life in politics, at least at the organizational level of local groups and social clubs.

In your romantic affairs you seek a partner who has both intellectual and physical interests. You need someone who is multidimensional and who can complement your nature by sharing a variety of meaningful interests. In this way you will both be enriched by each other's companionship.

You respect authority and accept the laws as your protection. Since you have the ability to do most anything you set your mind to, you don't accept defeat easily. You will impart this same attitude to your children and provide them with a good climate for development. You will never be too busy to listen to their problems and you will try to teach them the wisdom of your experience. You will be enthusiastic about their accomplishments although you may be conservative in displaying your emotions.

Mars Sextile Uranus

The sextile between Mars and Uranus shows that you have a restless, impatient nature and are constantly seeking outlets for your energy. Your curiosity is insatiable. You have strong opinions, which you are never afraid to state. Once you have determined what you will do, you act immediately. You cannot stand dawdlers and people who can't make up their minds. You are a strategist, and your plans are successful, but you always feel that a job you do can be improved on later. Although you have enormous energy, you must be careful that you don't bring on nervous strain by driving yourself impatiently to achieve your objectives.

You can work best in occupations requiring originality, intellectual skills, and alertness. Because you are aware of the present, yet compelled by the future, you are especially suited for work in research and development. Your excitement is knowing you've made a positive contribution to a better future for everyone's benefit. All levels of teaching would give you the satisfaction of making a significant personal contribution to others.

Your interests are varied, and you try to take part in as many as possible. You are likely to succeed in any activity you take up, because you invest a great deal of energy to increase the odds for success. You don't accept defeat. With your particular skill in argument and persuasive delivery, you can easily shatter any opponent's position.

An intellectual rebel, you are quick to challenge old ideas and doctrines that have outlived their usefulness. You demonstrate your concern for society by actively taking part in socially beneficial programs or by stirring up dissent to provoke necessary changes.

In your personal relationships, the one you love must have similar attitudes and mutual interest in order to avoid frustration when your partner tries to restrict you.

Kris

Mars Sextile Neptune

The sextile from Mars to Neptune shows that you understand the difference between passion and compassion. You realize there are times when you can assert yourself to satisfy your own desires, but that at other times you must yield to someone else's desires. You are intellectually aware of your responsibility to serve others when they are unable to serve themselves. You are imaginative in finding suitable means to express your creative abilities.

There are many ways to exploit your potentials. You are particularly suited to professions that satisfy important social needs. Medicine and related fields can provide you with a rich and rewarding experience. You have qualities that promote healing in others, perhaps through the soothing effect of your trust and sincerity. Also, your well-developed rhythmic sense lends itself to such artistic pursuits as dancing, physical culture, and acting, in which physical grace is a prime ingredient. You could work successfully in undercover enterprises involving classified material. Your psychic abilities would offer some protection even when conditions seem threatening.

You are a romantic in that you strive to find honest and refined ideals in everyone. You make allowances for the failings of others, and you expect them to be reasonably tolerant of your failings. In a romantic alliance you can always find positive qualities in your lover, even when certain traits rub you the wrong way. Above all, you insist on open and honest communication between the two of you. You detect insincerity no matter how skillfully it is hidden. Your strong emotional and physical desires must be satisfied, but you won't easily compromise your ideals by accepting a coarse or vulgar partner.

Your admirable qualities are much in demand today. You have a "feel" for social responsibilities and the pursuasion to do something about them. Through your efforts you raise the ideals of everyone you contact, in both your personal and your professional activities.

Mars Sextile Pluto

With Mars sextile to Pluto you are eager to know the truth, motivated by the realization that truth is more powerful than fiction. You are as persistent in your search for the facts as a detective seeking unassailable evidence. Forceful and articulate in conversation, you command the attention of your listeners. You know how to dramatize yourself to establish your position both to large groups and to individuals. You can effectively stimulate action to correct social injustices and will not tolerate weakness as a defense for inaction by anyone.

Because you are aware of other people's motives, you are rarely caught with your defenses down. In your personal contacts, you usually establish your position clearly so that no one has to guess about your intentions. In return you expect openness both from associates and from competitors. You deplore subtlety as unnecessary and indefensible.

You have strong physical desires, though you won't accept a merely physical relationship. To be acceptable to you, the relationship must include compatibility in other areas.

It may be necessary for you to yield occasionally to other people's opinions, for they are as valid as yours. You tend to be explicit in your expectations of others and may feel no need to make any adjustment in your attitude to compromise with theirs.

It is especially important that you do more than merely talk about your objectives. You must become actively engaged in pursuing them. You often talk as though you were involved in some activity when you have really only talked about it.

Mars Sextile Ascendant

With Mars sextile the Ascendant, you usually express yourself with persistence and determination. You are fearless in saying what is on your mind, and careless as well. You assert yourself enthusiastically but impulsively. This lack of temperance in expressing your opinions tends to put people on the defensive. Because you are somewhat of a "live wire," people come to expect the unexpected from you. With so much nervous energy, it isn't easy for you to sit still for very long. When your body isn't in motion, your tongue is, and this is how most of your problems in relationships begin. Although you may want harmony in dealing with people, it isn't evident from your actions. If you learn to reflect before you speak, you will avoid saying the wrong thing at the wrong time. You want to be admired by your friends for having a mind of your own and the courage to speak up when you feel you should. You need their support because you aren't always that sure of yourself.

You work hard at your career, perhaps doing more than is expected of you if you work under supervision, and certainly so if you are self-employed. There is some danger that you actually do more than you should, because much of your effort comes form nervous energy. You feel challenged by competitors and want to prove that you are more competent than they are. By being well-informed, you are prepared to take on any responsibility when the opportunity is offered.

You need greater self-discipline to get the full benefit of your creative ability. If you can consolidate your efforts toward a specific objective, you will always manage to succeed. Your zest for living is dramatically shown by your boundless enthusiasm in everything you do. Don't waste it in nonproductive enterprises or in a useless show of superior strength.

Jupiter Sextile Saturn

The sextile of Jupiter to Saturn indicates that your greatest asset is a vast reservoir of information. You are well informed, and your comprehension is excellent. You invariably find uses for the knowledge you've acquired, no matter how useless it appears to others. You belong to the classic tradition that considers *all* knowledge useful or at least broadening and enriching.

Because of your skill in planning, your creative ideas have an excellent chance of succeeding. Enthusiastic and optimistic, you believe in yourself, but you also realize that even the best-laid plans require hard work if they are to succeed. You are always searching for new avenues of expression, because you are determined to grow to your highest potential of development. You insist that your activities be entirely within the law, and you pride yourself on achieving your goals without resorting to questionable ethical practices. Your interest in philosophy has doubtless strengthened your conviction that honesty and sincerity pay the biggest dividends in the long run.

Many fields are suitable to your particular talents, including law, education, writing, journalism, politics, and the ministry. You would derive enormous satisfaction from efforts to improve a particular personal or social environment. You are especially concerned about mismanagement in government and could easily launch a campaign of writing and speaking to alert the public about such practices. You always make sure you have the evidence before communicating your information to the proper authorities; you take total responsibility for everything you do and will fearlessly challenge anyone to a debate on the matter.

You would make an ideal teacher, for you could dramatize your sense of history and the lessons learned from it in an exciting way. With young people you convey an intimate understanding that can stimulate them in their search for meaning in life. Your knowledge and appreciation of contemporary social structure are easily picked up by those who wish to learn and benefit from them.

In your own way you make a substantial contribution to society by your genuine concern for its members. Your depth of understanding might be the basis of a published work on some important issue that involves improving the management of social programs. Whatever gains your interest must have significance for you, and you feel responsible for communicating this to others. In many ways you are a standard bearer for the forces that spotlight social injustice.

Jupiter Sextile Uranus

Your Jupiter sextile Uranus shows that you are optimistic and hopeful about the future. You are foresighted about your goals in life and realize the necessity of planning for them. There are unlimited ways in which you can accomplish your objectives. Intensely curious and enthusiastic about everything, you are a glutton for knowledge, which you absorb easily and well. You rarely look back because the view before you is so exciting. You are a person with many ideas that merely need development. Your impatience does need curbing, but once established, you can go as far as you choose.

Professionally, you are best equipped to teach, but that should not stop you from going into other fields. Politics, writing, law, philosophy, religion, and the occult in general are areas in which you could excel. The sciences would also benefit from your creative talents, for the thrill of discovery keeps your mind razor-sharp. Your forward thinking adapts easily to the changing scene, so you don't have to worry about getting caught in a rut. Self-discovery is a continuing process that will never cease for you. You use your intellect inventively and are always uncovering new creative potentials that sustain your total interest in living. However, you need to share these experiences with others.

Honesty is so important to you that you quickly detach yourself from those who are not sincere. And this holds true for anyone in whom you are romantically interested. You insist on telling it like it is and openly resist those who resort to subterfuge. You have a broad circle of friends to whom you are reasonably generous, but you can quickly detach yourself if your trust is violated. You are mainly interested in people who openly resist the past because of its restrictions on future progress.

With those who seem obviously insecure in their own identities you should avoid coming on as an authority. Progress in your life depends on reasonable moderation.

Jupiter Sextile Neptune

The sextile between Jupiter and Neptune shows that you are imaginative, articulate, and extremely hopeful about the future. You study human nature, trying to learn the lessons of the past for guidance in solving the problems of tomorrow. Since you are mainly a theorist, some of your solutions may be realistically impractical. You recognize your social obligations but often dwell on them without taking any action. However, you will help publicize important social problems in order to arouse public response.

You are especially sensitive to negative political conditions and will offer your services to a candidate who promises to correct them. You are similarly sensitive to religious and social ideologies that don't seem to serve the public interest. An idealist, you are a champion for people who are too timid to voice their objections.

You are ideally suited to work in religious, social, or political enterprises, because you are not afraid to stand and be counted. With your imaginative understanding, you can be inspiring in your efforts to bring about social order by uniting its chaotic elements. You would also succeed at writing for the official magazine of an organization. You have the broad perspective to visualize how the individual can unwittingly be swept along by the tide of social, religious, or political concepts. Your sensitive delivery could help avert this kind of totalitarian effect.

Though you recognize the dangers inherent in social structures, you are still personally vulnerable to deception. You assign qualities to your emotional relationships that may be unrealistic. Because you want so much to believe you have made a good choice, you may be unprepared for deception and disillusionment. If you really want to know how someone feels about you, ask and find out! Be cautious and evasive when declaring your love for another; don't get yourself out on an embarrassing limb. Your best development will come through self-discipline and practical action.

Jupiter Sextile Pluto

The sextile from Jupiter to Pluto enables you to perceive truths that are hidden by appearances. Your curiosity often leads you to make a penetrating examination in order to discover the facts. Because of your high ethical standards, you align yourself with enterprises that act to improve social conditions in your environment.

You are concerned with injustices and will communicate your observations to the proper authorities, so that legal pressures can be brought to bear. Law and the administration of law are particularly suited to your basic character and integrity. You can be a champion to those who are unable to defend themselves or whose values need support.

You are also qualified to manage corporate financial enterprises successfully or to serve as liason in arbitrating disputes. Business administration could provide you with an excellent avenue of expression, regardless of your specific field. Medicine or psychology would also be satisfactory expressions of your personality, and you would enrich those you serve. Literally dozens of occupations could give you much fulfillment. You are a benefactor to those you contact through your profession. You enjoy giving your talents, because you respond to your fellow man with a sense of spiritual responsibility.

Your partner must share your enthusiasm for social responsibility, for serving whenever and wherever you are needed. Your mate will also have a mission to fulfill, and the two of you can be a powerful force to relieve society's burdens. You are especially responsive to anyone who is concerned with elevating people's sights for the future. Your optimism generates in others a desire to share your excitement as you philosophically "reach for the stars."

Your religious attitude requires you to actively participate in stimulating others to accept a spiritual obligation to mankind. Thus you will redeem the gift of your vast capabilities.

Jupiter Sextile Ascendant

The sextile from Jupiter to the Ascendant shows that you are enthusiastic in everything you do and optimistic that you will succeed. You enjoy meeting people, and your cheerful outlook on life makes you popular with your many acquaintances. You stimulate those you deal with to support your endeavors, and they cooperate whenever they can. You are generous with your possessions and always ready to lend a helping hand to those who need assistance. On many subjects, you can speak with authority because you are often as well informed as professionals in the field. You strive for excellence at all times and admire that quality in others as well.

People are generally impressed with the extent of your knowledge. With your depth of understanding, you are able to advise others in their affairs, for which they are usually grateful. You communicate well and express yourself eagerly in matters that are of great interest to you. Communications could be a rewarding medium for you; writing, public speaking, or education would be excellent outlets for your creative talents. You are also a good listener, realizing that continued growth depends on absorbing as much additional information as possible. Although you realize that you can never know everything, you intend to be as well-informed as possible.

It is difficult for you to say no when someone asks for help. But you occasionally try to do more than you should, so try to relax more frequently. You think of rest only as a last alternative to the many interests that hold your attention. In your eagerness to serve the needs of others, you tend to burn the candle at both ends.

You will always succeed in a partnership enterprise because you make such a heavy investment to assure its success. You don't shirk your responsibilities and may at times volunteer to make up for someone else's inability to do his share.

Saturn Sextile Uranus

The sextile between Saturn and Uranus represents deep respect for knowledge and the talent to use it. You realize your own self-worth and know exactly how to capitalize on your inner and outer resources. You instinctively seek the truth in all things and will persist until you gain it. Knowing that ignorance limits true freedom, you assert that you will never be tied down by being uninformed. Your intellect is highly developed, and your comprehension is keen.

You are more efficient and self-disciplined than most people in working toward well-defined goals. Therefore you can accomplish many tasks more easily. You waste little effort because you consider your time precious. Teaching is probably your best avenue of expression, although there are many other possible courses, such as science, math, research, the occult, astrology, politics, and the management of human resources. Whatever field you choose, you are not likely to stay long at your initial level. It is essential that you continue to progress in order to develop your maximum potential output.

Although you are reasonably sure of yourself (you know your self-worth, remember?), you may always have to make allowances in your daily associations for others who are less capable or less able to reason. What is obvious to you may be obscure to them. It would be advisable to play down how much you comprehend so you don't arouse antagonism in others, who may accuse you of being a know-it-all. This is also a good reason for going into education, where you are supposed to know more than others and cannot be criticized for it.

You relate more easily to people who have gained credibility through their intellectual development, as you have. Although ignorance is the catalyst for unleashing your knowledge for the benefit of others, you are nevertheless disdainful of it. Your general well-being can best be assured by associating with people who have established demanding goals for themselves.

Saturn Sextile Neptune

The sextile between Saturn and Neptune shows that your perception is keen. You use your inspiration skillfully and constructively for the benefit of yourself and others. You are deeply aware of and sensitive to your social obligations. Although you may not be prepared to actively participate in these responsibilities, you can offer your services to help others fulfill them. You may lay the foundation for action in planning or securing a sympathetic response from people in important positions. Your ideas are realistic and constructive for stemming the tide of social injustices.

In evaluating your environmental circumstances, you are thoughtful and reasonably profound, and you perceive accurately what is right and what is wrong. You deplore the waste of human resources and constantly strive for more efficient distribution of social programs and services in your community. This kind of work is especially suitable for you. You are willing to accept an unobtrusive position if the goals of the program will be better served this way.

Undercover work is something you could do well. You have the persistence and determination necessary to gather all the facts without being recognized. You can be trusted to maintain secrecy about confidential information. Your self-discipline and poise even under strain are admirable, and you would be extremely useful as a guide and advisor to individuals in power.

Your efficiency and organization may postpone permanent emotional ties, because you are preoccupied with social causes, through which you try to make a spiritual contribution. Your romance is in the broad perspective of human involvement. Your partner must feel the same way in order to gain and keep your respect. You won't sacrifice your ideals to gain anyone's favor.

Above all, you find it difficult to understand how anyone can tolerate the guilt of remaining passive to intolerable social ills.

Saturn Sextile Pluto

With the sextile of Saturn to Pluto, you realize that you must plan carefully in order to succeed. Knowing that nothing can depend on chance, you organize your resources in such a way as to achieve the best results. You understand your abilities and shortcomings and establish your goals and objectives accordingly. You are prepared to accept whatever responsibilities will enable you to grow into important positions. Success is not a surprise to you, since you have made an enormous effort for that very purpose. You aren't afraid that you will fail, nor do you feel threatened by anyone, because you've built your position on a firm foundation.

You know that experience is the best teacher, but you also value education and training as a means to expand your opportunities. These attitudes enable you to fill many positions. You realize that results are in proportion to your contribution, and this feeling is communicated to your superiors. Your good relations with them helps open access routes to promotion. You are humble enough to seek advice and guidance from more experienced people.

Although you are understanding of other people's motives, you aren't always tolerant of their negativity or incompetence. You expect a lot from those under you, and you can be vindictive toward an unqualified person who tries to gain a high position. But you prefer to discuss mutual differences rather than let a misunderstanding spoil a relationship.

Security is very important to you and is perhaps the reason for your urge to succeed. You also realize the danger of thinking that money is a universal solvent. You respect the power of money, but you won't be dominated by the extreme compulsion to accumulate a fortune.

Saturn Sextile Ascendant

Saturn sextile the Ascendant indicates that you take pains to express yourself clearly and thoughtfully. You realize that you are responsible for your conduct, and you act with self-discipline, knowing you will have to account for any failure to do things right. You are serious about everything you do. Because of your integrity, reliability, virtue, and sound moral principles, some people consider you self-righteous, but they also respect you. Basically efficient, you plan methodically before doing anything to make sure it is done right the first time. You are appalled by the effort others waste in nonproductive activities.

You know how to define your objectives and establish your priorities. In conversation you are a person of few but well-chosen words. People who speak without thinking seem very superficial to you. Because of your conservative manner, people may think of you as detached and indifferent. The fact is, you are busily trying to make sense from your observations, and you can do this only by being quiet and composed. Once you have formed an opinion, it is nearly impossible for others to make you change it unless they provide a compelling reason. You are very demanding but fair in your dealings, and you expect people to fulfill their agreements with you.

Your perspective may be narrower than most people's, but you are more profound in your understanding of people's motivations and deepest problems. Because you understand people so well, you can be effective in positions of leadership, matching the right person with the proper role as cleverly as a chess player.

You are quite concerned about security in your later years, so you plan to capitalize on every talent you possess to gain the optimum results. You strive for excellence in developing your personal resources.

Kris & Kathryn

Uranus Sextile Neptune

Uranus sextile Neptune indicates that you are part of a group consciousness that is intolerant of anyone who distorts the truth or withholds it from the people. You are especially suspicious of strong, established organizations that have powerful government connections, but you are similarly offended by the rigid control that organized religions have over their members. You prefer to decide for yourself what to believe and how to discipline yourself through whatever faith you've chosen. A revolutionary thinker, you resent the fact that you are expected to yield to the thoughts and beliefs of people you are suspicious of. The "establishment" represents a threat to your personal freedom. You insist that any commitment must be made voluntarily and without the slightest exercise of pressure. Fearful of the erosion of individual rights, you freely communicate this sense of danger whenever possible. You realize that people who follow others blindly are endangering their right to choose the path to their destinies.

From your generation will come the fruit of the seed that germinated between 1965 and 1968, when open hostilities were commonplace at many universities throughout the world. You will demand a say in the social, educational, and political systems to insure that your right to free expression will not be curtailed or denied. In everything that has a bearing on your future and that of the masses, you will seek the truth. You are not afraid to express your views because your opinion is backed by an arsenal of facts. You uphold the belief that every individual bears a spiritual obligation to his society, which you call the "Brotherhood of Man."

You hold that a societal structure based on materialism is an affront to the personal dignity of the individual. You aspire to a high degree of creative expression for everyone, regardless of the opportunities their material circumstances afford them.

Uranus Sextile Pluto

The sextile of Uranus to Pluto shows that you are shocked when you observe injustice and immediately voice your displeasure. You resent the fact that powerful forces such as government or private industry can apply economic pressure to gain public support for their goals. You object to those who use legal devices or political patronage to gain control of elected government officials, especially when legislation forces the individual to endure hardship and sacrifice, promising benefits that never materialize. Wastefulness in government is appalling to you, and you insist that those in charge be made accountable for their gross mismanagement of public funds. You have an uncanny ability to detect dishonesty and are never at ease unless government spending is essential and can be documented.

Uranus was sextile to Pluto from 1942 to 1946, which covers the period of World War II. At that time wasteful government spending was justified because of the greater priority for winning the war "at all costs." Enormous fortunes were made in the private sector as carpetbaggers emerged from every corner to reap vast financial benefits.

Born at a time of great international unrest, you are alert to the danger that your feedom may be abridged by selfish public officials or elected representatives who pass legislation that favors special interests. Luckily, you have the courage and determination to persist in arousing public attention to such developments. You demand that officials truly represent the public or else be removed from office. You encourage people to attend local or state government sessions when important bills are proposed. To you, freedom is so precious that you participate actively in order to preserve it.

Uranus Sextile Ascendant

Uranus sextile the Ascendant shows that you think like a rebel, whether you act the role or not. You are impatient with traditional concepts unless they bring results when you adhere to them. Fascinated by novelty, your mind races with high expectation when you encounter an ingenious idea. Although you are restless and like to be on the move all the time, you realize that you cannot hope to win any support for your creative ideas unless you convince important people that you are stable and dependable. Your greatest selling point is your original and progressive creativity. You are skillful in communicating what you know, and you freely share your ideas with anyone who will listen. Time means little to you, and you reject the limitations it imposes. You depend on intuitive hunches which are, more often than not, extremely reliable. Many times your statements are prophetic.

Because freedom means so much to you, your career must permit you some degree of independence and self-determination. Daily, routine jobs are too boring and restrictive for your creative talents. You bring ingenuity to any work you do, but research and development have a special appeal. If there is any way that new sources of revenue can be devised for the company you work for, you are the one who can find it.

You enjoy a wide variety of friends from different backgrounds. You are particularly fond of people who think for themselves and those whose interests are as novel as your own.

Among your associates, you sparkle. You enjoy competing with them, but you are not usually pompous when you win. Rather, you consider it a mutual victory, for you realize that your opponent helped stimulate you to win. You may be envied and even disliked by some co-workers, whose limited perspective prevents them from really understanding you.

It is unlikely that you will ever truly retire. Each day reveals new possibilities that continue to arouse your interest.

Neptune Sextile Pluto

The only aspect made by Neptune to Pluto in this century and into the next is the sextile. The influence between them began in 1942, when Neptune was in Libra and Pluto was in Leo. Although their positions in the signs will change, they will maintain a sextile relationship for the next hundred years. Therefore everyone born during that time will have this planetary combination. The signs they occupy will cause some differences in their effects, however.

The influences of these planets are global in effect and represent the evolutionary process by which man continually strives to achieve ultimate perfection. They indicate man's reaching out toward other dimensions of experience while trying to maintain order in the real world to which he is materially bound. People are becoming more aware of the probability that other worlds exist, and all our scientific skills will be used in attempts to reach them. A similar assault is being made in the quest to explore the vast inner world of man. Neptune represents that inner world, while Pluto refers to the outer reaches of infinite space.

Both worlds are truly infinite, and although man is pursuing similar goals in each direction, this author believes that neither quest excludes the other. It is suggested that the same goals will ultimately be reached regardless of which direction is taken. One either reaches out in the natural world in search of answers or seeks those answers in the inner depths of his own spiritual being. Man's familiarity with the physical world makes it the most plausible and safe area in which to seek tangible answers to the question of why he exists at all. While he struggles in this search, there is an equally courageous struggle to find answers through the occult. The increased investigation of extrasensory perception, alpha states of consciousness, psychokinesis, telepathy, and other such phenomena indicate that man senses that the answers may not lie outside him, but within him. There is no conflict between the two searches; in fact, they may well sustain and help control each other.

Although enormous benefits will be realized, there will still be many problems and difficulties for the world and its inhabitants before those benefits come about.

Between 1942 and 1956 Neptune and Pluto were sextile from Libra to Leo. The world was experiencing the terrible ordeal of global war. Pluto in Leo saw the rise and fall of powerful governments intent on world domination. Kings and queens were toppled from their thrones, and the spotlight was on the emergence of youth (Leo), which was to become a thorny element in postwar societies throughout the world. Accompanying this human development was the incredible power made available by the scientific breakthrough in harnessing atomic energy. Neptune in Libra provided advances in air power that served to alter the balance of power and thus end the global conflict when the first atomic bomb was delivered. This event stimulated a controversy (sextile) that would continue for many years. The peace that followed World War II was an uneasy one, and the sextile between these planets represents the endless meetings and conferences among the victors, who displayed a sign reading PEACE that covered a sign reading WAR.

Those born during this time eventually recognize that understanding and compromise are not enough and that scientific progress must be depended upon to maintain peace. Even as hostilities ended, new leaders emerged who would continue to threaten the peace.

You will always be suspicious of your leaders. You want them to establish the kind of government that will truly serve the public and in which you can have complete confidence. Your continuing suspicions will serve to produce greater honesty in government, but with Neptune in Libra it will be difficult to really know if honesty has been achieved.

Kris & Kathryn

Neptune Sextile Pluto (1957 — 1970)

Neptune in Scorpio sextile Pluto in Virgo produced significant advances in medical research. New drugs helped control the population explosion following the war, but along with this positive development was the increased use of illegal drugs by youth, which resulted in many deaths. You were born during a time of important changes in human priorities. Sex was an enticing area of exploration, and virginity became so unfamiliar that you would have to read about it in history books or look it up in a dictionary.

You have learned to resent the fact that organized religions could dictate people's beliefs or that marriage was ever necessary if two people loved each other. In maturity you resented the power accumulated by the industrial giants and took issue with how the universities and colleges were being run. You are among those who feel that the world is becoming too materialistic, that society lacks any feeling for the individual and his personal dreams.

You feel the need to serve society. You deplore the quality of life that is available, for you consider life very precious. Horrified by what industry is doing to nature, <u>you support legislation that will conserve the natural resources that remain so that your children can inherit it</u>. You will also support funding for continued medical research to find cures for killer diseases such as cancer, heart disease, etc. <u>You will advocate continuing research to develop safe and effective methods of birth</u> control.

Neptune Sextile Pluto (1971 — 1983)

Neptune in Sagittarius sextile Pluto in Libra shows that those who have just been born and those who will be born until 1983 will have completely revised attitudes about religion, philosophy, education, and human relationships. Religion will be restored to a place of usefulness in the daily lives of those born during this period. It will hardly resemble the religion of your elders, but it will be a far more vital element in your life. You have faith not just because your forebears accepted it, but because it adds meaning to your life and makes you responsible to others for your actions. Your faith adds to your search for perfection while you make any contribution to society that will help to bring about that state. You are deeply concerned for your fellow man and are willing to make compromises in your desires if it will prove beneficial to others in the long run.

You will insist on the integrity of those you select for your leaders and will demand that they truly represent the electorate. You will want schools to re-emphasize the humanities in education and give students the opportunity to choose professions that serve man rather than the tight, confining specialization of industry.

You will also show increased interest in the occult and be responsible for major developments in the fields of ESP, extrasensory perception, and alpha states of consciousness. You will open new dimensions of the mind and explore them for unlimited resources, which are denied the more materialistic investigator.

Neptune Sextile Ascendant

Neptune sextile the Ascendant shows that you have difficulty in expressing yourself and often give people the wrong impression. You have a fertile imagination, and you usually embroider your accounts with embellishments that distort your meaning and confuse your listeners. Because of this, people are guarded in dealing with you. In your eagerness for conversation and attention you unconsciously create situations that don't exist or invent stories about incidents that never occurred. You can put this talent for imagery to better use if you apply it to constructive activities such as writing, public speaking, or acting.

Although you downgrade your abilities, your friends recognize how inspired you are in your creative expression. They find you charming and friendly but also rather naive and defenseless. You show an interest in the conditions of your immediate environment and feel some pain of guilt if you fail to do something to correct negative conditions. In spite of this, you may give endless excuses for neglecting to take action. Your reasoning may be that since other people seem unwilling to make a contribution, you need not feel badly about your negligence.

You get along well with most people because you never seem to threaten them by competing openly. People are misled by your sympathetic and docile nature into thinking that you won't challenge them.

It isn't easy for you to make decisions. You find it difficult to isolate the most important facts so that you can arrive at a sound judgment. When you fail at something, you may indulge in self-pity for your incompetence. It is especially important for you not to compare your performance with anyone else's. If you do, you will invariably assume that the other person is superior to you. Your self-confidence can be improved only if you take on tasks you know you can handle successfully. You can do a lot if you stay within your limits. As your confidence increases, you can add more demanding duties. It is important that you approve of what you accomplish.

Pluto Sextile Ascendant

Pluto sextile the Ascendant shows that you have a deep understanding of the important role you play in the lives of the people you deal with. You know you can influence them to do what you want. Some people may be wary of you because of this power. You willingly accept challenges, especially from adversaries who demonstrate their competence. You are direct and blunt in expressing yourself, and you win many admirers for your courage when you are right. When you are wrong, however, you defend your position argumentatively. You are not as sure of yourself as you appear. Knowing that you can be overcome if competitors learn of your weakness, you always try to make the first move and put them on the defensive.

You have big ideas about the future you want to carve out for yourself, and you are willing to work hard to realize your desires. Your deep concern about social, religious, and political upheavals that might interfere with your goals motivates you to do what you can to ensure competent leadership in these areas. You might express your thoughtful opinions in order to arouse public interest in sound social programs and genuine concern for effective political leadership. In any case, you are not content to sit idly by and see your future dreams shattered by self-seeking officials.

In a crisis situation you are dependable and will go to the assistance of anyone needing it. You respect those with the courage to stand firm in their convictions, and you are exasperated with those who are too indolent to defend themselves against oppressors. You are almost obsessed with the idea that unless you challenge those who try to deprive you of your individual rights, you will lose your freedom. You consider any such public servant as a parasite who must be exterminated for the public good.

Chapter Three

Squares

Next to the Conjunction, the Square is the most powerful aspect between planets. Its dynamic influence exceeds that of all other aspects, and it surpasses even the Conjunction in stimulating human reaction. It is the aspect that denotes action and reaction at the most refined level. The planets involved are almost always in signs that are naturally hostile to each other. Because of this fact there is little harmony, unless the individual reacts in a harmonious way to their combined influences. Positive human reaction is essential if there is to be any constructive effect.

The workings of the elements in the Square are analogous to the effects of fire and water. It is obvious that these two cannot occur simultaneously without adapting in some way. Water can put out fire, or fire can reduce water to vapor. When both elements are handled judiciously, the results are constructive. Water can control fire and prevent a holocaust, while fire can heat water to produce energy as steam. A similar process takes place when two planets are separated by an angle of 90º in what is called a Square aspect.

The initial effect of a Square is to cause frustration when the psychological factors corresponding to either of the planets are involved. Some adjustment must be made before one can use the energies positively. This aspect shows that there are lessons to be learned about how to use the energies constructively; otherwise, negative effects are certain. The Square aspect presents a test which, when passed, builds character and infuses it with increasing perfection.

The greatest tests in life come through the Square aspects. They generally occur as crosses that must be borne in the struggle to gain mastery over the unconscious. They show the major crises that must be dealt with for the soul to evolve and grow toward greater self-conscious awareness.

Sun Square Moon

The square from the Sun to the Moon means that you will have some difficulty in using your resources to satisfy your desires. You bitterly resent that you must make enormous adjustments in order to get what you want from life. It seems as if you never have quite the right training for what you want to do, but you make only half-hearted attempts to acquire the training you need to succeed. Although you want the "good life," you aren't willing to discipline yourself to get it. You are at odds with important people who will not accept you unless you can prove yourself by demonstrating a willingness to work. Your negative response distorts the information you receive which makes it more difficult to learn from your experiences. Generally you react to stimuli in a way that is not consistent with achieving the recognition you want. The frustration you feel has inhibited your character development and is a problem in other areas, including domestic matters, social relationships, emotional interests, and professional affairs. Your lack of success in these areas shows that you have a lot to learn before you can expect to reap any rewards.

You must learn to bring your emotions and your will into line and subdue them with intellect and organization. You seem to think that any response will satisfy the will to achieve significance, but you will have to realize that only hard work and self-control can get you what you want. What you gain from your habitual actions is inadequate to your needs, as can be easily demonstrated. For one thing, you haven't progressed from obscure positions to positions of increased responsibility. Also, you either haven't been able to win favor with people in high places, or you've done so by making concessions to them. If you will get your ego out of the way, you can accomplish many things.

You may have some problem in relating to the opposite sex. Comfortable domestic conditions may be impossible unless you can get that chip off your shoulder. You are argumentative and defensive, probably because of your emotional insecurity. This can be reversed if you will change your fighting attitude and become more compromising. You have a serious misalignment between what you want and what you are willing to do to get it. The possibility of realizing your dreams is in direct proportion to the investment you make.

Sun Square Mars

The square from the Sun to Mars gives you much enthusiasm and energy to carry out your tasks, but under prolonged pressure you periodically need to wind down and get away from your work. You must try not to drive yourself so hard in fulfilling your ambitions. When your efforts don't yield the expected results you become annoyed and fly off the handle in disgust. Experience will probably teach you that you did not plan your actions carefully enough, so that you got exactly what you deserved under the circumstances. In time you should learn to meet obstacles by anticipating them and taking steps to overcome them in advance; in this way you will avoid the frustration of resistance. Think before you do anything, and you will save the precious time that is wasted in doing it over. You need to learn patience in handling difficulties and to conserve your energy for constructive purposes. When challenged, you react with indignation, feeling that your competence is being threatened. You would be better advised to observe and learn how others conduct themselves under pressure. This is better than indulging in senseless argument or a bitter display of temperament.

There are many fields in which you could successfully apply your talents, such as teaching, writing, sports, military service, medicine, law, and police work. However, you would have to understand the limitations to your freedom that these careers involve. Because you value your freedom, you should determine your priorities before indulging in any worthwhile endeavor. You must be willing to make that investment if you expect to gain prominence and recognition.

You are fairly good-natured and enjoy the company of many friends whom you admire for their own accomplishments. But you can be overbearing in demanding attention and trying to focus discussions on subjects that you are especially knowledgeable about. You have to learn to be a good listener too.

Although you have a highly developed sexual nature, you aren't too successful in overcoming the frustrations involved in satisfying it. Either you want what you can't have, or you've grown disinterested in what you do have. It is obvious that you will have to compensate as much as possible by diverting your energies into satisfying and enjoyable activities. The mate you are looking for is one who can match your physical needs and also be a companion in your other interests.

Somewhat careless about safety precautions, you invite accidents. Take care of any cuts as soon as they happen in order to reduce the possibility of infection.

Sun Square Jupiter

The square from the Sun to Jupiter indicates that you are extremely immoderate in your actions and attitudes. You are aware of this tendency, and it bothers you. Learn to examine your priorities carefully before you act, or you will waste a lot of effort and time. You tend to bite off more than you can chew and then desperately try to cope with the situation as best you can. You don't plan your affairs well, but you are annoyed when someone offers a suggestion, even after you've asked for advice. It is pompous and arrogant to presume that you can accomplish what you want without self-discipline. Only experience will subdue this arrogance, and you will realize that everyone depends to some extent on others in the struggle to gain significance and recognition.

After you learn to accept reality and gain some degree of self-control, you can assert yourself toward any goal that you choose. You could attain excellence in education, the media, theater, law, philosophy, or public relations. Your desire to exploit your creative potentials must be accompanied by a full realization of the responsibilities this entails. You have to accept both good and bad, successes and failures, advances and setbacks, because they are all part of the tapestry of accomplishment. Through the problems you encounter you can make your greatest development, if you are willing to learn from your mistakes. You want to succeed so much that you can fairly taste it, but unless you plan your moves carefully, the taste of success may be bittersweet.

In many ways you are a wheeler-dealer and enjoy becoming involved in manipulating people in their human situations. You are not afraid of a good fight that tests your competence in the open market of human frailties. You enjoy challenges, but you may have to endure failure before you eventually succeed. Communication is one of your strongest talents, but you must be properly informed before you attempt to present your ideas. You may sometimes bend the truth to achieve your objectives, which can lead to unhealthy complications later. You tend to push your luck unwisely, but hopefully you will learn greater discretion as you grow in experience.

You demand a lot from the person you love. You expect devotion, approval and, if possible, admiration for your efforts. You want your mate to indulge all your considerable desires, and you expect that person to stand by you through all your high and lows. You make promises you can't always fulfill, although you may fully intend to at the time you make them.

Self-indulgence is basically the cause of your physical problems. Too much food, drink, and pleasure need to be balanced by moderation and sufficient rest. Avoid doing things on impulse, because this planetary combination inclines you to accidents, especially during periods of relaxation when you may be engaged in sports.

Sun Square Saturn

Because of the square of the Sun to Saturn, you have had to resolve many conflicts about your self-worth during your early years and even into adulthood. You are naturally defensive and fear rejection by people you think of as superior. Success will not come easily because you underestimate your potential and don't assert yourself when you should. You must be willing to suffer the pain of rejection and the frustration of not reaching your goals. From these experiences you will learn, and your judgment will be sharpened so that you can make decisive plans for success. You just may have to fail in order to succeed.

Your qualifications show that you are suited to make achievements in teaching, philosophy, industrial management, conservation, or any occupation that requires methodical application of knowledge and experience. You must expect to begin at the bottom in your chosen field and plan your rise to prominence one step at a time. You must also learn to like yourself so that you can successfully meet competition as you continue to grow.

Your present lack of confidence can become self-assurance later. And this applies to your personal relationships as well. In your early years, you tended to assume that others would not welcome your company, perhaps because you were not as aggressive and compulsive as they were. But then you realized that not everyone admires people who come on strong and that you could relate to many people after all. You will undoubtedly choose a partner who can accept you as you are. Your mate will recognize that your potential is much greater than you know and will believe in you.

Try to maintain a positive outlook on life. By talking to those you admire, you'll discover that they too have apprehensions and fears, and you are not alone.

Sun Square Uranus

The square from the Sun to Uranus shows that you are eccentric and sometimes unprincipled in your behavior. You insist on being allowed to do anything you want, even when you know you're wrong. You have a strong desire for power, and you persist even when it is clear that others won't grant it to you. Basically an upstart, you always have to express an opposing point of view, if only to cause dissension. Learn to base your position on sound, realistic values so that you aren't unjustifiably at variance with the majority.

Before you can succeed, you must re-examine your attitudes about authority in general. You must get over the idea that people are deliberately trying to restrain you, or that others are treated better than you. Your arrogance and unwillingness to follow rules will restrict your development. Humble yourself when necessary and learn how to grow one step at a time. You will earn the respect of others if you don't seem to threaten them. Although you doubt your own competence, you direct your anxieties toward other people.

Once you realize that others may be as sensitive about their own egos as you are, you will have established a solid foundation for realizing your objectives. Compromise will assure mutual benefits for everyone. You do have leadership ability, which you can use dramatically in dealing with large numbers of people. Teaching, the physical sciences, politics, or government service at any level will provide you with the creative expression you want and need.

Socially, you are at odds with anyone who challenges you, and you may be referred to as a "troublemaker." Although you have many friends they are mainly those who are willing to submit to you. This facet of your individuality colors your romantic affairs. You demand subservience from others, but lose respect for them if they submit. You will have to make many adjustments in your outlook before you can attain emotional satisfaction. Your strong will may disguise the depth of your emotional feelings.

Sun Square Neptune

The square between the Sun and Neptune indicates that you may suffer from an inferiority complex. Because of early conditioning by your parents, your faith in yourself is seriously undermined. They completely misunderstood you and could not see that you were asserting your own individuality. As a result, you began building protective neuroses to defend yourself against continued emotional harassment. As you matured you continued to shield yourself against people who seemed to be trying to undermine you. You are creative, imaginative, and eager to express your potential. But because of your rejection of reality, it is extremely difficult for you to find avenues for self-expression. You create images of failure and construct impossible dreams to justify your inability to succeed.

You must define your ambitions within the framework of probability. Your sensitive nature does not allow you to challenge those who may compete with you, for two reasons. First, you underestimate your ability to succeed, and second, you don't want to feel responsible for hurting anyone. You seriously need counsel to help you get over your hang-ups, to accept reality, and to assert yourself even in the face of certain failure. Your greatest liability is that you run from duty. You feel guilty because of what you don't do, but until you are willing to risk failure you will never know success. Learn to love yourself so that you won't continue to take a back seat to everyone else.

Become involved in professional activities that require minimal responsibility at first. You will learn through this experience that you can capably fulfill responsibility. In time you will grow more aware of your abilities and will be able to define even higher goals and ambitions for yourself. There is no better way to become independent and to express yourself with satisfaction and confidence.

You are especially vulnerable emotionally and must extricate yourself from relationships with people who may try to use you. Be prepared to withdraw when you sense that others are trying to exploit you.

Sun Square Pluto

With Sun square Pluto you tend to be extremely willful, sometimes constructively but more often destructively. No one feels the pressure of frustration as much as you do, and when the pressure become intolerable, you explode. You have difficulty in maintaining moderation in relationships with others.

At some time in your past you adopted the attitude that "might makes right," and that you must strike first to gain victory. You seem to have a chip on your shoulder and to be on the prowl looking for adversaries. You arouse the worst qualities in others, as they try to defend themselves against your apparent abuse of authority. This makes you your own worst enemy.

You are an enigma even to the people who are closest to you. On occasion, you demonstrate amazing self-control, but at other times a minor incident will put you in a tailspin. This is probably why friends and associates deliberately keep their distance from you. You are psychologically defensive about forming close emotional ties and equally apprehensive about achieving your goals.

You do have executive ability and the talent for managing ambitious enterprises. But you must realize that others have usually made some contribution to your success. Learn to accept advice from people who are temperamentally equipped to make decisions based on the evidence rather than on personal feelings. Take care not to become hardened and insensitive to the feelings of those you must deal with.

Try to compromise. Recognize that you alternate between being receptive to worthwhile suggestions from others and expecting their complete submission to your demands.

Professional and domestic crises should help you realize that you must work hard to gain mastery over your powerful ego and drive. Moderation in everything you do will bring more benefits than you can imagine.

Sun Square Ascendant

The Sun square the Ascendant indicates that when you express yourself you unknowingly cause others to react negatively. You tend to get off on the wrong foot because you have trouble convincing people that you are sincere and honest. You come on a bit strong, which just doesn't set quite right with people, and they resent you for it. All the endearments you use never quite offset your suspected lack of sincerity. You should ask your closest friend about this, because the chances are that you will resent and reject what is said here.

You will compromise only when there is no other alternative. You have an incredible inability to face the facts about yourself, although they are painfully obvious to everyone else. You want to win everyone's approval, and you can do so by asserting yourself more modestly, so people don't feel that you are forcing yourself on them. The same holds true for associates with whom you are in close contact for extended periods of time. People will appreciate you more if you let them make willing gestures to you. In that way they can feel that they are the aggressors. It is better to attract them to you than to demand their submission.

In spite of the foregoing, you are accustomed to resistance when you try to do something. Knowing that nothing worthwhile comes easily, you are ready to endure frustration at times because the experience is valuable in building character. You had to overcome difficulties with superiors in your formative years, and as a result you may have grown up with a chip on your shoulder. You also know that you will have to rely on your own resources if you want to succeed. The difficulty comes in dealing with people in authority who expect you to recognize your inferior position. If you realize that it's not your creative abilities but your attitude that offends people, you will succeed in winning complete approval for your competence.

Moon Square Mercury

The Moon square Mercury indicates that you have difficulty in making reasonable judgments, because your feelings are usually involved. It can be disturbing to find out later that your actions have shown incredible immaturity. It isn't easy for you to be completely rational or objective, for you are overly sensitive and cannot remain impartial in what you say or do. You sometimes have difficulty in separating fact from fancy and may unfairly assume that people are criticizing you when this is not the case at all. Because of this, you get involved in gross misunderstandings with many people and can become very unpopular.

You are sentimental about those close to you and attach great importance to the things you own. Preoccupied with trivial matters, you waste a lot of needless effort and energy on them. Your problem is that you dwell to excess on yourself, for you are insecure and fearful that people won't appreciate you, no matter what you do. In a sense, you are selfish; you need to devote as much time and concern to other people as to yourself. Try to rechannel your interests outside yourself. Just the effort of trying will help reduce your almost neurotic attitude about your personal affairs. It would not only be healthier but would enable you to observe that the problems others have are not very different from your own.

After you realize your shortcomings and can relate to people more easily, you can look to the future with optimism. You should find some comfort working with young people or children. But stay clear of people in your own age group until you learn to withstand their criticism, which you see as a put-down. Once you are truly secure in what you know and what you can do, you should think about competing with your peers. Be careful you don't cut people down when they challenge you. Before you launch a verbal attack, reexamine the facts to see if it is justified.

You communicate well with those close to you, because you don't feel insecure. It is quite different with strangers, though, for you feel threatened by them. This is why you don't make friends easily. You resent having to make adjustments or allowances for other people, preferring that they adjust to your particular frail and vulnerable personality. You hold fast to your opinions and are defiant when anyone suggests you are mistaken. Unbend a little—it will be a lot less painful for you and will encourage others to be more sympathetic and understanding.

Moon Square Venus

The square from the Moon to Venus means that you are apprehensive about forming close emotional ties because you fear the responsibilities they bring. You are defensive in admitting your feelings for others, fearful that they will make demands on you if you do. Your deeply ingrained ties with the past were probably etched by your relationship with your parents. No doubt you were expected to show undying loyalty to them, to the complete exclusion of anyone you might choose. It is wrong for you to feel any guilt about trying to transfer your personal feelings, for your parents should not try to hold you to a total commitment to them. Your priorities are distorted, and a change of attitude is in order; otherwise, the danger is clear.

Your rebelliousness can introduce problems in your personal relationships. In an attempt to get away from the restrictions that you feel closing in on you, you may indulge in an affair that is less than desirable. You could become the dumping ground for the emotional anxieties of others, and you would be abused and deceived into thinking that the feeling toward you was genuine.

It would be advisable for you to become independent as soon as you can earn a living and take care of your own needs. You need the companionship of people who don't expect anything from you except friendship. You should develop a new perspective so you can relate to people with greater understanding and mutual trust. If your intense emotional nature requires that you become involved, be hesitant about making any binding commitments. Marriage could be a disaster if you have not overcome the subtle distortions of your early conditioning. You would in a way be "getting even" with your partner for damages wrought by someone else; you would be punishing the wrong person. You are enormously vulnerable to manipulation, because you tend to be indiscriminate in satisfying your emotional hunger. Be assuming that everyone is honest and sincere, you could be left high and dry when you most need cooperation.

Time is the factor you have going for you, because in time you will gain maturity and judgment. Don't take a shortcut and avoid the laborious process of learning to understand people and their motivations. That would be asking for unhappiness. Become involved in group endeavors that will bring you into close contact with people so you can learn how they behave and how they are motivated in their objectives. You will also learn to understand human failings and to judge more clearly anyone to whom you are affectionately drawn.

Moon Square Mars

The Moon square Mars indicates that there are great obstacles in the way of successful interhuman relationships. You resist making any adjustments to other people for fear they will take advantage of you if you seem to compromise. Your feelings are vulnerable because you are so sensitive; you are always defending yourself against threats that never materialize. To justify your uncalled-for emotional outbursts, you assert your right to use any necessary tactics to protect yourself. Your lack of control creates problems where none exist and complicates those that do. There are times when you are simply contrary in your dealings with people. You are satisfied only when others give in to your lack of maturity and indulge your need to feel you've won when you've been challenged.

Eventually you will have to grow up, or you will always suffer from the problems that arise from your lack of moderation in dealing with people. If you can understand this problem, you can learn to be more compromising and derive benefits from meeting others halfway. Until you do, you will have a hard time achieving your goals because you will waste so much effort in endless arguments with your competitors. You consider an opinion that is different from yours an affront to your intelligence and competence; those who voice such opinions are assailed with your arrogant and abusive displays of temper. If you are competent, what do you have to fear? Do you need constant reassurances to bolster your sagging opinion of your own worth? If you are not competent, get the training that will enable you to stand your ground with competitors. Your greatest drawback is your lack of self-discipline.

Your professional distress tends to cross over into your domestic life and cause painful situations to develop between you and your partner. Unless you take steps to relieve these pressures, the scars may heal with great difficulty. It is important to maintain complete separation between your domestic and professional lives to avoid contaminating both of them.

You are forceful in making demands of others, but you are not equally prepared to fulfill what is expected of you. This double standard irks the people who have to work closely with you.

The constant strain of argument and the resulting distress cannot fail to have an effect on your physical constitution. Stomach and intestinal disorders could easily develop from the keyed-up tensions and anxieties of your daily affairs.

Moon Square Jupiter

The Moon square Jupiter inclines you to react to your experiences with excessive emotion and to fail in making intellectual appraisals. Consequently, you jump to incorrect conclusions, which causes difficulties in solving your problems. Your reasoning is based on such scanty evidence that you often have to withdraw any statements based on it. The fact is, you lack the emotional stability to pursue your investigations and really get at the facts. You are self-indulgent, not too ambitious, and sometimes irresponsible, preferring to live on the fringes of involvement with people and situations. Your fickleness does not endear you to those who support you because you don't seem to really care whether they support you or not. But if they turn from you because of your indifference, you could become bitter, feeling that you've been deserted. Because you lack emotional maturity, you will be passed by when opportunities come up, especially if they are of a serious nature.

You are generous to excess, so you may find that you are always short of funds when you need them most. Taking a course in financial management would teach you not to indulge in reckless credit buying without any means for repayment. This planetary combination means you prefer to take the easiest route to satisfy your desires, and your planning probably does not go beyond the immediate purchase. Credit buying should be avoided or, better still, completely eliminated. Money burns a hole in your pocket because you have very little sales resistance.

You vacillate between periods of intense enthusiasm and periods of complete apathy. You have creative inspiration but are not willing to make the necessary effort to develop and apply it. You feel sorry for yourself because you are getting so little from life, but on the other hand, you won't make any investment of yourself.

You should develop a program that will give you strict rules for your financial affairs and help you accept responsibility and plan for the future. There is no other way to get your faculties in proper working order. Once you do this, you won't have to settle for routine menial occupations that bore you and infest you with additional lethargy. You can look forward to such interesting fields as law, medicine, home economics, restaurant management, or education. An even better occupation would be in rehabilitation of the handicapped or physical therapy. In such areas you could compare your own situation with the lives of people who have genuine liabilities. That may give you the determination to accomplish some objectives and light the fuse of your creative abilities.

Your physical problems are almost completely the result of overindulgence in food and drink. Avoid rich foods altogether; they only bog down your already sluggish constitution. When you run, let it be as an exercise, not an escape from responsibilities.

Moon Square Saturn

The square between your Moon and Saturn indicates that you find it difficult to let go of the past and anyone associated with it. Because of your early conditioning, you are overwhelmed with guilt when you express disloyalty toward someone you have known a long time. Family matters are therefore very important to you, and you forget few birthdays or other commemorative events. These tendencies show that you are emotionally trapped; it is difficult for you to establish your independence outside the confining circumstances of the home and family.

Your parents were especially responsible for your feeling of dependence and your inability to stand alone. Unfortunately, parents sometimes don't realize how damaging it is for their children to be dependent on them. Your creative expression will be deeply limited by your emotional restrictions.

The most likely fields of work for you are those that serve the needs of the elderly. Such fields as nursing, physical therapy, housing, geriatrics, food, and public assistance programs are some possible avenues of expression. These areas of endeavor emphasize domestic circumstances or identification with individuals who bring to mind your parents. You could perform excellent work and be amply rewarded for your efforts, and at the same time know that you are filling an important need.

Your own romantic satisfaction may not occur until you have fully realized how meager is the scope of your own life. Only when you become aware that time is passing and that fewer partners are available to you, will you scramble to find a mate.

Try to become interested in some avocational activity. Your normal inclination to melancholy and depression will be reduced as you become involved in creative functions. Children could also be a source of great joy to you and relieve the lonely hours by their frivolity and endless curiosity. You might join an organization that helps youngsters who need a big brother or sister or someone who can substitute for their parents.

Eat wholesome food and avoid eating on the run in the fast food service places that today's hasty social structure offers. Try not to eat cold food, and if you can, make it a point to eat with others.

Moon Square Uranus

The square from the Moon to Uranus shows that you are emotionally impulsive and erratic in your behavior. If someone crosses you, you reply abruptly and may even be bad-tempered with those you love most. Your hair-trigger temper literally fires away, especially when you are emotionally aroused. You must exercise greater self-discipline in order to control your outbursts, many of which are unnecessary and unjustified. Because you are accustomed to having your own way, you can't stand being challenged. You have many lessons to learn, and the first is submission. The freedom that you demand you must give others as well, or you will encounter many problems in your relationships.

You are bright and ingeniously clever. When you gain more self-control, you can become a smashing success. Your talents are suitable for teaching, writing, research, or politics. You have the ability to successfully handle or represent groups. A born fighter for equal rights, you can vividly depict to others the freedom that they have been denied.

Your impatience and impulsiveness may make you accident-prone. You lack caution in judgment, which encourages accidents. Your restlessness may be the result of early conditioning, when you weren't allowed to assert yourself at will. You tended to defy authority by rejecting responsibility. If others preyed on your feelings to make you yield to them, you may have responded with emotional arrogance.

Marriage can succeed for you only if you are willing to compromise. Because of your eagerness for personal freedom and your rejection of responsibility, you would be totally unprepared for a union except on your own terms. Your concept of marriage is of the old style in which one partner is the sole authority. But this structure has little chance for success today. Actually, you have a desperate need to relate to your partner on an equal basis. If you do, you will delight in your gain rather than malign your loss.

Moon Square Neptune

The Moon square Neptune shows that you have difficulty in separating fact from fiction. Your highly developed imagination causes some confusion when you are faced with reality. You often "adjust" the reality to what is emotionally tolerable to you. When this is not possible, you may artificially create an environment to which you can escape. You tend to reject your responsibilities, feeling that you are being persecuted by them. Your negative reaction to socially acceptable behavior may cause you to become a parasite and wastefully allow your vast potentials to disintegrate. If you will use it, your extreme sensitivity could be put to use in developing organizations to relieve socially depressed conditions. No one needs to study human nature more than you, and for this, an education is absolutely necessary.

Your early parental conditioning has not prepared you to accept the challenges of the harsh outer world of competition. Fear of the unknown is the greatest deterrent to your success. Your professional activities should relate to earthly enterprises in which your decisions must be approved by someone else. Be especially careful not to become involved in any suspicious alliances. When in doubt about such an alliance, reject it immediately. You are vulnerable to treachery from others who won't hesitate to dump their negative results on you. Be realistic in your ambitions and aim for goals that can be attained within the near future. Proceed with caution, one step at a time, knowing you can redefine your goals as you achieve them.

You should ask a trusted confidential friend or professional advisor to help you find the proper perspective for your creative potentials. Don't trust to luck to see you through the initial stages of your personal or professional relationships. Believe only some of what you see, and none of what you hear.

Your greatest guilt results from letting misunderstandings grow and fester between you and your mate. What you don't know *can* hurt you. Eat nutritious food and be especially careful that cleanliness is a habit, not an accident. You are more open to infection than most, and must take precautions to maintain good health.

Moon Square Pluto

With Moon square Pluto, you are a deep-feeling person who finds it difficult to let go of the past. You are apprehensive about the future and often withdraw defensively. Early parental conditioning may have been responsible for the way you anticipate danger as you face life's problems. Perhaps the relationship with your parents was strained; you felt rejected because you could not discern the love behind their discipline.

You tend to be a loner, but when you do relate to others you often force yourself on them. The result is that they become intolerant of your demanding nature. You expect others to make adjustments to satisfy your expectations of them. You have a lot to learn about human nature; until you do, you may suffer defeat and emotional anxiety. Try to examine situations intellectually and judge them fairly.

Emotional responsibility tends to be a burden. You want to enjoy the pleasures of love without having any limitations imposed on you. With your ardent nature you are inclined to form close but temporary ties based on physical expression.

You are an extremist in your relationships, and you need to learn the art of tender loving care. You must give others the opportunity to show they care for you without forcibly extracting this response from them. If you can modify your rather negative attitude, both you and your partner can derive mutual excitement and reward.

You should seek occupations involving the public so you can observe how people deal with one another. Learn to compromise when it will help you reach your goals. Recommended fields include rehabilitation and physical therapy, welfare programs, social security, or any occupation that helps the disadvantaged to reconstruct their lives in spite of severe limitations. As you assist others, you will realize how useful you can be when motivated by a concern for others. If you can redirect your self-preoccupation toward others, you will be enriched more than you know.

To stay in good health you must occasionally unwind and get away from it all. Problems may develop in the generative organs, and you should have periodic check-ups, if only to keep your mind free of anxiety.

Be cautious about indulging in any aspect of the occult. You may be unable to keep the information that you gain in proper perspective without becoming confused.

Moon Square Ascendant

The Moon square the Ascendant shows that you are emotionally biased in your reaction to events and experiences with people. An impressionable person, you have difficulty in realistically evaluating the conditions you react to. Perhaps you are aware of this tendency and are annoyed with yourself for not being more objective. You are a victim of habits that have become so deeply ingrained that they are difficult to change. Emotionally vulnerable to strong character types who try to mold you to their liking, you are often powerless to do anything but submit. Your difficulty in facing reality increases your problems in relationships, because people are never sure how you will react to them. You are a sentimentalist with strong ties to family and home. It is not easy to transfer those ties to other people with whom you can associate in a personal, emotional relationship. But it is important for you to break away from the past and the limits it imposes on your freedom. You will then be able to develop on your own without feeling that you must get someone else's approval.

The abrasive conditions of open competition will always be painful unless you can insulate yourself by learning to cope with people and circumstances intellectually. You will thus learn that everyone has certain feelings of apprehension about meeting challenges and that you are not alone with this problem. If you talk with your friends about this, you will see that they too have similar anxieties. Knowing this might comfort you. Don't take on more burdens than you need to, especially in your career. Get an education, if you don't already have one, for it will help you succeed in meeting competition. Be wary of associates who may try to get you to compensate for their lack of ability and then leave you holding the bag if things don't turn out as expected.

Above all, keep your personal affairs to yourself. Don't give adversaries the opportunity to learn your weaknesses. And stop feeling sorry for yourself.

Mercury Square Mars

The square from Mercury to Mars gives you enormous mental energy for tackling arduous tasks, but you may lack the determination to persist and complete them. You are strongly opinionated and get angry when your views are not accepted. People may avoid getting into a conversation with you because you will start an argument at the slightest provocation. You are not a good listener if the opinions being expressed are different from yours. You find fault with just about everything, and no situation is too insignificant to escape your notice. Your rudeness to others is tactless and abusive, and you don't even realize it. You should learn to be silent when you are not fully informed on a subject, or you risk being ridiculed by those who know what they're talking about.

Your imagination is highly developed, and you only need to apply it constructively. You will have to make many concessions to others before you can succeed in any profession. Other people need to express themselves just as much as you do; until you learn to adjust to their needs, you will encounter severe obstacles to your desires. You will meet a lot of competition in seeking your goals, but most people are willing to compromise if you give them the opportunity. If you are wrong, admit it. If you are right, say so diplomatically. By doing so, you will come through with flying colors. No one likes a braggart, and everyone admires a person with the strength of character to admit human failing.

When you have dealt with the need to concede to the rights of others, you can achieve success in such fields as law, management, teaching, writing, drama, public relations, or any other communicative endeavor. You could also find satisfaction in sports, either as a performer or in related functions. You will win sometimes, but you must learn to be a good sport when you lose.

Many of the points mentioned in relation to social contacts can also be applied to your romantic interests. You tend to be bitter and vindictive when your attentions are not welcomed. Try to be gracious and shrug off the disappointment. Although you may think you want your partner to be submissive, you would lose respect if that were the case. You need someone who will challenge you to demonstrate your maturity and character.

Mercury Square Jupiter

The square from Mercury to Jupiter shows that there is some discrepancy between your beliefs and the truth. You are eager and enthusiastic to know as much as possible, but you lose interest before you have acquired all the necessary information for practical use. You are impulsive in judgment, and your decisions are often based on insufficient information. You always want to find the easy way out of a dilemma, never wanting to accept responsibility for your actions. The greatest obstacle between you and success is that you expect to start at the top. You lack the self-discipline to apply yourself to your goals and to plan each step along the way. Although you visualize yourself as an informed person at the height of accomplishment, when it is time to plan for that goal you become lazy and sluggish. You've always asked questions in your quest to become a knowledgeable person, but if you don't like the answers, you alter them to suit yourself. You could be called a pathological liar because you don't realize how you have distorted the facts.

Your intentions are not bad, you are only misinformed and lacking incentive. You are sloppy in managing your affairs and unforgivably naive in your dealings with people. You have very little sales resistance, which makes you easy prey for the wily salesman selling the Brooklyn Bridge!

Getting an education is your highest priority, and it is your only chance to avoid a lusterless life with endless detours that lead nowhere. When you are trained you can achieve success in public relations, education, travel, or even writing. Education will help sharpen your judgment and teach you to plan your climb to achievement. You have no other alternative available. However, it might be advisable to postpone your education until you've had an opportunity to feel the abrasive competition of the open market. It might prove to be the most constructive lesson you ever receive and could convince you that without training you belong to the masses who have no advantages.

You are likely to suffer from nervous disorders caused by mental anxieties over your life direction and the pain of competition. Frequent rest and avocational pursuits are recommended. You cannot be forced to change your attitude, but it is hoped that you will, for your own benefit.

Mercury Square Saturn

The square from Mercury to Saturn indicates that your early conditioning has inhibited you from using your imagination in exploiting your potentials. Somewhat traditional in your thinking, you find it difficult to stay in the mainstream of current ideas or develop new ideas. You may be narrow-minded in your opinions because you fear change and the insecurity it represents to you.

In school you were slow to learn because it required so much effort. You felt you were being punished because you were expected to maintain your grades. It's not that you are incapable, but rather indolent and mentally lazy. When you don't succeed with a minimum of effort, you quickly become depressed. The result is a lack of enthusiasm in developing your creative potentials. Your conservative attitude is a liability, because today's society demands personal assertion in order to succeed. Your fear of competition means you cannot prove to yourself that you are capable of meeting challenges. Unless you adjust your thinking to the rapid changes taking place in the world, you will greatly limit your progress.

Once you get over feeling negative about everything, you can make plans to see that your ideas are acted on. This planetary combination gives many advantages. Instead of fear, have courage to accept the obvious. Replace negative thinking with plans that will allow you to face your obligations with optimism. Look to the past, of which you are so fond, for the lessons you need to adequately cope with problems of the present and future. You don't really have any alternative if you want to achieve your objectives in life.

You could achieve success in education, science, politics, conservation of natural resources, government service, industrial management, or architecture. As you can see, some of these fields, especially science and education, require that you be willing to accept change. You need only the determination to succeed and the ability to capitalize on your creative potentials in order to rise to prominence in any of these occupations.

Be careful not to sign legal documents without reading the fine print, and avail yourself of legal counsel. You can be vindictive if someone tries to take advantage of you. In your job you are resentful of authority and complain bitterly when someone else gets the promotion you feel you deserve. You must demonstrate your superiority in order to attract attention. You may just have to try harder than others to succeed or gain recognition.

Try to look at the bright side of life and admit that if you are having difficulty, perhaps you haven't made as much of a contribution as you could have.

Mercury Square Uranus

With Mercury square Uranus, you are mentally alert, bright, and ingeniously talented. You are also eccentric in your thinking, and your opinions are usually dramatically at odds with prevailing beliefs. You are a rebel with causes that most people find obnoxious or belligerent. In seeking to obtain truth, you often bypass logic. Your extreme impatience with established facts often forces you to create whatever truths require the least commitment from you. The problem is your refusal to accept responsibility for what you say.

Your arrogant "know-it-all" attitude makes it very difficult for you to succeed at occupations in which rules must be observed. You take rules lightly and openly protest to the person who constructed them. The first lesson to learn, then, is humility. When you have learned this you will be readily accepted and will have the opportunity to demonstrate your vast intellectual talent. You can rise to the top in many fields, such as science, education, social services, and even politics.

Only time will convince you that it is foolish to project yourself prematurely and run the risk of being discredited. Experience is what you need to sharpen your deductive ability and reward you for using your talents wisely.

Your personal relationships often don't last long, because you are unable to compromise. Often, what you say is not what you really feel which makes anyone who is emotionally involved with you feel unsure. Problems between you and the one you love aren't easy to resolve. You don't want to give in, yet to obstinately stand firm is completely unrealistic. You are obviously exciting to have around, but perhaps it would be wise to choose someone with a more stable temperament as your lifetime mate.

Try to slow down and maintain a moderate pace if you want to avoid nervous problems. Don't stay keyed-up for prolonged periods.

Mercury Square Neptune

Mercury square Neptune shows that your imagination often gets in the way of logical thinking. Your fear of responsibility causes problems in both emotional and material affairs. You seem unable to view life realistically and by supposedly logical arguments can convince yourself that an unbearable reality doesn't exist. The resulting distortion further complicates matters so that the truth is completely hidden. You are an escapist, a problem partly caused by your early parental conditioning.

Until you face up to the harsh realities of the world outside, your progress will be limited. Because of your extreme sensitivity, superficial problems become exaggerated. You have talent to express, but you must prepare for occasional setbacks when you expose yourself to competition. The challenge of competition can threaten your success unless you exercise self-control and become more confident. You must train your intellectual abilities in order to gain self-confidence. Be honest with yourself at all times as you develop your capabilities so that you will understand your limitations.

Eventually you can succeed in writing, acting, education, art, or in social programs to benefit others. You must clarify your objectives and learn to focus your attention on one specific thing at a time. This is important: too many interests at once only bring out your weakness under pressure, which will defeat you.

Your best bet is to involve yourself in activities that serve other people's needs. Exposure to their problems will help you solve your own as well.

Be cautious or conservative in your romantic alliances, for your imagination can play tricks on you. If you interpret a person's casual interest as an indication of love, you could be disappointed. Above all, don't make any commitments to others until they establish their sincerity. You are easily victimized by your desire to experience an ideal relationship. Develop your creative talents so that when you are occasionally alone you are not lonely.

Mercury Square Pluto

The square from Mercury to Pluto indicates that you must learn to concentrate and apply self-discipline in mental pursuits. You find prolonged study painful and demanding, so you may resent anyone who forces you to persist. This was probably more apparent in your early years when schoolwork seemed so laborious. In spite of this, you have the self-determination to accept responsibility, although not under the watchful eye of someone else.

Your manner of speech is penetrating, and you express yourself so harshly that you seem almost insensitive. This arouses bitterness in others. You are undeniably bright and keenly perceptive, but you rarely feel obligated to other people. You are inclined to pessimism. Your behavior is extreme; at one moment you will criticize others with brutal frankness, and the next moment you will show amazing skill in maintaining your poise under pressure. It is truly difficult for people to know how you will react, so some may avoid getting close to you.

Though you are fearless by nature, you demonstrate an incredible lack of common sense in dangerous situations. You take unnecessary risks just to prove to others how courageous you really are. Because of this, you may seek occupations that involve hazards. You are prone to accidents from equipment that uses or contains pressure, such as heating systems and boilers. Observe all safety precautions in handling them.

Before you decide on any profession, you must develop self-control and responsibility. You are more inclined to make errors in judgment than the average person, especially in handling large sums of money. Avoid getting into debt unless it is absolutely necessary.

You might be interested in such fields as crime detection, research and development, chemistry, pathology or medicine, but you must be prepared to yield to the authority of your teachers. It is essential that you pay attention to detail and work hard to gain the expertise required. Although you prefer to avoid reality, you must live with it. When you realize this, you will begin to grow and develop.

In your immediate environment you can make enormous contributions to the socially disadvantaged. You are not afraid to speak up and challenge authorities when you learn they have abused their positions of trust. Just be certain you have all the necessary supporting evidence in order to avoid being ridiculed. This would bring out the worst in you and could result in violence.

Although you certainly know better, you sometimes have an obsession to shape other people's lives. You use cunning schemes to gain their submission. Because of your intolerant attitude, you should study human nature and learn how to effectively motivate others.

Mercury Square Ascendant

Mercury square the Ascendant shows that you are often misunderstood when you express yourself. People tend to react negatively when you talk with them and resent what you say, though they may not show it. You are unable to project yourself with confidence, and this lack of assurance is unwittingly transmitted to your listeners, who find it hard to believe you. Your air of superiority doesn't quite hide your feelings of inferiority. Hoping to win the approval of those you deal with, you appeal to their emotions, but your flattery is obviously tinged with insincerity. People are never really sure what you mean and may ask you to repeat yourself so they will know whether they heard you right the first time.

You want your friends to like you, and you willingly do favors for them, hoping they will show their appreciation. You are guardedly optimistic about gaining your objectives, because your early home life taught you to seek only those goals that your superiors would approve of. This condition delayed your development as an individual, which would have enabled you to be independently secure on your own merits. You tend to compare yourself with peers who have succeeded while still relatively young, and you resent the fact that you did not have the same opportunities to become successful.

Your education may have been delayed because of family priorities. But a late start doesn't deny you success; it only means that you will have to work harder to catch up, if that's so important to you. It may also mean that you will feel frustrated when challenged by well-educated and trained competitors. Don't give anyone a chance to demonstrate superiority over you. You *can* succeed in competition by getting the education you need and by working hard to gain experience. You can train yourself and acquire a reputation for excellence in everything you do. If you think positively about developing your creative potentials, you will learn to like yourself for what you can accomplish. Also you will win the admiration you deserve.

Venus Square Mars

Your Venus square Mars indicates that you have difficulty in maintaining harmonious relations with people. You are not the easiest person to get along with; you expect others to make concessions to you, but you refuse to make any compromises without being pressured to do so. You have a strong desire nature and use all kinds of clever tactics to get what you want. People may accuse you of using others to gratify your desires by taking advantage of their feelings for you, especially when you don't have similar feelings for them. You greedily assume the privilege of indulging yourself at every opportunity, expecting no interference from anyone.

This planetary combination indicates that you are not really happy with yourself, so you provoke trouble with others in order to blame them for your inability to resolve your personal conflicts. You are indifferent to the feelings of others because you don't really think they are worth it. The problems you have in relationships should cause you to wonder whether you are worth it to them as well! Somewhere there is a solution, and it would certainly help if you toned down your desires and adopted a more compromising attitude. Accept the fact that few people get everything they want, and when they don't, they turn their attention elsewhere. You cannot force yourself on people and not expect some resentment for it.

Until you work out these personality difficulties, you will have problems with your family, friends, and associates on the job. If you can become more compromising you can be successful in any occupation, even those that bring you into close contact with people. You have magnetism, and you tempt people to want to be close to you. You are certainly not dull, and excitement goes wherever you go. Just be sure the excitement doesn't become turmoil. Don't complain about negative human qualities—you have a fair number of your own.

Make an effort to broaden your perspective by learning something about art, literature, music, and the social amenities. This aspect tends to produce a coarseness of manner that requires refinement and polish.

Venus Square Jupiter

Your Venus square Jupiter indicates that you are a bit indulgent and careless in attending to your responsibilities. When things are going your way, you are outgoing and personable, but you can be difficult to deal with when you run into opposition. In your relations with people, you may indicate that you will make adjustments, but this is often an empty gesture. You resent being forced to do anything and wish that people would realize this before attempting to get you to act. You feel that antagonistic feelings between you and someone else are largely the result of the other person not understanding you. You are generous mainly when it satisfies an ulterior motive, and you may withdraw an offer to help someone at a later time by saying, "It wouldn't have been appreciated anyway."

You have the potential to fill any of a variety of occupational positions if you learn to accept responsibility. You may not be free to engage in other activities that you would prefer, but you must be realistic in determining your priorities. You must discipline yourself to earn your living first and indulge yourself only when your duties are fulfilled. It is indeed almost impossible to have it both ways. In all your affairs, including personal relationships, job opportunities, or frustrations, you tend to exaggerate your plans for the future. You make it seem that everyone is beating a path to your door for your attentions. But the truth is that you are desperate for attention and will resort to all sorts of deceptive tactics to gain it. You must come to grips with these problems before you can expect to be successful. Once you do, you are well on your way to achievement in such fields as travel, public relations, guidance counseling, etc. Communication is your greatest asset, and you can use it skillfully to gain your objectives. Stop being so defensive; most people are willing to meet you halfway if you give them the chance. You feel that you attract more than your share of hostility from people who are trying to take advantage of you.

If you present yourself honestly, you will attract individuals whom you can relate to romantically. Learn to be generous to others, even if it hurts to know that the generosity may never be returned. You may be surprised to discover how many people are naturally generous. Certainly you sometimes hate yourself for being cantankerous with people who don't deserve this treatment. When you indulge the needs and desires of others, it pays big dividends in goodwill.

Your greatest problems are learning to be less suspicious of people when they extend themselves to you and to be less demanding of them in their relationships with you.

You may have a problem in keeping your weight down because of your self-indulgent habits. Rich foods are not for you, and a low-carbohydrate diet is recommended. Rest is also very important, and if you cannot get extended hours of sleep, try taking frequent short rest periods.

Venus Square Saturn

The square from Venus to Saturn indicates that you have difficulty relating to others. As a result, you may feel left out of the mainstream of social relationships. You are basically unwilling to accept the responsibility that is established when two individuals meet in a more than casual way. You tend to be on the defensive, as if you feared that the other person would make impossible demands of you. Perhaps in your early life you felt rejected by someone you really cared for, even a parent. As you grew you sheltered yourself more and more from outside communication, always afraid of rejection. This conditioning may have produced the feeling you have that you are not destined for happiness in your relationships. If you accept others for themselves, realizing that everyone has to make concessions and adjustments to others, then happiness can surely be yours. Remember that even people who seem happy have difficult moments in relating to others; your predicament is not at all unique.

Perhaps your most significant lessons will be learned in relationships with others. If you will meet people halfway, you'll find that most of them will do the same. If you are attracted to someone whom you can admire and respect, isn't it worth adjusting to that person's peculiarities? You will find your own identity by being willing to identify with others in mutual responsiveness.

Before you can hope to succeed in any occupational capacity, you will have to solve your problem in relating to people. Otherwise you will create a difficult environment in which to work. Most people will not tolerate someone who is cantankerous or difficult to please. You have the talent to achieve rewarding and satisfying goals, once you learn to meet people halfway.

You could find satisfaction in banking, finance, law, insurance, real estate, buying and selling, or designing. Your sense of order and balanced judgment could prove useful to you in any of these fields. But it is essential that you recognize your self-worth before you implement your talents. You must gain the recognition of your employers for your honesty, integrity, and good judgment because these are the good qualities that will help you achieve success.

Try to become more optimistic and give yourself a greater chance for happiness. Feeling melancholy and sorry for yourself stimulates some physical problems, such as high blood pressure caused by tension and anxiety. Learn to relax and let go. Life is too short to let it become unnecessarily burdened by unimportant matters. Try giving instead of complaining about what others demand of you.

Venus Square Uranus

The square from Venus to Uranus shows that you tend to be fascinated by individuals who have unusual qualities. You remain infatuated until the person begins to be seriously interested in you. Then you find ways to detach yourself from any permanent tie, because you enjoy being a free spirit. You are not really sure you can ever accept the responsibility of belonging to one person. The fear of responsibility is unrealistic, but it is consistent with your figuratively promiscuous temperament. You defy convention and deliberately show your disdain for those who submit to it.

You refuse to compromise with tradition because to do so would mean that you had no individuality of your own. There is much confusion in your mind between love and friendship. You win friends easily but you aren't committed to them, except socially or superficially. Love, however, is more difficult, because of the demands involved and the limitations on your freedom. It is extremely impractical to expect others to make adjustments that allow you to preserve your freedom, while you contribute nothing in return. Even friendship requires that you meet others halfway.

You can enjoy exquisite thrills in the total fulfillment of a true love relationship. In a merely casual contact, however, "If you settle for less, you will get less."

If you apply the same attitudes to your professional interests, the results can be devastating. Promotion is unlikely unless you slow down your breakneck social pace, to show that you are sufficiently stable to accept greater responsibility. You must also be more discreet in your private affairs, which you tend to flaunt carelessly.

Nervous irritability often results from this planetary combination, especially if you are immoderate and don't get sufficient rest.

Venus Square Neptune

The square from Venus to Neptune means that your imagination may cause you some difficulties. Your defenses usually go up whenever anything or anyone seems to challenge you. They may not in fact be threatening you, but you still respond as if they were. It is not easy for you to see things clearly, and you are often ill-advised in your judgment. Instead of rose-colored glasses, you have blinders that block out the truths you can't accept. Your outlook on life needs great adjustment if you wish to avoid the many problems that are sure to develop.

You are best suited to self-employment. You are so sensitive to people that occupations involving others can produce much anxiety and stress. Because you can't handle frustration, it is doubtful that you could succeed in any competitive function. You will tend to get into disputes with co-workers or make accusations you cannot sustain or justify. You must reconstruct your attitudes so that tolerance is a feature, not an accident, of your behavior.

Find an individual outlet for your enormous creative ability so that when problems occur it must be your responsibility alone to resolve them. In this way, you will avoid the complexities of guilt or condemnation that can result when others are involved. In time you will learn from your experiences and know how to cope with reality when escape is not possible. Meditate seriously so that you can be spiritually prepared to endure external abrasions with dignity and self-assurance.

Discipline yourself in your personal relationships and romantic ties. It is one of your failings that you tend to encourage others to take advantage of you. Be cautious about making any emotional commitments unless the other person has shown solid proof of honesty and sincerity.

Your lack of concern about material matters can prove costly. Don't overmortgage yourself so that you are caught in a financial trap, and resist buying on credit. You are easily entranced by appearances and often ignore the harsh reality of paying for what you have purchased.

Venus Square Pluto

As a result of Venus square Pluto, you may find that your emotional life brings you more problems than satisfaction. You are deeply aware that any benefits you receive are always accompanied by some negative effects. What you want is often not what you need, so that as you strive to satisfy your desires you also have to endure suffering in some way. These desires cast you into relationships that eventually frustrate your real need for a permanent and serene partnership.

You tend to give of yourself in order to get what you want and may even profess love for someone in order to marry. You could be obsessed with using sex as a device to obtain financial security or material comforts. It may also be that you really love someone who is already attached, or that your lover may be taken from you by a new interest in someone else.

There will be a major upheaval or serious crisis in your life, which could easily transform your preoccupation with personal, physical relationships to a broader love that includes spiritual and intellectual companionship as well.

You can be sure that if problems persist in your domestic and professional relationships, you have not successfully resolved your personal conflicts. To demonstrate your worth you must learn to fulfill your responsibilities. Don't wait until you are sure you will benefit from a particular course before you start, or you never will accomplish what you want. Make sure that your behavior is above reproach so you can attract people for what you are. This will also encourage the kinds of circumstances you can deal with, at home and on the job.

You need to change your attitudes in order to significantly improve people's feelings about you. Patronizing people is a poor substitute for being honest with them. Friends thus gained will never respect you, and you won't respect them either. Don't make promises unless you intend to keep them. People will think you are a poor loser or that you make gestures of compromise only when there is something you want. You are inclined to take when you should give, to make accusations without thinking and to feel offended when your sincerity is challenged. All these qualities make others behave offensively to you. Try to develop warmth, sincerity, and compassion. The revised image will miraculously transform your personal and social affairs to your benefit.

You may experience some malfunction of the generative organs. Periodic physical examinations are recommended.

Venus Square Ascendant

Venus square the Ascendant shows that you are a sentimentalist and too attached to your early home life. Your still-vivid memories of that time interfere with your becoming independent and secure enough to stand on your own feet. You feel that if you assert your freedom, you are being disloyal to the past. It should be apparent that unless you let go of binding obligations to those you love, you will never succeed in realizing your personal goals. To justify your difficulty in transferring loyalty to yourself, you devise all kinds of excuses for holding on to your obligations.

You can gain the security you need if you capitalize on your creative ideas. Not having sufficient financial reserves is especially painful for you. You know how to make money but you don't enjoy making any physical effort to earn it. You love your comforts and don't like to be disturbed unless it is absolutely necessary. Perhaps it seems easier to let someone else provide for you, so you prefer to live at home with your parents in a ready-made environment.

At times you are ungracious to your friends when they ask favors of you, probably because you don't like to extend yourself unless it will benefit you in some way. You are generous when you talk about what you would do with a huge amount of money, but if you had it you probably wouldn't follow through. You admire people who are skilled in accumulating capital in their endeavors, but you resent it when you cannot induce them to assist you in your efforts.

Hard work seems worthwhile to you only when your future security is at stake. Your goals are not well-defined, because to define them would burden you with responsibility. You avoid making a personal commitment in using your creative talents unless there is no other alternative, or if your source of sustenance is cut off.

Mars Square Jupiter

Your Mars square Jupiter indicates that it is essential for you to discipline yourself in using your abundant physical and intellectual resources. Everything you do must be planned, or you will waste a lot of energy in nonproductive enterprises. You want to emulate those you admire for their professional accomplishments, but you may not be willing to endure all the hard work required to succeed. You make valiant efforts to acquire knowledge, but when there is no immediate reward you quickly lose interest. Once you acquire faith in your ability to succeed, persistence and determination will come. You are impatient to an extreme, but with some contact between Saturn and Mars or Saturn and Jupiter, this will eventually be corrected.

In spite of the sloppiness resulting from your careless use of your energy, you will nevertheless benefit somewhat from the lessons learned. Only time can refine your manner of applying yourself. You need to define your objectives clearly and then establish a program for realizing them, a schedule you can adhere to. You need to consolidate your resources to make a massive assault on your most important priority. To do anything less than this would be a sheer waste of energy. Diversification is fine, if you take up each subject exclusively, but not if you attempt to develop a variety of interests simultaneously.

You are almost certain to have domestic and professional difficulties when you first set out to make a life for yourself. This planetary combination inclines you to some difficulty in dealing with people. You feel threatened by competitors and unfairly treated by superiors in your job. You don't accept criticism gracefully. Your domestic tranquility will be disturbed because you complain so bitterly about the way you are treated that your partner becomes bored with it all.

You have the potential for excellence in law, government, teaching, writing, public speaking, sports, acting, and the communications media in general. This aspect gives you the necessary drive to accept challenges, for you realize that they are the only way to determine your competence. You are probably more likely to avoid a confrontation when you suspect that your opponent is expertly trained and has a greater advantage than you. With experience, you will meet any challenger with complete assurance of success. Even if you don't succeed, you will know you have given your best, and that is all that can be expected.

This configuration indicates that you are accident prone because of your reckless disregard for safety measures. You tend to act impulsively, not taking time to consider whether any danger is involved. Because you do everything to excess, you need frequent rest to restore your physical reserves.

Mars Square Saturn

With Mars square Saturn you alternate between periods of aggression and periods of recession and apathy. You are constantly at war with yourself because you cannot resolve this problem, which is not an easy one, as your experience has shown. Even when you gather the will to assert yourself you are apprehensive that your timing may be off. Likewise, when inertia prevails, you realize you should have taken advantage of an opportunity earlier. Only time will improve your capacity to correctly judge when you should take action.

You will have to be very careful not to become embittered by your occasional setbacks. If you can learn from them, you are ahead because of the experience. Potentially you can accomplish much, once you know your limits. You can excel in occupations requiring endurance and follow-through, as in the fields of military service, land development, sports, and physical therapy. In whatever profession you follow, you must be willing to start at the bottom and work your way to the top. There is no easy way to gain a position of authority—you must earn it. Any shortcuts to the top are at best hazardous, because your position will be insecure.

Your greatest lessons in life will probably be learned through your relationships with others. You don't always know just how much you can assert yourself in your associations. You especially need to develop your opinion of yourself by learning to use your talents so skillfully that you never need to feel threatened by anyone else. You must develop self-confidence about meeting challenge and competitors. When you say NO! you must mean it, and when you say YES! it should be with firm conviction based on reason. You must especially avoid vacillation and indecision, because they raise doubts about your credibility.

Your romantic relationships are ensnarled with inconsistencies of temperament and emotional intent. You suffer deeply if your advances are rejected by someone. It is possible for you to become vindictive and even use physical violence against people you don't really want to hurt. You tend to hurt the one you love without realizing it.

Caution in all physical activities is advised, because this planetary combination inclines to accidents and broken bones. Be particularly careful around machinery, and when you are unsure whether you can do something that requires considerable physical strength, don't.

Mars Square Uranus

The square from Mars to Uranus shows that you have a strong desire to be free to exploit yourself without hesitation or restraint. However, the fear of emotional or material losses reduces this drive to prudent levels. You must have self-control in order to conserve your personal resources, and you should have some guarantee of safety in any deliberate action that you take. You may feel much anxiety and apprehension for accomplishing less than you could if security were not an important consideration. Before you begin any contemplated action, you must be assured that the effort will not have been wasted.

An undercurrent of measured caution always accompanies your professional activities. Because of this, it will take longer to realize your goals. Once you achieve your objectives however, they will be far more permanent because their foundation is solid. You will still be impatient, though, for postponing projects can be aggravating. There is no alternative, unless you go ahead, taking the chance that others won't resist you and challenge your desires.

Your romantic needs are strong, since your desires are well-developed. But the responsibility associated with emotional satisfaction may deter you from ever marrying. If you readily accept responsibility, then the urge to marry may occur early in life. Otherwise, you will have to relate to someone who can accept an arrangement without legal sanction.

You should avoid machinery until you learn to protect yourself. You must acquire a healthy respect for safety. Try not to exceed the limits of your physical capabilties, and if you are in doubt about whether to indulge in a physical activity, your decision should be negative.

If you are in charge of others in your work, don't expect them to perform as you would. They may not have your drive. Above all, moderation in all things should be your guide.

Mars Square Neptune

With Mars square Neptune, it is difficult for you to assert yourself without causing some turmoil. You fluctuate between an intense desire for action and complete apathy. The unconscious or vague reasons that prompt you to act are in conflict with your aggressive feelings. You also have deep anxieties in your sexual life that are a constant source of annoyance. Your needs are considerable, but obtaining the satisfaction of sexual release is often complicated by your inability to face reality. You may be attracted to someone who is already attached, so that you experience guilt in fulfilling your desires. Early parental conditioning may have tried to repress your desires, and now you suffer from the results of repression.

With your temperament, you should work with as few people as possible to minimize the subversive factors others sometimes use to gain control over you. Self-employment would be even better. You could function well in the field of medicine and satisfy your need to render service and still remain detached. You need to develop your ability to plan and control events in order to determine the effects you hope to achieve. Leave nothing to chance. When things don't go well you tend to blame others, diverting criticism from yourself. You defend yourself against imagined abuses as if you were looking for ways to persecute yourself.

Because you are somewhat accident-prone, you should avoid machinery and mechanical devices. You are also more susceptible to infection than most people and should follow hygienic rules strictly in preparing your food. The same attention to cleanliness should prevail in all of your activities.

The crises in your relationships may be caused by your casual attitude about your lover's credentials. Sometimes you lower your standards and attract negative types whose primary interest is sex. When such disappointments occur, you may become bitter and resentful, but you have only yourself to blame.

Mars Square Pluto

The square of Mars to Pluto provides you with an overly forceful nature. You are inclined to be extremely aggressive in pursuing your desires, and your behavior is often foolish and reckless. If you assume that you can assert your will on others with impunity, you may discover later that you've created a problem you can't handle. The embarrassment of such an incident can make you angry, and you may even resort to physical violence in retaliation.

When frustrated, you can become abusive, which will cause problems in your relationships with others. The result may be domestic difficulties and antagonism from your superiors, which could jeopardize your income. You must learn to curb your temper under stress, or you will bring yourself more grief than any temporary satisfaction would warrant. Once you learn this, you will find that you can accomplish what you wish because of your courage, determination, persistence, and self-driving ambition.

You have a highly developed but unrefined sexual drive. When your advances are rejected, you overdramatize and exaggerate the importance of the incident. The sexual drive is significant, to be sure, but you need to assess its value in relation to your total life direction. Make sure it is balanced by other facets in your relationships with people.

When you are unhappy with disagreeable elements in your environment, examine these elements realistically, not emotionally. Get someone else's opinion and then submit the problem to a person with the authority to do something about it. If you attempt to take matters into your own hands, they will only get stained in the process.

A final word — try to be *for* a cause with the same enthusiasm you show when you are *against* something. Love works wonders in getting people to work voluntarily with you. Resist issuing ultimatums when you run into resistance.

Mars Square Ascendant   *Kathryn*

Mars square the Ascendant indicates that you show no moderation in asserting yourself. When you feel the urge to take action about something important, you usually do so without polish or refinement. When you act this way, people resent it and find you offensive. When reminded of your shortcomings, you are offended because you feel you should not have to answer to anyone for your actions. It is nearly impossible to stop you from expressing your opinion, and you don't care where you are or who hears you. Anyone who provokes you invites your immediate reaction, usually a negative one.

You seem to enjoy watching people become upset by your display of bad manners. You delight in putting people on the defensive and watching them squirm as you antagonize them with your tirades. Because you aren't really convinced of your superiority, you have a chip on your shoulder. Only winning in a show of strength can satisfy your ego.

Your parents probably tried to stimulate you to do the things they were unable to accomplish in their lives, and you became annoyed by this pressure. Disagreements and bickering in your early home life have caused you to become bitter and resentful of authority. Although you want your talents to be recognized, your inability to submit to authority creates problems and restricts the progress of your career. Problems may also result because your parents could not provide you with an education. If you have received an education, you have done so by your own efforts.

You admire people who can translate their capabilities into financial gain. But if you are willing to endure the self-denial and sacrifice required, you can accomplish the same thing. You know your future security depends on successfully developing your potentials. You are willing to work hard to realize your goals, but there are times when you wonder if they are worth all the effort and the frustrations you must endure.

Jupiter Square Saturn

The square from Jupiter to Saturn indicates problems in self-awareness. You tend to put yourself down when you compare your capabilities to the skills of other people. The fact is, you are trying to avoid your responsibilities to yourself and to those persons who depend on you. Parental influence played an important role in your lack of self-esteem; your early conditioning led you to believe that you were less competent than others and that you had to yield to those who were "obviously" more talented. Now your actions show that you lack the courage to persist in spite of adversity. You feel you don't have the right to expect anything worthwhile for yourself. You have little hope for success, but this is just lazy self-indulgence and is inexcusable.

Stop making comparisons with other people's accomplishments; you have your own. You have a vast storehouse of information with which to gain your objectives, but you must formulate them yourself. Once you've extablished goals, prepare a program for achieving them, and adhere to it. Try to focus on one thing at a time and direct all your resources and energy toward that. Stop making excuses for yourself and realize that only hard work will pay you any dividends.

You could become successful in such fields as law, education, physical therapy, or the ministry. The demands of these occupations may tax your endurance and cause periodic setbacks, but you must persist with great determination. It is important for you to be able to look back with satisfaction on occasional successes and realize that you are capable of much more. You will encounter resistance from superiors, and you may have to endure many indignities for the sake of job security. Acquiring the credentials that attest to your competence will mark a milestone in your development.

You will have to learn the hard way that accomplishment comes from a lot of hardship and self-denial. There is no easy road to victory for you. Don't make any agreements that you can't fulfill and don't sign any contracts that go beyond the limits of your abilities. Give yourself the opportunity to reach your goals. Yours is a bittersweet destiny with many highs and lows, progress and reversals, but you will always move toward realization and fulfillment.

Faith is your greatest ally when nothing else seems to work for you. It can sustain you through your most difficult periods and comfort you when you reach your goals with assurance that you have done your job well.

Jupiter Square Uranus

The square from Jupiter to Uranus indicates that you have some powerfully inhibiting conflicts, which limit your goals. Perhaps you simply bite off more than you can chew, taking on more burdens than you can satisfactorily handle at one time. You are quite able to do whatever you set your mind on, but you strive to do too much at once. You need to establish priorities and exercise self-control so that you can complete one thing at a time. It is easy to see that if you mobilize your efforts toward a single objective you can get results that would otherwise be difficult or impossible.

Because of your enthusiasm you could achieve success in politics, education, law, religion, or the occult. Your greatest problem, though, is your motivation for success. If others see that you are motivated by the desire for recognition and accolades, it could interfere with your objectives. Your plans are only as good as your purpose. Unless you include others in the benefits of your efforts, you may suddenly encounter severe reversals that could shatter your dreams.

You are inclined to want to start at the top, but you aren't likely to be tolerated there unless you are well equipped and have good credentials. Your growth and development depend entirely on your willingness to submit to rigorous preparation. Learn the basic foundation well before trying to implement your talents. Learn to stop, look, and listen before you do anything, and you will avoid many embarrassments.

Your pretentiousness also leads to disappointments in your romantic affairs. Has it occurred to you that not everyone finds you irresistible? Many will, of course, but be cautious with those who don't. Try to construct your goals, both emotional and real, according to their probability of success. Be moderate in your enthusiasm, so you can enjoy the elation of happiness when success is realized. Learn to expect failure; it's where the greatest lessons in life are learned. Your future happiness can be planned; don't make it an accidental process.

Jupiter Square Neptune

The square from Jupiter to Neptune shows you have creative potentials that need only self-discipline and control to become activated. You are excessively self-indulgent, so the dreams you create never have the slightest chance of being realized. You tend to reject any social burden as being too demanding of your time. Yet you casually waste your time elsewhere and offer yourself to projects of questionable validity, although you don't see them in that light. You are gullible and easily influenced by others to adopt their attitudes.

Your greatest problem is in overextending yourself in buying on credit. There is no excuse for not using your intellect to determine how far you can indulge yourself before you land in trouble. Your higher mental faculties are in good order, but you don't want to face reality and responsibility. Your lines of reasoning are somewhat distorted, and your vision is clouded. Don't be a sucker for deceptive advertisements — they're designed to sway you and others with your vulnerable temperament.

You are sympathetic and kindly toward others, but it may be a mistake to extend yourself for people who will take advantage of your unselfish nature. In your professional work, be extra careful and *don't take any chances*. If an accident *can* happen, it will happen to you. Openly discuss who will be permitted to have classified information and rigidly adhere to the decision. You could easily be the fall guy when there is an infraction of the rules. Mind your own business, and don't discuss your personal life with anyone. When you speak you often reveal secrets without realizing it.

It would be wise for you to avoid any discussion about religion or occult matters in general. You are not temperamentally equipped to defend your position in such a conversation. Be hesitant and cautious in everything you do, and try not to emotionalize your romantic attachments. When you do, others may get the impression that you would indulge in escapades even with someone whose ethics and spiritual values were unacceptable.

Jupiter Square Pluto

The square from Jupiter to Pluto inclines you to rebel against existing codes of ethics. You may challenge authority in your efforts to find easier ways to realize your goals. Your greatest problem is in expecting a large return from little or no investment on your part. You exaggerate your burdens to justify your unwillingness to accept responsibility. Often misguided in contributing too much to questionable enterprises, you can suffer bitter disappointments in this way. Don't count too heavily on others to come to your assistance when you are in trouble. It is especially important not to overextend yourself when buying on credit, hoping you'll have the money when payments are due.

You lean toward professions associated with large-scale enterprises that affect many people and in which substantial financial returns are likely. In other words, you enjoy wheeling and dealing. Yet you know that you walk a tightrope in these kinds of activities. You seem to tempt fate by seeking out risky schemes that could run into legal difficulties. Money-lending, political maneuvering, and professional gambling are some of the activities you may get caught up in. You could unscrupulously exploit others for your own gain, and you may find yourself similarly victimized.

Your romantic interests could come about through your business functions. You may go to extremes in your romantic conquests, from the coarse and vulgar to the polished and refined. The people you admire are those who yield to momentary impulses and don't care about propriety. You live for the moment and avoid looking back.

Unless you recognize your frailties and shortcomings, you must expect to be severely dissatisfied with your goals. It is imperative that you examine your life in retrospect and honestly realize how you have shortchanged yourself by rejecting rules to live by. It is difficult for you to learn from experience, but until you do, your future hopes must remain empty dreams.

Jupiter Square Ascendant

Jupiter square the Ascendant shows that you never act in moderation and are self-indulgent to an extreme. Lacking sufficient self-control, you do everything to excess, and only realize later how much time and effort you've wasted.

You have big ideas that you want to work out and capitalize on. Although you hope that your parents will provide the funds you need to develop your ideas, you are prepared with other alternatives if they can't help you. You understand the importance of having financial reserves available. You also know that you can always convert your creative abilities into cash by developing and using them constructively.

Secretly you long for the time when you can enjoy all the comforts and benefits that you have denied yourself in pursuing your goals. This longing drives you to get the largest possible return from your creative talents so you can enjoy your retirement years free from financial worry. You are willing to make whatever contributions in effort and hard work are required to achieve that objective. You also have a big heart, and people take advantage of you without your realizing it.

You need self-discipline so you don't take on more obligations than you can handle. You know how to fraternize with important people to gain favors and access to important positions. You want to reach the top in your career as soon as possible, but you may not fully realize how unstable a top position can be. Remember, it is only as secure as your willingness to endure self-denial in holding it.

It is important for you to work in partnership with others so that you can consolidate all your talents and resources. However, you will have to modify your desires to be consistent with group objectives.

Saturn Square Uranus

The square between Saturn and Uranus refers to the difficulty you have in making decisions, especially when old attitudes must yield to the process of change. It is the kind of apprehension you may have experienced when you learned to drive a car after going everywhere on a bicycle. Your fear in unfamiliar situations is really the only deterrent to your progress.

Perhaps you were so conditioned by parental discipline that you still look for approval before asserting your creative potentials. It is probably more difficult for you to break with the past than for most people, but it is imperative that you do. Your future depends on successfully breaking old ties, even if it means alienating others. You may be "reminded" that you can't do this or that because you're not old enough or you lack the experience, but you must persist. Once you overcome your fear of the untried, you can climb to any level you choose.

You are especially suited to work in large organizations where the sky's the limit for your potentials. You have sufficient self-regard to know your limitations, and once you recognize your own worth, success will be yours. Your respect for the lessons of the past should serve you well in the pursuit of your goals. Politics, industry, science, research, and even the occult fields would benefit from your contribution.

You must be prepared for occasional setbacks and reverses, but these will make your credentials more secure and establish your worth in the eyes of those who need your talents. Success sometimes is made more precious by the failures encountered along the way.

In your personal relationships, this dynamic planetary combination suggests that you will seek out people who will give you approval. Don't underestimate your virtues, which include a sense of responsibility and the ability to give form to your ideas.

Saturn Square Neptune

The square from Saturn to Neptune indicates that you are sometimes given to unrealistic fears about poverty or personal incompetence. You are often overly anxious in matters over which you have no control and for which you should not bear any guilt. You become emotionally disturbed about them, and yet you do nothing to relieve your anxiety. You feel inadequate to deal with negative environmental conditions that you experience or observe, and this can cause you to become depressed. Actually you are afraid of responsibility and have doubts about your competence to deal with it effectively.

Your negative attitude may cause difficulties as you seek a professional career. The real problem is your lack of self-love, which often results in underachievement. Avoiding challenges may lead you to believe that you really cannot accomplish anything. It is imperative that you be willing to fail occasionally in order to find out where and how you can succeed. Being indifferent to duty and obligation doesn't solve anything. Withdrawal only further deepens your feeling of incompetence. You must be prepared to face competition so you can sharpen your talents for future use. Remember that those you meet in competition are also being tested by you, because they do not know your abilities.

You must come to see your fear of encounter and failure as an avenue of opportunity for development and progress. Small but increasingly significant successes can restore your self-confidence. You won't become so overconfident as to be arrogant, but you will know what you can and cannot accomplish.

You should seek the services of a trusted friend to show you how to manage your potentials efficiently and gain the most from them. Be discriminating in selecting your friends, and refrain from discussing your personal problems with others. They probably have a sufficient number of their own.

Saturn Square Pluto

The square from Saturn to Pluto shows that early in life you became a "sore loser." If you thought you couldn't win at a game, you just wouldn't play. Later, you associated with kids who were either weaker or younger in order to guarantee your supremacy over them. You lacked the generosity to admit that others might be more qualified than you. This attitude, in time, has become unacceptable in your relationships with others. You are emotionally insecure, and your value-judgments are unrealistic.

You are inclined to defensively avoid social responsibility, viewing it as an obstacle rather than an opportunity. You overdramatize the loss of personal freedom in fulfilling your duties. If forced to submit to them, you may become bitter and resort to extremes to get out of your obligation.

Your professional life will be full of difficulties until you change your attitude. Your superiors will not tolerate your attempts to grasp control. If you are willing to serve until you can demonstrate your readiness to handle authority, you may be accepted. But you are impatient and resent the time-consuming effort required to reach the top by the usual methods.

You need advisors to assess your capabilities and help you determine what your goals should be. Your desires are unrealistic in light of the resources you have to satisfy them. Status and its accompanying security have a high priority in your life. But resisting the demands of your superiors will only complicate getting what you want.

You are envious of those in powerful positions who have wealth and social status. You project this resentment, and others feel threatened by you. Correct this by developing skills through education. In this way you will meet and associate with co-workers on a mutual level. Also you will clarify your goals and be able to work out a methodical plan for success.

Saturn Square Ascendant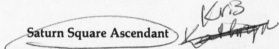

Saturn square the Ascendant shows that you are basically apprehensive about asserting yourself because you are afraid that you will encounter a lot of opposition. You underestimate your capabilities. In competition with others you prefer to move slowly at first, in order to gain self-confidence. When pressured excessively, you tend to withdraw rather than fight. You avoid challenges whenever possible and are defensive when you do accept them. If forced to defend yourself, however, you will use every trick you know to protect yourself.

You are a late starter in defining the goals you hope to achieve. Because you are too cautious and self-disciplined for your own good, you deprive yourself of many opportunities. Some people may think of you as cold and indifferent, but in fact you are serious and responsible. From your experiences you have learned that you have to earn everything you get, and you don't expect to get any rewards without making a substantial contribution. A perfectionist, you aren't content unless you can do your very best at all times.

Your early home life was probably an austere experience. It would seem that there was little warmth between you and your parents, and you were expected to perform your duties without question. Though you respected your parents or guardians, it is not likely that you felt any great tenderness for them. The result is that now you are extremely cautious and reserved when dealing with people in authoritative positions.

You are very preoccupied with achieving a position that will reasonably assure your financial security. You are far more talented than you know, and you will eventually realize this as you gain the success and recognition you deserve. In your determination to realize your goals, you persist in spite of setbacks. The security you gain in your material affairs compensates for your emotional insecurity about meeting someone who will share your life completely.

Uranus Square Neptune

Uranus square Neptune shows that you belong to a group consciousness that is in constant rebellion, but isn't quite sure of the reason. Although you feel the oppression of ignorance, you will have to do a lot of hard work to make clear exactly what you are going to do about it. If you are guilty of rejecting your social obligations, you may refuse to demonstrate your opposition to the corrosive effects of political subversion. Or you may decide that your professional status and personal security are too much to risk for the sake of that faceless crowd of humanity from which you've become detached. If you do decide to participate, it may be through an intermediary, because you say, "I don't want to become personally involved, since I have so much to lose if I'm discovered." This is an understandable position, but it is also indefensible. You would be the first to cry out in anger if your own personal freedom were being taken away. In the past, millions refused to "rock the boat" for fear their own security would be jeopardized. How many of them gained the security of a roof over their heads—in prisons, detention camps, and the like? If freedom is truly important to you, then you must have the courage to fight for it.

Lacking the courage of Uranus, you have consented to live in bondage at the hands of leaders who lust for power and who consider you expendable. On the other hand, you can challenge those who abuse their leadership positions and demand that they be held accountable to everyone for their deeds. You have the ability to arouse others and to stimulate them to action when mere words will not suffice. If you cannot personally supervise the action against oppressive conditions, you can at least support those who will.

Your future objectives are always weakened by a tendency to take a laissez-faire attitude toward the political motivation of existing government officials. You cannot afford to relax your attention to this danger.

This combination occured between 1952 and 1956; anyone born during that period of time will have this combination.

Uranus Square Pluto

The square from Uranus to Pluto shows that although you know there is much you can do to preserve the freedom you enjoy, you prefer to let someone else do it. You assume there will always be people with the courage to accept this responsibility, so you don't need to add your contribution. But if developments in your immediate environment threatened to curtail your liberties in any way, you would be the first to react. This planetary combination shows that you would be directly affected by such changes, if you are apathetic about preventing them, you are at fault. An example of such apathy is the fact that many people do not exercise their right to vote and then complain loudly when an ineffectual candidate wins the election. On the other hand, you could be so concerned for your fellow man that you would become a servant of the people, such as a fireman, policeman, or public official. In that way you could do something positive to improve the general welfare of society.

Uranus and Pluto were in this relation from 1931 to 1934, when dramatic events stirred the world. While people were deeply preoccupied with the Depression, trying to find work and food, Hitler made his move. He effectively restored order amid the chaos in his own country and stabilized its economy, but the price paid by the people was extremely high. He enslaved them and gained domination over those willing to serve his madness.

You must be constantly alert to the price you will pay if you fail to respond to the danger signals of any popular movement or political development. There will always be individuals who will try to rise to power when the public is apathetic.

If your instinct for self-preservation is strong enough, you will protect yourself against such tyrants by taking an active role to establish legal safeguards. You will also urge others to join with you in resisting domination and seeing that such individuals are removed from office.

Kris   **Uranus Square Ascendant**

Uranus square Ascendant shows that you are a rebel at heart. When your independence is denied even momentarily, you are defiantly abusive. You feel you have the right to do anything you want without adhering to any rules or regulations. In general you are irresponsible and find it difficult to learn anything from your experiences. You were at odds with the rest of your family when you were growing up, and you will always strike others as being different from the average person. But you do have a mind of your own and insist on finding for yourself the best way to capitalize on your wealth of ideas.

Generally indifferent to money, you prefer to devote your efforts to enterprises that are characterized by such cliches as "relevant" and "meaningful." What you do is far more important than what you are paid for doing it. Your modernity is repelled by tradition, and yet you conform to another kind of tradition that is consistent with the values of your generation.

You refuse to stay confined in a career that does not give you some degree of freedom and mobility. A nine-to-five routine would be positively crushing to your individuality. The only reason you want an education is so you can make a better contribution to society, but you must learn to be wary of people who will take advantage of you and deprive you of even basic necessities. Giving is noble, but in this case poverty is stupid. You are not likely to seek a binding partnership unless it is by agreement rather than by contract. You remember rebelling against the close confinement of your youth, and you have no intention of repeating that experience.

You are disturbed by social injustice and hope that some day you can contribute substantially to eliminating those injustices. You need to know that your life's work is serving a wide human need. Closely identified with youth in society, you try to help young people exploit their creative potentials.

Neptune Square Ascendant

Neptune square the Ascendant shows that you are overly sensitive to criticism. Because of this, you often fail to assert yourself when you should defend yourself against adversaries. You are never sure of your ability to

172

succeed in competition, and you may choose to avoid challenges until you feel more competent. The line of communication between you and your parents was faulty, which made it difficult for you to win their support and encouragement for a specific career. It will be a long time before you really know what you want out of life, so choosing a career will be difficult. You tend to daydream instead of doing something to actively express your creative ability. Always seeking the ideal, you are disappointed with anything less.

Your imagination is well-developed, but you lack the determination to benefit from it. You consider yourself far less talented than your competitors and tend to relegate yourself to a position of unimportance beside them. Although you have a high regard for education, you are lazy about finding the means to get one. You have to work doubly hard to compensate for your lack of opportunities to develop your potentials. Your efforts are often unrewarding because you tend to spread your interests too widely. You must confine yourself to specific fields of endeavor if you want to derive any benefits.

You are easily victimized by the people you deal with because you are too willing to believe them, and you always give them the benefit of the doubt. You often misunderstand those who have authority over you because you don't want to hear the truth if you suspect it might be painful. In the same way you may be misunderstood by others, who will question your motives in dealing with them.

You should try to find a career that ties in somehow with the needs of the masses. You are very sensitive to observed social injustices and feel that if you can correct them, you will earn the appreciation of others and gain spiritual credits too.

Pluto Square Ascendant *Kris*

Pluto square the Ascendant shows that you feel you are destined to have a powerful influence on the lives of the people you contact. Overly impressed with your righteousness, you feel that you alone can properly control their affairs. Nothing you observe is ever to your satisfaction, so you want to make alterations to suit yourself. Apparently your early training led you to assume that the world was waiting for you to grow up and restore order to it. With such an incredible belief in your own omnipotence, you are sure to run into major problems with those who have authority over you.

A major issue in your life will be learning to accept traditional chains of command, especially in organizations. You make an arrogant display of showmanship by assuming command that doesn't belong to you. This quality is extremely irritating to those who have to deal with you. Your behavior is probably a direct reaction to your feeling that your parents or guardians had supreme authority over you. Because of this, you became insensitive to the way people react when you assert yourself. You often show bad judgment in making decisions, but because you are convinced that no one should question what you do, you persist even when your error is quite obvious. You have a lot to learn about how much pressure people will tolerate from you.

Once you learn how to exercise good judgment, you can truly achieve greatness with your skillful ability to organize others to achieve your objectives. You are gifted in maintaining composure under trying conditions, and you never back down when challenged, even by the most competent adversaries.

You may have trouble in personal relationships because your demands are sometimes oppressive. Your lust for power and recognition seeps into all your affairs, so that compromise is nearly impossible.

Chapter Four

Trines

The trine aspect is formed when two planets are separated by an angle of one hundred twenty degrees. A positive aspect, it has the nature of the Sun and of Jupiter and the qualities contained in Leo and Sagittarius. It stimulates activity in the circumstances associated with the fifth and ninth houses of the horoscope.

Although the trine is a benign aspect, our experience compels us to view it with reserved optimism. In a horoscope that shows serious psychological misalignment from difficult planetary aspects elsewhere, the trine is often unable to compensate by providing constructive alternate avenues of expression. It lacks the power to counteract the intense pressure of the negative aspects, but it is available to soften their effects when used with understanding and willful deliberation. When there is adversity, the trine is a creative and sustaining aspect and builds hope that conditions will improve.

When two planets form a trine aspect and a third planet is also one hundred twenty degrees from each of the first two, a Grand Trine is formed. It is traditionally regarded as a difficult configuration because it produces apathy and indifference to responsibility. A Grand Trine is commonly found in the charts of criminals. Two noted murderers, Henri Landru and Albert DeSalvo, better known as the Boston Strangler, had the Grand Trine well represented in their horoscopes. Landru had a Grand Trine involving all but three planets in his chart, and DeSalvo's Grand Trine involved six planets. These are extreme examples that gained publicity, but it serves to remind us that we must determine the extent of influence of every factor in a horoscope. Sometimes environmental conditioning or circumstances alone trigger the planets to function, and the manifested effect can be positive or negative, depending on the degree of rapport between the planets and the available circumstances.

In general, the trine is a beneficent aspect and tends to integrate the natures of the planets involved. However, this summary oversimplifies a problem that is actually far more complex than the ideal suggests. As with all of the aspects, it is the natures of the planets involved, not the aspect, that determine the ease or difficulty of synthesizing the psychological dynamics they represent. For example, it is very difficult for Venus and Saturn to establish a mutually satisfying meeting ground. Planetary protocol forces Venus to submit to Saturn, and even the trine aspect requires Venus to make enormous concessions, because there is so little rapport between these planets. Under Saturn's watchful discipline and cautious reserve, the romantic nature is chilled, and realization is far less than expected. But even though they lack the excitement and fascination of more glamorous encounters, romantic alliances are reasonably secure.

Sun Trine Moon

The trine of the Sun and Moon indicates that there is a harmonious balance between your will and your habits and emotions. You naturally react to stimuli in such a way that your ego can continue to develop properly. There is a good balance between the lessons you have learned from your past experiences and your ability to use these lessons to realize your destiny. Your relationship with your parents was generally favorable to your continued growth. They might even have inspired you to assert your own individuality so that you could become your own person rather than a reflection of their desires. You should enjoy a pleasant relationship with them and with other members of your family throughout your life. Only stress contacts between the Sun or the Moon and other planets in your chart could complicate the foregoing. In such instances, you would be responsible for the difficulties; the favorable influence here would still hold true, as you would eventually realize.

Your greatest problem, if it can be called that, is your tendency to be apathetic when you could deliberately assert yourself. You have an abundance of creative talent that can be usefully applied in situations that involve people in close relationships. Young people and children are comfortable with you and are on their best behavior because they want to please you. They respond to your attitude of protective caring for them, and they would never forget your contact with them.

You have the opportunity to rise to prominence if you want to. There is a luck factor in your favor, but also you have the temperament to feel completely at ease in positions of authority. You always exercise your will with an understanding of how people will react to it. Persuasive but not offensive, you have a knack for getting people to do what you want without appearing domineering. Your refined nature is a decided asset if you choose to pursue a professional career.

Your sincerity and honesty make you attractive to both sexes. You are warm and friendly toward casual acquaintances as well as close friends, and wherever you go you leave a lasting impression.

You underestimate your potential to climb to the top in any endeavor you find attractive. You should choose a field that has possibilities for growth. Land or land development, homes, and domestic enterprises in general are some of the areas in which you could build a very rewarding future. Working with the public is advised because you have the calm disposition to cope with any situation that could develop.

Sun Trine Mars

The trine from the Sun to Mars shows that you have leadership ability and the self-confidence to use it creatively and fairly. Your courage and endurance enable you to accomplish very demanding tasks. You have faith that you will always be able to succeed without resorting to deception or dishonorable practices. Not only are you honest in your dealings, you pride yourself on competing successfully with those who aren't so honest. Although you may behave impulsively at times, on the whole you plan your actions efficiently and purposefully. You can always express your creative abilities in such a way that you benefit from it. If anyone dares to question your ethics, you rise in anger, generally with the support of those who know you well.

With an abundance of energy to sustain you as you seek your goals, you won't be greatly restricted in expressing your talents in the life work you choose. In performing your duties you don't challenge or threaten people, and you get along well with most of them. You like everyone, and other people think well of you too. When someone needs assistance you will provide it, since you are secure in your own destiny and no one can seriously deter you from it. You mind your own business and maintain privacy in your affairs.

It is possible for you to gain prominence in the fields of law, management, or sports, in creative activities such as acting and the communications media, or in working with young people as a teacher or guidance counselor. Guidance counseling is especially suitable to your capabilities. You easily win the approval and admiration of youngsters because you accept them at their own level of development, not expecting them to behave as adults.

Your emotional interests are average, so you will be able to adjust your desires in order to encourage a partnership with someone who fulfills all your expectations for a mate. You accept people for what they are and expect the same treatment.

Your life is apparently untroubled, and you take care of any problems without fanfare or publicity. You are content to let those with driving ambitions have all the rope they need, but you don't need that kind of anxiety to spoil an otherwise tranquil existence. Not that your life is uneventful, for you work diligently and play enthusiastically. But because you don't have high expectations, your investment is less burdensome.

Kris Sun Trine Jupiter

The trine between the Sun and Jupiter gives you abundant creative potential, but in order to benefit from this potential you must use it. You are inclined to be apathetic so that you don't take advantage of your assets. Although you are intelligent, optimistic, responsive, articulate, and well informed on many subjects, you don't seek challenges. It never seems important to assert yourself toward a specific goal. You prefer to live outside the painful pressures that characterize the "rat race." You like to play a comfortable role that doesn't cut too deeply into your freedom and makes only moderate demands. This is a lazy planetary combination, requiring the stimulus of a strong Saturn relationship to either your Sun or Jupiter. This would fortify you with the courage and faith to take on massive burdens, knowing you have the intellectual skill to handle them.

Many fields of endeavor are suited to your creative talents, although there is no way you can be forced to apply them. Suggested fields include medicine, law, philosophy, writing, education, theater, working with large animals (animal husbandry), or any field in which you could set your own level of application. This aspect inclines you to seek less demanding occupations, but you could still pursue your destiny in any of the above fields. You are not a trailblazer, because you lack the necessary incentive to take on arduous tasks.

You are indulgent to yourself and similarly generous toward others. Your air of self-assurance is comforting to those nearest you in their times of stress or difficulty. Young people and children are drawn to you because you don't expect a lot from them and don't challenge them. You are doting rather than stimulating.

Relating to people is relatively easy for you because you are not selective in your circle of associations. Since you tend to give everyone the benefit of the doubt, you are vulnerable to those who capitalize on your good will. You are especially fond of individuals who are psychologically uncomplicated and live simply.

You are direct and forthright in seeking your mate. Your partner must be reasonably polished, have good moral fiber, and uphold good taste in conduct. A person's level of educational accomplishments is less important to you than the degree of good common sense and understanding.

Sun Trine Saturn

The trine between your Sun and Saturn shows that your drive to achieve success will be easier than for most others because you do not find it difficult to accept responsibility. There is no need to struggle for mastery over the circumstances of your life because you inherently know how to take advantage of opportunities when they arise. Almost without effort you can mobilize your talents creatively to gain your objectives. You know you are loved, and you know you have talent. Because you are reasonably sure of yourself, there are few impediments to your rise to success.

There are a great many occupations in which you can express your creative potentials and become successful while making an important contribution. Conservation, law, politics, industrial management, architecture, market speculation, land development, or park and recreational management— these are only a few of the fields to which your talents could be applied. You are only moderately ambitious, but you can climb to important positions as long as you know that your abilities are needed.

You may not be lucky in the usual sense of the word, but you have a knack for doing the right thing at the right time to achieve the best results. Regardless of the partner you choose, you will bring much stability to the relationship. Your partner must be sincere, creative, and self-disciplined, and have reasonably well-defined goals. If your partner has to work hard to get anywhere, you will be the sustaining force, because of your attentiveness and your faith in the good outcome of such a quest.

This planetary combination shows general good health, probably because you care enough about yourself to pay attention to good healthful habits.

Sun Trine Uranus

The trine from the Sun to Uranus indicates leadership ability, creativity, and the inspiration to use them effectively. You have a quality of personal magnetism that delights others with the joy of being in your company. Your liberal outlook on life and your understanding of people bring you much satisfaction. You are talented at finding ways to exploit your considerable creative abilities. Luckily, you are not too impressed with your own accomplishments, so you should never be accused of being an egotist. You understand both your capabilities and your liabilities, but you have learned to accentuate the productive qualities.

There is little you can't accomplish if you set your mind to it. You have an endless fund of ideas that can be promoted and developed successfully. Success comes easily to you, unless there are barriers elsewhere in your chart to frustrate it. Human service enterprises such as education, group encounter therapy, social functions with a spiritual motivation would give you the inner satisfaction you want. Knowing that you have made an important contribution to others is sometimes all the reward you need.

People are attracted to you simply because you are more interested in them than in yourself. You give others an enthusiasm they often need, injecting a kind of life-force without realizing it. When others need you, you are intuitively aware of it, and you generously give of yourself. You are never superficial, and you don't assume that anyone else's problems are trite.

To the object of your affection, you bring much enthusiasm and optimism. You continually keep your lover's interest alive and exciting with your meaningful contributions to the relationship. Your openness in expressing your feelings is warmly welcomed and makes the relationship easy.

Sun Trine Neptune

The trine from the Sun to Neptune means that you have enormous talent to express, but you may never find the energy to exploit it. You take up ideas with enthusiasm, then drop them right away. Your mind has a precocious quality, in that you learn quickly and with deep comprehension. You respond to what you learn both emotionally and intellectually. In reality, you are extremely psychic, and much of your knowledge has been acquired through this faculty. This may have been the reason you were bored, as a child, by teachers who were giving you information that you already knew intuitively. Because you learned easily and didn't have to overcome the usual obstacles, now you don't readily take on duties unless you want to very strongly. You may avoid involvement in the affairs of the community, for it is almost impossible for anyone to provoke you to respond to your social responsibilities.

You can write your own ticket to your professional ambitions. Probably you will never encounter a challenge that you can't successfully meet. You are extremely creative and will be able to perform most any task assigned to you. Your greatest problem is dawdling when time is urgent or schedules must be met. Consequently, it is better for you to be self-employed, so you can work at your own pace, and others don't have to depend on you. Art, drama, education, writing, and medical research would all provide you with a field for creative expression. Even though your ambitions may not be defined, others will benefit from your efforts.

Your personal relationships are characterized by permissiveness between you and your mate, a freedom based on mutual trust. You and your beloved enjoy a blissful, romantic love and can indulge in escapes to Shangri-la. You can be devoted to your mate and know that indiscretion will never come into your life. Your family will be warm and tender toward you, and your children will be a source of endless joy to you as they grow into maturity.

Sun Trine Pluto

With the Sun trine Pluto you are courageous and determined and have a talent for mobilizing your resources to achieve personal goals. Motivated by social conditions, you can use your creative potential to stimulate improvements in your environment. Your innate vitality stirs others to support you, and your sense of purpose and dedication to your objectives inspires them. You assert your will generally because of a spiritual motivation.

Although you are a born leader, this seems unimportant to you. Your interest is focused on solving challenging external problems. Your attitude is one of righteous indignation toward those who attempt to "bend" the truth or take liberties with the law. You are incredibly perceptive, and your intuitive insight enables you to function well in a crisis. Because of these qualities, others may suspect that you have been given access to privileged information.

You are especially skilled in handling the financial resources of others and could easily become a financier. Your deductive abilities would be useful in a career devoted to exposing criminal activities. Other investigatory occupations would also suit you, such as psychology, medical research, penology, or rehabilitation. You would do well in any profession, in fact, in which the desired objective is to restore order from chaos. There is a magical property in the way you can transform others merely by your presence, and you probably have healing abilities that you're not even aware of. This is essentially what you accomplish when you solve the problems of others.

Wherever you go and whatever you do, luck seems to follow. You will gain from other people's losses and will probably receive an inheritance. Your enormous creative potential may not develop completely until you have endured some frustration, because you are in some ways a spectator. You may even choose to avoid important issues in your life. This would be a tragic waste, though, since you have tremendous power and the will to achieve goals that most people only dream about.

Sun Trine Ascendant

The Sun trine the Ascendant shows that you have a generous disposition, and you are self-confident about your ability to succeed in almost everything you do. You are generally optimistic about all your affairs and easily win the cooperation of the people you deal with. Creative by nature, you use your talents with such imagination that it seems inspired. Although you have abundant vitality, you are inclined to be apathetic about taking full advantage of your potentials, so you shortchange yourself of the benefits you could derive from them. Possibly you are even lazy at times, feeling that there is plenty of time to do what you have to.

You have inherited good resources of character from your parents, but you still have a mind of your own. If you will accept the responsibility for it, you can successfully seek your own fortune. You give too much attention to your shortcomings and failings, and you do not react well to criticism. You like to believe that you do everything as well as the next person, and for the most part you do.

Your future is very important to you, and you seek a career that will allow you creative expression and give you security in your later years. Because you prefer a career that makes demands on your talents, you will probably become a professional in the endeavor you choose. You want to be admired for performing your job well, and you expect to be well paid. You need the challenge of competition in order to strive for excellence in your craft.

You should find a partner who shares your enthusiasm for the good things in life; such an alliance would make working for your goals and security worth the effort.

Moon Trine Mercury

The trine of the Moon to Mercury indicates that you are willing to accept all your experiences as ways to enrich your consciousness. You evaluate your reactions to people, events, and situations quickly. Since you derive more significance from your response to stimuli than most people do, you accumulate a vast storehouse of information. This forms the basis for your creative development and expression. Your emotions are well integrated with your intellect. You are warmly sympathetic toward everyone and show a high degree of comprehension in your dealings with people. You have an amazingly retentive memory, and your ability to recall past incidents is remarkable. However, you don't allow the past to distort your reactions to current events; instead, you make good use of the lessons you have learned from the past. You show great eagerness to make your life useful and expressive. You search for new ways to exploit your talents and usually find them.

Your circle of friends is large because you are flexible enough to make allowances for people's undesirable traits. You earn the affection of everyone you deal with because you are fair and never too busy to offer assistance when they need it. Young people are especially attracted to you, and you make them feel quite comfortable with you. Because you don't expect more trom them than they can do, they don't feel threatened. You are never so preoccupied with your personal affairs that you can't spend time with them.

You can succeed in your professional interests because you know how to apply your knowledge to get the best results. You look at problems objectively and are willing to ask for help if you cannot solve them. Realizing that you don't know everything, you are not afraid to admit it.

You may have some emotional anxieties, but you are completely aware of them. You don't generally reveal your personal problems to anyone except your most intimate and trusted friends. You don't dwell on negative thoughts and with your compassion and sincere concern, you can often help those who do.

Your life should be happy and filled with close friends, pleasant social activities, and comfortable domestic conditions. You will probably realize the goals you only dreamed of yesterday. You may have periods of difficulty, but you have the ability to cope with them, so they will not be long-lasting.

Moon Trine Venus

The trine between the Moon and Venus shows that you have a gentle and harmonious disposition. Optimistic about the success of your relationships, you feel reasonably secure that your trust in people will not be violated. You are probably an attractive person, either by your physical appearance or in other ways that make you seem so. You don't have to work at having good intentions, because your motives are rarely less than honorable. You are imaginative and inspired in using your creative talents. You have faith that other people can succeed, just as you believe in yourself and strive for excellence in everything you do.

You can achieve prominence in work that involves handling people, and your talents would be best suited to public relations. You should always remain exposed to the public, where you can assert yourself warmly, sincerely, and imaginatively. Your presence in a group is always desirable, since you energize others when they lose interest. You have a calming effect on people who are distressed because you refuse to be negative. Your peaceful demeanor is infectious, and an otherwise dull day brightens when you come on the scene. Your judgment is good, but you don't try to override anyone else's opinion. Your values are well organized, and integrity keeps you from forming an alliance with anyone whose integrity can be questioned. You are never offensive or coarse, and vulgarity is something you cannot tolerate. When a vulgar incident occurs, you simply walk away and detach yourself from those who indulge in it.

Your emotional satisfaction is derived from relationships that are honest and sincere. You don't bore people with details of your private life, and you are not interested in invading their privacy. Your mate should be interested in having children, for they would be a source of much joy to you. Young people are drawn to you as if fascinated. You make them feel perfectly at ease because you show that you care for them.

You could find additional pleasure in avocational pursuits such as theater groups, interior decoration, artistic endeavors, or craftwork with children and young people. Sunday school might also be a rewarding way to spend leisure time, and your participation would enrich the lives of those involved because of your effective delivery and sincere interest.

Moon Trine Mars

The Moon trine Mars indicates intensity of feeling and emotion, which you relieve by applying yourself to creative activities. You do more than just what is physically required whenever you can. If necessary, you are willing to compromise your desires by making adjustments. You meet people halfway and enjoy good relationships with a large number of friends, associates, and relatives. You may not be satisfied in all areas of your life, but then, who is? On the whole you should be able to deal with people more easily than most. You have mastered the art of relating to people and can even chastise someone without being abusive or violent. Even when you display temper or fight for your rights, you don't give an impression of hatred. You don't generally interfere with others and prefer that they respect your right to privacy as well.

Your psychological alignment allows you to function easily with the public and in personal relationships. You are sufficiently sure of yourself that you don't feel threatened by associates or competitors. You have faith in yourself and in those with whom you enjoy a close emotional contact. When challenged, you quietly accept it and cope as best you can, but you don't get uptight if you don't succeed. Your "easy come, easy go" attitude helps conserve your abundant energy for important matters. You have a good imagination and the energy to express it well in your job and in avocational interests. Children respond well to your influence because you don't expect them to act older than they are.

You are not afraid to express your feelings toward those you care for because you don't have any hangups about your affections not being returned. People can't help but be impressed with your attitude and behavior. You put others at ease and make them feel welcome in your company. But you don't warm up to persons who are dishonest with you, for they are not worth the effort. You are reasonably independent, because you don't feel emotionally obligated to anyone. Nor do you hold others to account, unless they feel it naturally. Permissive to a fault, you enjoy warm, personal relationships with many types of people. You give everyone the benefit of the doubt in fulfilling what you expect of them, but you don't ignore them when they fail. You find qualities to admire in everyone, and you don't categorize them in neat little pigeonholes.

Moon Trine Jupiter

The Moon trine Jupiter gives you a glowing personality, ease in relating to people, and generosity. You have a vivid imagination and much creative potential. Even when circumstances seem dismal, you always look at the bright side. Your hopeful outlook brings optimism into the lives of everyone you contact, especially in your own family. Your infectious enthusiasm generates a feeling of well-being among the people you are with. You are very sensitive to outside influences, but you always attempt to understand their real significance. You work out solutions to your problems as quickly as possible because you don't tolerate complications in your life for very long. Confident that you can cope with any situation as it arises, you don't try to cross a bridge before you come to it.

Because you are well informed on many subjects, you can hold your own in just about any conversation. Civic affairs hold an interest for you, and you may hold some elective position in your community. You would support programs for solving social problems, because such projects are especially interesting to you. However, you might not become personally involved in their administration, because your day is already filled with matters that need your attention. Knowing how to determine priorities, you become totally absorbed by whatever heads the list.

You enjoy the many avocational interests that fill your life with purpose and accomplishment. Your activities enrich those close to you by stimulating their continued development. The spiritual fortitude that you radiate is comforting to them. Because of this, you might find that you are the advisor whom everyone seeks when they have problems. You apparently have a capacity to take on these burdens without laboring under them. Your opinion is highly regarded because of your vast experience and good advice.

Such fields as public relations, civic functions, travel, or physical therapy could serve as a platform for your creative talents. Working in these or similar areas would benefit others and give you a sense of accomplishment. You are inclined to be self-indulgent, though, and you should limit your activities to a selected number of interests. It would seem imprudent to sap your physical reserves by taking on more tasks than you can handle easily.

You are romantically interested in persons of good moral character who are sincere, honest, and spiritually motivated. A peace-loving person, you enjoy being with people who are untroubled by tension and pressure in their personal affairs. You are greatly devoted to the one you love, and your relationship will deepen with each passing year.

Moon Trine Saturn

Although the Moon trine Saturn makes you conservative and cautious, you are nevertheless very creative and for the most part optimistic. Your parents have given you a solid background in training so that you possess a reasonable degree of common sense. You maintain a respect for tradition, but also appreciate the value of change when it seems productive. You are emotionally stable and resourceful and realize that to benefit from something you must make an investment in personal effort. You don't expect to get anything without making a contribution for it. Your friends always know how you feel about them, and you never knowingly violate their trust.

Engineering, industrial management, politics, education, law, and public relations are some of the professions you could follow with reasonable assurance of success. These fields would give you many opportunities to demonstrate how useful you can be even under very demanding circumstances and responsibility. Your retentive memory is a great help at such times. You appreciate any job in which you can exploit your considerable potentials, but you may lean toward accepting a position of leadership, for which you are suited. In fact, the chances are good that you will gain a position of authority in any field you select.

Though your circle of friends may not be wide, you enjoy the lasting friendship of those friends you have. The mutual trust and understanding between you constantly enriches your life and theirs. You respect only those who have self-respect, and you look for the same quality in a prospective marriage partner. You do not make any decisions without a careful investigation, especially where your feelings are concerned. Always one to observe the rules, you are unlikely to consent to a permissive relationship without some binding agreement. But you would agree to a marriage contract only if your partner realized the full implication of such an agreement. Because you bring so much creative effort into a relationship, its success is practically assured. Your mate must also uphold the contract you've made together and be willing to work to sustain your mutual interests above everyone else's.

As a parent, you would be a disciplinarian, but merciful and loving. You would encourage and strengthen the individuality of your children, as long as it is positively directed.

Moon Trine Uranus

The Moon trine to Uranus shows you are inquisitive and eager to know all you can about everything. You are mentally alert and absorb knowledge easily. Your perspective on life is broad, and you rarely concern yourself with superficial matters. Your sparkling personality attracts a wide circle of friends. Since you are a willing listener, you don't threaten anyone's identity, but you can still hold your own in an argument because you are well armed with facts.

Your early conditioning prepared you to accept your future and made you aware that you could cope effectively with any situation. You have a healthy respect for legitimate authority but will challenge anyone who assumes power irresponsibly. Your temperament draws you to occupations that serve the group rather than the individual. You are thus especially suited to teaching, politics, and broad social programs. When you speak in public, your delivery, which is usually dramatic and to the point, stimulates positive reactions in your listeners.

Your outlook is toward the future, and you can easily establish the proper foundation for logical development in the future, to everyone's benefit. Others will thirstily seek your help in defining the goals they should strive for in their lives. Without even trying, you utter profound truths that sometimes reveal spiritual wisdom.

In your thinking, the past is well integrated with your desires for the future. There is no conflict in your circumstances that cannot be resolved easily. The answers you need always seem available, because you are emotionally prepared to accept the truth. Study of the occult would open vast areas of additional knowledge to you. You could also succeed in the professional application of this information.

The mate you choose should also function at your high frequency, or the relationship will dissolve from sheer boredom on your part.

Moon Trine Neptune

With the Moon trine Neptune you sometimes express your creativity in a prophetic way. Your inner and outer selves are well integrated. In other words, you react to outside stimuli imaginatively and creatively. You are inventive in the artistic sense and can dramatically communicate your aesthetic experiences. You are deeply appreciative of the finer things in life, for they enrich you in many ways every day.

In your professional activities, you generate warmth and genuineness. You radiate affection and appreciation for creative efforts. Spiritually you are "in tune," although you are not necessarily a religious fanatic. You are dutiful and aware of social obligations in your church, social club, civic affairs, or programs that serve worthwhile causes. However, you do not necessarily feel within yourself the need to help those who won't help themselves. Apathy is your singular liability.

On the domestic scene, you would particularly enjoy observing and nurturing your family's creative potentials. However, you may choose not to have a family, merely to keep your present mobility and freedom. Young people are sensitive to you and can gain much from your participation in their affairs. They feel comfortable in your company and will cooperate with your efforts to assist their developing talents.

In personal relationships, you usually require that others have a variety of interests. You offer much to those who interest you, and you are willing to serve their desires if your efforts are appreciated. You are drawn especially to educated and refined individuals. Although you find the negative elements of your environment distasteful, your activities are not inhibited by them. You may even cultivate programs to bring about more acceptable social conditions. Your best development lies in actively contributing your vast resources for the benefit of others.

Moon Trine Pluto

Moon trine Pluto shows that you are a deep-feeling individual, but you generally keep your emotions under control. You do not usually waste your feelings on casual acquaintances, although you are friendly and sociable. You give others the benefit of the doubt when you decide how you feel about them. The friends you do have can count on you for help when needed.

Yours is a special kind of spiritual loving that is not cast freely to the winds. You love people for themselves and not for what they outwardly represent. You have high expectations of meeting the right person who will encompass all the virtues you expect in true love companionship.

You have a fondness for children and young people, for they provide you with much contentment and joy. You put them at ease and bring out their affectionate feelings. In your care they feel comfortable, for you are naturally protective of those in your charge. The young are a source of creative expression for you.

Your capacity to care for others is boundless, and you could express this by serving people who have physical liabilities or social disadvantages. Fields such as public relations, physical therapy, social welfare, financial advice, or creative avocational work would be congenial to your interests.

You have great insight into the uses of power and the effective management of money. Your understanding of the motives behind people's behavior is a protection for you. Working in personal contact with other people would be an excellent medium for you.

You are enthusiastic and optimistic that any problems you do have will eventually be worked out. This is a sign that you truly enjoy life.

Moon Trine Ascendant

The Moon trine the Ascendant gives you an easy-going disposition and allows you to derive much pleasure from creative expression. You are imaginative, sensitive, emotionally poised, and articulate in expressing yourself. You appreciate the sense of values that your parents have instilled in you, and you are prepared to take advantage of your sensitive intellect and develop your own mental resources and ideas. Being resourceful, you will find the way to capitalize on your talents, even though it may be difficult to find the necessary funds to accomplish what you want. You may be forced to do without some necessities, but you feel it is worth it if your main objectives can thus be realized. Unless you are alert, people will try to take advantage of your good nature to benefit themselves. You should require your friends to prove their worth before accepting them completely. You cannot afford to be indifferent to your own needs in relationships, whether casual or intimate.

You have sufficient talent to make a substantial contribution to your career. You realize that in order to succeed, you must make sacrifices in your personal affairs. This might mean deferring marriage until you can get the education you need to succeed in your professional endeavors. You want to know that you've exploited your creative potentials, and you want the fulfillment that this brings.

Your marital partner must always remain a lover, so that you will continue to make substantial contributions to maintain the fascination and excitement of your first encounter.

You need to know you are wanted, and you are crushed if your efforts are unappreciated, especially by those to whom you've been the most generous.

Mercury Trine Mars

Your Mercury trine Mars shows that you have a lot of creative energy and the imagination to express it in many ways, although you sometimes lack the enthusiasm to do so. You know your capabilities and limitations and have enormous potential to succeed in most anything you attempt. However, success never seems urgent enough to instill in you the desire to achieve. You cannot be forced to do anything you don't want to do and no one can deter you from what you want.

You have considerable depth of understanding and the ability to concentrate when it is important. Well-informed on many subjects, you can hold your own in any conversation. You are inoffensive and friendly to everyone you meet. You can be trusted with classified information and would never reveal someone else's secrets.

There are many fields in which you can apply your skill in communication. Some of these are law, politics, public relations, education, writing, acting, and military service. Another endeavor that would prove rewarding is working with young people or children. You have the patience to cope with their boundless energy and the enthusiasm to stimulate them to achieve on their own. Whatever occupation gives you the most satisfaction is yours to choose. You are not intimidated by the excellence of your contemporaries, and you don't threaten those who are less skilled than you. You are equally at ease working alone or with people in large groups. But you can achieve the most worthwhile effects by working with groups, since your temperament lends itself to this.

You may also enjoy many avocational interests, especially crafts. You could become so competent in a craft that eventually you might make it your primary occupation. You have the talent for this kind of work and the imagination to succeed.

You enjoy the company of people who are not troubled with psychological hangups. Not one to interfere in the lives of others, you demand that others give you the same consideration. You will probably respond emotionally to a person who is creative and inspired, someone who would cooperate with you in a mutual endeavor suggested by either of you.

Mercury Trine Jupiter

Mercury trine Jupiter shows that you have a high level of comprehension, and your inspiration actively provides you with ideas for fulfilling your creative potentials. You have an optimistic and fresh outlook on life and an explicit belief in your capacity to succeed. You are already a veritable encyclopedia of information, and merely need some direction for applying it. You are indulgent and sometimes pompous about your knowledge, but you will be criticized if you do nothing with it. There is so much you can accomplish with a minimum of effort that it would be sad indeed if you did not distinguish yourself in some achievement.

Education is especially suited to your talents, but journalism, foreign correspondence, law, or counseling young people and children are all avenues through which your creative abilities could be expressed. In any of these fields of endeavor you would rise to prominence quickly. You learn rapidly and retain what you learn, so you would be a valuable asset to any company that hires you.

You are a person of integrity, with high standards of behavior. Because of this, you can win the esteem of persons in high places, who could safely delegate you to represent them. You would handle the opportunity well, for your manners are good, and you can fit in easily with any level of society. Your polish and sophistication do not alienate you from the average person because you never lose the "common touch." You are probably sought after to grace important local and state functions, and you are on a first-name basis with important political personalities.

Your breezy manner endears you to a wide circle of friends. You are tolerant of other people's weak moments, knowing that time will eventually straighten things out. You stimulate the best in people, and they are impressed with your kind and affable disposition.

You are an enjoyable partner to the one you love because you have a good sense of humor and enjoy a variety of interests. Life is never boring when you are around, and everyone who knows you delights in your company. Children love you and are comfortable with you, for they know that you don't expect them to behave as adults. You are like a big brother or sister to them.

This combination of planets does not have any negative physical effects.

Your general feeling of well-being comes from being optimistic and not allowing problems to fester in your imagination.

Mercury Trine Saturn

Your Mercury trine Saturn shows you have a well-developed intellect, are mentally organized, and precise in your opinions. You have considerable creative ability, which you can express whenever you choose. Never at a loss to exploit your potentials, you create opportunities if they aren't available otherwise. You are able to solve problems easily because you use every fragment of information you have. Your conservative mentality allows you to accomplish a great deal with the least amount of effort. You are extremely efficient and know how to dispense with nonessentials. You know your worth and can assume important tasks that others fear they can't handle. Not that you are immodest. You are a good learner with considerable power of retention. Even under pressure, you are patient and self-disciplined.

There are many occupations you could follow with very good chances for success. Your enthusiasm for the creative opportunities they provide could be the determining factor. Education is high on the list of probable fields, in addition to construction, architecture, drafting, design, politics, industrial management, government service, science, research in various fields, or writing. You would do well in studying languages, deciphering symbols found in archeological excavations, or in teaching history. In whatever interest you follow, you can always derive something meaningful and concrete. You are usually content in your work because you bring creativity to it and you know you will succeed. Because you make enormous contributions to your work, you will receive many benefits from your investment.

You don't indulge in daydreams, because you realize that you can obtain better results by establishing realistic goals. Knowing your limits, you confine your objectives within them.

You are courageous and willing to stick your neck out to defend your integrity. You are morally upright and demand that others behave honestly in dealing with you. When you have been deceived, you utterly reject the person who violated your trust. Only those with strong moral fiber have a place in your life. You insist that others keep their agreements, but you will make an exception for someone's honest inability to keep a promise, if the circumstances justify it.

As if you were a confessor, people seek to unburden themselves to you. Your understanding and wisdom encourage them to reveal themselves.

Your later years will be enriched by the memories of what you accomplished during your active life. At that time you will turn to writing as an avocation; it may be impossible for you to truly retire because life will always have so much meaning for you.

Mercury Trine Uranus

The trine from Mercury to Uranus shows that you have a fertile, intuitive mind, which you express creatively. Your opinions are always based on sound principles, and you speak with conviction. You rarely make superficial statements because your mind does not dwell on trite matters. You seek after the truth, knowing it is the only way you can feel free. And freedom is very important to you.

You understand occult matters and may become involved in some facet of this field as your life's work. Your flashes of intuitive insight are amazingly accurate, and you could excel in the study of psychic phenomena. Mysteries fascinate you, so you might also become proficient in solving problems of the scientific world. You find the human factor equally interesting, and you could master the fields of psychology, philosophy, or social programs.

Although you have carte blanche in deciding what to do with your vast resources in human understanding, teaching should be high on the list. The truth has been revealed to you, and you could communicate it to those who are eager to share in your good fortune. You have leadership ability, but your best choice would be to stimulate others to develop their own. You are way ahead of your time in comprehending matters that usually require many laborious years of study.

Your spiritual values are highly developed and well integrated with your material responsibilities. There is no conflict between your inner and outer lives, since each sustains the other.

You are restless with those who are satisfied with knowledge for its own sake. For you, the only justification for increased knowledge is in reaching toward human perfection.

Mercury Trine Neptune

With the trine from Mercury to Neptune you have enormous creative abilities and the inspiration to use them successfully. You communicate effectively and have a flair for dramatic delivery. Because your intuition is highly developed, you understand what motivates others in their relationships with you. You have an artistic imagination and the skill to express it well. You are sensitive and intelligent and prepared to accept your social responsibilities without question.

Because of your talents and temperament, you are much in demand and can succeed in many occupations. Since you adapt easily to your surroundings, you can work creatively in any environment. You are innately tolerant of human imperfection and do not make excessive demands on others. Your hopeful disposition, even when you face difficulties, stimulates others to have the same attitude. Your artistic appreciation and creative ability can be expressed in such endeavors as art, music, writing, design, or social functions.

Your social life satisfies your need for a warm and friendly atmosphere. As a speaker, you easily gain your audience's attention. You are persuasive and convincing because you can "tune in" on what your audience will respond to.

Superficial matters don't clutter your life. You focus on the important issues that have social implications and tend to ignore other issues. You are ever hopeful that others will become spiritually responsive to injustices and will make some contribution toward correcting them.

Although you respond to refined persons and enjoy their company, you don't necessarily need personal contacts in order to be happy. You are rarely lonely, and your inner life is richly satisfying, because you are able to express your creative potentials in so many ways.

Mercury Trine Pluto

The trine from Mercury to Pluto indicates your ability to concentrate, a fascination for the unknown, creativity, and depth of understanding. These intellectual assets merely need to be developed realistically and used effectively. Your understanding of cause and effect will give you an advantage others lack when you apply your talents to the profession you choose. Your wealth of creative ideas is some guarantee of success, if you exploit it.

Crime detection, medicine, research and development, engineering, analysis, chemistry, pathology, and surgery are some of the occupations that are suitable to your talents. Your financial management skills are excellent. You enjoy the challenge of competition and can take on a heavy burden of responsibility without tiring because you become absorbed by whatever interests you. You always choose a subject that requires complete participation. As a writer, you might write technical papers or mystery stories. Your capabilities are so wide-ranging that you can discuss corporate finances as easily as the mysteries of the occult.

In a personal relationship you expect a lot from the other person, but you are willing to make a substantial contribution too. You have the inner perception to "see through" appearances and understand what motivates people. You are alert to the potentials of others and can stimulate them to use their talents better. You speak with persuasion and authority, and both unschooled and learned people are fascinated by your delivery. You focus on people's needs and their level of comprehension.

Be watchful, though, that you don't provoke resentment by seeming to know all the answers. Give others the chance to demonstrate their understanding.

Your greatest problem is apathy and lack of interest in important environmental and social issues, where your talents would be of great use. You could be extremely useful in organizing group enterprises. The success of their efforts would be assured, for you can coordinate individual talents to meet the most demanding objectives of any group endeavor.

Your methods of pursuing goals are generally within the guidelines of sound personal convictions and ethical standards. You must know that you are capable of many accomplishments and that in realizing them you sweep others along to their goals.

As an avocation, you could indulge in market speculation. In your free time you might also contribute your talent to youth programs such as Junior Achievement, in which you could offer sound guidelines in marketing, finance, and investment. Without much effort, you can offer your services in many ways to produce substantial benefits.

Mercury Trine Ascendant

Mercury trine the Ascendant shows that you know how to express yourself. You are rarely misunderstood because you dramatize what you say and get the full attention of your listeners. You know that you are creative, perhaps because your parents encouraged you to develop your creative potentials and even provided opportunities if they saw that you would use them. In any case, you do understand your enormous capabilities and only have to decide that you will capitalize on them. You know what you can accomplish as well as what your limits are. You speak optimistically about your goals in life. With your enthusiasm, your chances for succeeding are good, but if there are setbacks or reversals, you will simply start anew, because you don't accept defeat. You learn from every experience and find new ways to use your talents. Determined to succeed, you will always find people who will support you in your endeavors.

You know how to convert your creative resources into cash. Not the most ardent laborer, however, you try to find effective ways to make money with the least amount of physical effort. You are not afraid to take chances in order to attract attention to your ideas. But you don't trust only to luck, for you know how to examine the details of any proposal and logically evaluate its chances for success.

You know how to deemphasize your negative qualities and overplay the positive ones. You seek the approval of your friends and generally get it, because of your views on matters of current interest. You let others think you are primarily concerned for their welfare and best interests; with your superiors you use this tactic with masterful skill. Although you recognize the importance of getting an education, you depend more on effective communication to help you get what you want. You don't like to be challenged by competitors if you are uninformed and know you can't win.

Venus Trine Mars

The trine from Venus to Mars shows that you are warm, affectionate, and congenial. You have a happy disposition and look for the better qualities in the people you relate to. You eagerly project yourself toward others and generally get the response you hope for. The demands you make on others are no greater than you would be willing to have them make. You have sex appeal, but you are not preoccupied with sex to the exclusion of other kinds of human contact. Your willingness to compromise encourages people to make concessions to you when it seems the right thing to do.

You are creative in entertaining friends at home, and people seek you out for their own social activities. Your creative talents could also be developed in the arts, drama, music, and appreciation for the dance. Any of these could prove rewarding to you either as a primary interest or as an avocation. You express yourself easily and could succeed in occupations that require you to appear before the public in some capacity. Public relations would seem particularly appropriate. With your congenial disposition, you can handle the most inflexible individual you might meet in carrying out your duties. You might also achieve success if you were self-employed.

Children find you a delightful companion, and you stimulate them to achieve because you believe in their individual capabilities. You also know how to win people over to your point of view by dramatizing your own position and not casting aspersions on theirs. You don't generally arouse criticism from those you deal with because you don't appear threatening to them. You tend to bring out the best in people.

You probably had a fairly happy home life that conditioned you to maintain happiness. Your own children will benefit from this too.

Your belief in yourself allows you to give others the benefit of the doubt in your relations with them. You have a deep understanding of human nature and usually try to be helpful when people need help. But you don't assume that you have the right to interfere unless asked.

A fun-loving person at heart, you enjoy a good time. You may run into problems with romantic partners, who will assume by your nature that you won't care if they take liberties with you; for the most part, they would be mistaken.

Venus Trine Jupiter

The trine of Venus to your Jupiter shows that your inner poise enables you to view people and circumstances optimistically. You are rarely disturbed by negative elements in society because you have faith that everything will eventually turn out right. Most of the time you are cheerful, but when conditions warrant it, you can be serious. Your happy disposition bolsters people out of depression, and they feel they are not as badly off as they had thought. You meet people more than halfway because you are generous, understanding, and sympathetic. Others are not aware that you are not always as trouble-free as it seems, for you do not wear your problems on your sleeve. You don't share your difficulties with those who have enough problems of their own. Nor do you attempt to fight "city hall," preferring to quietly take care of your affairs with little or no fanfare. You may gain attention, but you don't seek it.

Your talent in handling people suits you to work in public relations, social organizations, artistic endeavors, or any occupation that serves the public needs or desires. You have a great appreciation for art and could find much satisfaction in some aspect of that field. Perhaps decoration, design, and fabrication could provide you with meaningful employment.

You have a strong sense of ethics and social decorum. You always try to put your best foot forward and reach out to people with sincerity and honesty. You disdain anything vulgar or obscene and abhor being with individuals whose attitudes are perverse. You prefer to associate with well-mannered persons who conduct themselves with propriety. Music, art, drama, and dancing are delights that enrich your everyday existence. You enjoy good food, the company of friendly people, and pleasant social activities.

You are drawn to individuals who are traditional in their conduct. In a romantic relationship you are especially fascinated by persons who are not pretentious about their expectations of you. You want honesty between you and your lover and above all, sincerity. You want to be respected and admired for not indulging in public displays of love, for you feel that such things should be reserved for the intimate moments when you are alone together.

You seem self-assured about what you want most in life, and you should enjoy marital and domestic harmony. Because you are able to make adjustments to get what you want, you are likely to get them.

Venus Trine Saturn

The trine from Venus to Saturn shows that you have good judgment about people, and you always know who to turn to when you need help. You are optimistic, understanding, and responsible in your dealings with people. However, you hestitate to project yourself toward others unless you know you will be welcomed. You know that even the best relationships require mutual adjustment.

Your early years helped to prepare you to accept self-discipline as a necessary factor in achieving success. You are tolerant of the needs and desires of others and offer assistance when they require it. You are not necessarily generous, but you certainly will give if you know it will be beneficial.

You have artistic potentials, although you may not actually pursue them, and a deep appreciation for all kinds of art. Music, writing, poetry, painting, sculpture, and the graphic arts can enrich your life and surround it with comfort. You could also achieve success in any occupation that requires balance, order, design, and utility. Fields such as banking, law, real estate, insurance, finance, buying and selling, and architecture could provide you with suitable expression.

Your avocational interests could be with children or young people. Teaching crafts and art appreciation would give you much enjoyment and provide release from the inner tensions that might develop in your business. You could also find release for your creativity in pleasurable activities such as dancing or working in social organizations and clubs.

You are moderately enthusiastic in your romantic pursuits. If attracted to someone, you evaluate that person cautiously, examining all good qualities and noting liabilities in temperament to which you will have to adjust. Above all, there must be mutual respect. You are loyal in your affections and can anticipate a durable relationship.

You will make a good parent because you understand that every individual needs to develop within the guidelines of discipline and respect for others. You truly want what is best for your children and know how to help them develop and express their individual potentials. Your later years will be satisfying, because your children will continue to show their appreciation for the role you have played in their lives.

Venus Trine Uranus

The trine from Venus to Uranus shows that you are usually optimistic and cheerful and thoroughly enjoy life. You express your love for people without great fanfare and can usually detect insincerity in others. You make necessary adjustments to people, which endears you to them, but you are quick to see when others are abusing your affable nature.

Because of your sense of values, you strive to enrich the lives of others by sharing your good fortune with them. In the past you accepted your responsibilities and now you can enjoy the rewards. You realize that what you give is returned in abundance by others, to your mutual benefit.

Your well-developed sense of harmony and appreciation of beauty may be expressed through the arts, music, design, or drama. You radiate warmth in everything you do and are rarely negative in your social contacts. You can work effectively in occupations that involve the public because people feel comfortable with you.

Children are especially appreciative of your truthfulness in dealing with them. As a teacher, you would instantly capture your students' imagination because you have a talent for making a subject come alive. Your unique talents could prove rewarding in financial work. Your intuition would be an asset in speculating on the stock market.

Because of your innate self-control, you will probably marry well. You can look forward to satisfying romantic experiences based on mutual trust and understanding. You expect a lot from your partner, and you are willing to do whatever is expected of you. You have high hopes for a future rich with inner contentment. Your excitement and joy in living are the keys to much happiness.

Venus Trine Neptune

The trine from Venus to Neptune means that you use your creative imagination in an inspired way. Through your sensitive and romantic nature you respond to the highest ideals of others, and you are enriched by them. You have artistic talents and a deep appreciation for all that is refined in art, music, and literature. Generous in your judgment of others, you are kind even when they disappoint you. You are reasonably permissive with anyone who fails, as long as he is earnestly trying to succeed. When you become aware of negative elements in your environment, you may look the other way, for you can be complacent about such conditions, not wanting to get involved.

There are many ways you can express your creative talents, although you are particularly suited to artistic endeavors. In the performing arts, you could succeed in drama, dance, or in choral groups. You might dramatize your abilities by teaching young people to appreciate the finer things of life. You have a refined and personable nature that makes your company soothing and enjoyable. People are often hypnotized by a kind of mystical quality in you. Because you generate trust, you may be given a great responsibility that others cannot be depended upon to fulfill. Your delicacy and charm endear you to your superiors, and yet co-workers rarely feel threatened by competition for favors.

You easily form attachments with individuals who strive to improve themselves and who voice displeasure for anything unclean, sordid, or coarse. An idealist, you have well-defined spiritual convictions, which make life truly meaningful to you.

You may choose to assert yourself creatively or elect not to involve yourself, but it would be a waste of talent if you didn't.

Venus Trine Pluto

Your Venus trine Pluto enables you to enjoy the highest creative experiences that love can bring. You derive spiritual benefits from your social and personal contacts, and you stimulate others to emulate your attitude about love, which benefits them too.

You will control your ardent love nature until your intuition signals that you have found a suitable partner for creative expression of your passion. You may have love interests, which can be more romantic than real love, but when you meet the one special individual, you will respond with undeniable persuasiveness. The chances are good that the feeling will be mutual. There is a quality of fate in the chance encounter that defies all logic; this love will grow until you both feel as one.

You can be extremely effective in teaching others about moral and spiritual values and how to enrich their lives by adhering to the highest ethical standards. Young people especially will relate to you; you can teach them to stand on their own feet, secure in their values and commitments and in their eagerness to be loving in spite of adversity.

Any profession that you follow, you will be dedicated to. You are honest and would probably quit your job if you had to bend your ethics in performing it. Some fields that are especially suited to your capabilities include investment, insurance, financial management, and sales. Selling would be especially rewarding because your sincerity would encourage customers to buy your product. You could also function well as an analyst because you can focus on people's needs. You are understanding, sympathetic, and yet strong enough to persuade people to accept your suggestions for their own good.

You have a quality that is essential to success — you believe in yourself and in the potentials of others. Your basic integrity is solidly founded. You could make a substantial contribution to society through government service or political activity, probably in the financial management of someone in office or seeking it. You could also find satisfaction in working for the Internal Revenue Service or as a private citizen conducting your own tax service. It would be difficult for anyone to pull the wool over your eyes because you are keenly perceptive of dishonesty.

Whatever course you follow in your private and your professional life, you will be amply rewarded for your efforts. The love principle you project to all has the peripheral effect of bringing abundance into your life. This aspect usually means you will inherit something, and it is almost a certainty that you will be named in someone's will because of your unselfish contribution.

Venus Trine Ascendant

Venus trine the Ascendant gives you a charming and conciliatory manner that generates warmth in the people you deal with. Usually you are sociable, refined, and gracious, but at times you artificially turn on the charm to win someone's support. Although you enjoy receiving gifts, you prefer to reciprocate with favors rather than gifts; you don't often spend money, except on yourself. If you do buy a gift for someone, you would rather deliver it personally than send it.

You deliberately avoid discussing other people's negative qualities for fear your own bad features will be mentioned. Because you cannot stand criticism, you don't like to hear what may be the truth about yourself. You try hard to win the approval of your friends, and you make concessions to them so they will think well of you.

You may have to work harder than your co-workers to please those you work for. Perhaps you don't take your work seriously enough to satisfy your superiors, so you make the extra effort to prove that you are responsible.

You probably did receive an education, and you especially enjoyed the social aspect of college life. You also were looking for someone who was as career minded, refined, and socially oriented as you are. You must respect the person you are attracted to, and that person must want to improve on the traditional life style of the past. In other words, you want someone who will be eager to succeed and to acquire the comforts of success.

You win friends easily, and you make it a point to hold on to those who can be helpful in your career. You usually make encounters with people who may become important social contacts, and you genuinely like these people as much as everyone else.

Mars Trine Jupiter

The trine from Mars to Jupiter indicates that you apply your physical resources in a well-integrated way. Because you have a good blending of intellect and physical strength, you will be able to achieve your goals with only a moderate amount of effort. However, you may not rise to the challenge of competition because it doesn't seem worth the effort. You are creative and sometimes even inspired in accomplishing tasks that would overwhelm others. Luck seems to play an important part in your successes, although talent is applied too. You have the knack for doing the right thing at the right time, or of being in the right place when an opportunity is presented. You never have to resort to subterfuge to get what you want. Honorable in temperament, you uphold the law in your dealings and trust people without question. Your "easy come, easy go" attitude makes you a bit careless about spending money. You have amazing optimism about life, and it never occurs to you to fear that you won't gain what you want.

Such fields as law, government service, sports, working with children, teaching, exploration, writing, or arts and crafts seem appropriate to your talents. Success of itself is not terribly important to you. You merely want to express yourself to the fullest through work that you enjoy. The "rat race," in your opinion, takes too much effort for the returns you get. You are too self-indulgent to deprive yourself of the many pleasures you enjoy by mortgaging yourself to limiting endeavors.

You enjoy the company of a variety of people who lend interest to your life. While you don't make excessive demands on people, you will not submit to such demands by others either. You prefer to enjoy your friends freely and always maintain the right to end any association that tries to bind you.

You are not especially disturbed by current changes in attitudes toward organized religion. You are privately secure in your beliefs, regardless of the prevailing dissent among theologians and philosophers.

You are romantically attracted to persons who are similarly turned to an untroubled existence. Your physical desires are strong, but even these are reasonably controlled. You expect more than physical expression from the person you love. You are an idealist who will not settle for less than a mate who shares your needs and wants in mind, body, and soul.

Mars Trine Saturn

With your Mars trine to Saturn, you know how to assert yourself dutifully. You use your energy efficiently, wasting little of it on nonproductive endeavors. You are a fine disciplinarian because you don't expect the impossible from anyone under your authority, and in fact, you are often helpful in giving assistance. Your temper is generally under control and you don't fly off the handle when someone performs a task unimaginatively. You are a good teacher because you are creative and enthusiastic and care enough to use your talents wisely.

There are many professions you can follow, such as teaching, exploration, law, police or military service, forestry service, and ecological enterprises. All endeavors in which conservation is an important factor would be suitable for you. You would excel in industrial planning and control (efficiency). The areas in which you could apply your talents are almost unlimited. In any occupation, you would eventually rise to a position of authority, because you have exceptional managerial skills.

You should get along well with everybody. You respect others for what they are and accept them at their level of development. You really know how to get people to accept their responsibilities through careful planning. You show them that success is rarely an accident—and you are the best example of this. People in difficulty may seek your advice because you always seem to succeed, in spite of temporary setbacks or reversals. In other words, you tend to do the right thing at the right time, so people value your judgment. You are guardedly optimistic in all your affairs, whether in personal relationships or material concerns.

You are moderately aggressive in your romantic pursuits. You relate well to responsible, mature people, and you are particularly attracted to individuals who have well-defined goals and want to make something of their lives. Your sexual needs are average, and you generally satisfy your physical needs in traditional ways. Though others may consider you a "square" in this respect, you are convinced that a binding emotional relationship should include other, more important matters. A family and its security, objectives and goals, respect in the community, and the satisfaction of a job well done are more important to you than the mechanics of lovemaking.

Mars Trine Uranus

The trine from Mars to Uranus shows that you act with originality and creative enthusiasm. There is a feeling of drama in the way you express yourself. Although you are impatient, it is only because you are always excited about what interests you. You demand freedom in order to exploit your creative potentials and to indulge yourself when you choose. Your energy is boundless, and you have innumerable projects to keep you busy. You feel sorry for people who are trapped in limiting circumstances, because you realize how these can destroy creative development.

You are best suited for occupations that give you mobility and self-determination. The nine-to-five scene is just too routine and full of restrictions. You should become involved with group activities, where your leadership qualities can be used to best advantage. Exploratory enterprises, research, invention, travel, industrial sales, and engineering are some of the occupations that could provide you with the kind of incentive you need.

Even politics could be fascinating for your abundant creative talents. You enjoy being with people who are exciting, progressive, and interested primarily in the developments of tomorrow.

You do need to learn greater moderation though, and you must be patient if others don't act with your decisiveness. Occasionally you need to unwind to ease the nervous tension that frequently builds up. You may not realize how abusive this can be to your physical condition, for you pride yourself on getting along with no let-up and little rest.

In your romantic affairs, you are impulsive and restless. It goes without saying that you have strong sexual needs. You don't tolerate rejection with grace. The limiting ties of marriage are not of much interest to you, and you disdainfully view the conventional life as a relic from the past. You prefer to enjoy a wide circle of firends who can give you a variety of pleasures. Others may envy you for your exciting life-style.

Mars Trine Neptune

The trine between Mars and Neptune shows that you have successfully integrated your aggressive and desirous nature with your social responsibilities. You can satisfy personal goals and objectives without sacrificing your impersonal obligations. Because you understand your deepest biological urges, you are able to control them, realizing there is a time and a season for everything. You are sympathetic with those who are less fortunate in managing their impulses and readily "lend an ear" when others want to unburden themselves or discuss their problems. Your inner perception is highly developed to detect sincerity or dishonesty in people.

Your inspiration and driving ambition to serve others are particularly suited to welfare programs, medicine, law, or physical therapy. Your healing abilities would astonish even a professional practitioner, who may not realize that your success results from helping people cope with spiritual as well as physical problems. You would bring special insight to psychology, group encounter therapy, and other rehabilitative techniques.

If you are motivated to seek personal acclaim, you could pursue a theatrical career as an actor, dancer, or stage designer. You have a flair for effective delivery, and your sensitivity brings out a warm, emotional response in others.

Your romantic life is uncomplicated but still very exciting. Because of your poise and personal dignity, you enjoy warm and tender relationships with the opposite sex. You maintain honest and sincere ties with those you love, and willingly sever ties with those whose interest in you seems to be waning. Their love may fade, but they will never fail to respect you completely for all your good qualities. You hold others simply by your magnetism, charm, and sociability, and you know how to bring enthusiasm and joy into the life of the one you love.

Mars Trine Pluto

With Mars trine Pluto your aggressiveness is well aligned with your dedication to causes. You can be effective in solving awesome problems in society because you have a deep understanding of those problems and their origin. You offer your services out of a spiritual conviction that you are obliged to do something constructive about your surroundings. You may even feel that as a member of society you have contributed to the problems. On the other hand, the ease of this planetary aspect may enable you to dispassionately detach yourself from any responsibility and remain simply an observer.

Your ardent sexual nature is reasonably under control. You are intensely concerned that the object of your affection truly cares for you in more ways than just as a lover. You expect more than a plysical expression of love and you offer more than this in your love. The physical release you seek is enriched by a shared spiritual union. Your loving nature extends in many directions to transform those you contact socially and emotionally.

You aren't preoccupied with power as an instrument for gain but see it rather as a force for continued growth. You realize that life is a continuing spiritual process in which patterns of ever-increasing awareness unfold. Recognizing that everyone has their own level of development, you are tolerant when they occasionally stumble. You will offer your hand in assistance when you are needed, but rarely interfere except to avert an impending tragedy.

You are fearless in defending your rights and may surprise your friends with your ruthless courage in the face of overwhelming odds. You can draw on vast sources of spiritual energy to sustain you through the most difficult crises.

Mars Trine Ascendant

Mars trine the Ascendant shows that you assert yourself positively and aggressively. You have much enthusiasm, which you transmit to others in such a way that they are aroused to support you in your actions. Although you may not always be right in what you do, you are certainly willing to take that chance. You enjoy taking chances anyway, and luck seems to hold out when you do. You have a mind of your own and are determined to express yourself when you feel the urge. You have the gift of gab and know how to gain the advantage in a conversation. Being competitive, you enjoy both mental and physical challenges. Sports give you the opportunity to let off steam, either as a participant or as a spectator. You delight in winning, but whether you win or lose, you take tremendous pleasure in the game.

You need a considerable amount of money to support your pleasures, and you can dream up the wildest schemes to get it. Because you are inclined to spend much more than you earn, you must learn to be more moderate. You find it every embarrassing to be without money, but you should avoid money lenders, if you can.

You don't pay enough attention to planning for the future. Your motto could be, "Live today, for tomorrow you may die." But with this attitude your security is always in doubt. In your job, you give an impression of great activity, so that your superiors think you are making an enormous contribution. When it comes down to reality, however, you may fail to prove your worth. You need greater self-discipline so you can harness your creative enthusiasm to specific tasks. You would like to be independent, but because of your inclination to spend, it may be difficult to accumulate enough money to function freely. Your personal affairs tend to get in the way of your professional endeavors, and you could end up relying for assistance on the generosity of others.

Your success depends on your willingness to work at developing your talents. Hard work will bring you the results you want, as well as satisfaction for not having to depend on others.

Jupiter Trine Saturn

With your Jupiter trine Saturn, you integrate the lessons you have learned through past experiences with your designs for the future. Your goals are within the guidelines you've set for yourself. Success is not a surprise; you expect it because your proposals for yourself are responsible and within your capabilities. People may think you are inspired because things always come up roses for you, but you know differently. You have access to useful information and are skilled in evaluating the details on which you base your actions. The outcome of this planning is generally a sure thing even before you become involved; you don't really take chances on anything.

Having great faith in yourself, you project a wholesome expectation of success in all your endeavors. You don't waste precious time and effort on trivia, but you are thoughtful in applying yourself to the matters that you feel are important. You might succeed in law, finance, physical therapy, counseling of young people, education, or the ministry. You are creatively inspired in using your talents for working with people, especially in religious endeavors. In making any public presentation you dramatize yourself effectively. You are fairly easy-going with co-workers and don't challenge them if they are less competent than you.

You could become apathetic and indifferent to success, since this planetary combination gives you the luxury of such a choice. But it would be a loss to society if you elected to detach yourself in this way. If you choose, you can be the catalyst for the development of other people's talents. People without dreams of their own can achieve with your prodding. Their destinies would be immeasurably benefited by contact with you.

You may decide to avoid the hostile world of professional endeavors. If so, you might devote your talents to such areas as recreation, physical development, or training young people in need of a strong adult who believes in them. Participating in Junior Achievement programs would be a useful way to offer your expertise to those desiring it. You would be of great value and would be enriched by the results of your efforts.

Jupiter Trine Uranus

The trine between Jupiter and Uranus shows that you have enormous creative ability and can also mobilize your talents to gain whatever goals you desire. You are mentally alert to every opportunity that presents itself. There is a decided luck factor operating in your life, which enables you to accomplish more than most people do with the same creative potentials.

Your professional activities should relate to education, law, politics, religion, or related fields. In any of these you could succeed without too much effort. You also might be interested in working with young people. You have the flair for gaining their interest and stimulating their enthusiasm. Your intuition is highly developed, and your sudden flashes of inspiration enable you to work wonders, especially with children.

Your participation would enhance the efforts of organizations, societies, clubs, or religious group endeavors. Just by your presence you can dramatize the purposes of such groups. You are a good leader with a deep understanding of other people and their desires. You know how to make problems seem less difficult or even disappear. Consequently you are warmly received and encouraged.

Freedom is very important to you, and you resist those who may try to fence you in. The experience of travel would broaden your development and be especially enriching.

You are warm toward your friends and sincere even with your enemies, if you have any. You have enormous faith in your own abilities and are optimistic about the potential success of other people, whom you will help when necessary. But you are impatient with pessimists who fail before they even try to succeed.

You expect honesty from your lover and offer spiitual strength and integrity with your love. People admire you for your unselfishness.

Jupiter Trine Neptune

With the trine between Jupiter and Neptune you have the inspiration and integrated knowledge to make your life rich and contented. Your deep spiritual understanding of life and people will give you moments of serene contemplation. Being aware of the coarse realities in your environment, you may offer to make some contribution to refining them. You can see good where others see evil, constructive potentials where others see decay, and restored order where others fear utter chaos.

With your sophistication, you should participate in activities that benefit the public. Your efforts could stimulate social programs for developing the productive potentials of poor people. Education, art, religious interest, and writing are some avenues for expressing your enormous creative talents. These would prove successful to you and immeasurably beneficial to others.

You have the deepest respect for religion and philosophy because they bring order to the lives of those who respond to them. For yourself, however, you are fascinated by the occult and have a deep understanding of mystical matters. Your psychic abilities are considerable, and much of your knowledge comes through this faculty. Others sense your strength when they seek comfort from you. Permitting others to benefit from your tender, loving care helps relieve your spiritual anxieties.

Your greatest fulfillment is through service to others, especially when your efforts result in lasting benefits. There are always causes to which you can make a significant contribution. Even if you are not gainfully employed, you will be involved in useful activities, such as art or fashion shows or a benefit for a needy cause.

Your refined nature is comfortable in romantic attachments with others of similar persuasion. You never sacrifice your ideals to satisfy a physical need, for you respond only to people who have meaningful spiritual values.

Jupiter Trine Pluto

The trine from Jupiter to Pluto indicates your interest in stimulating individuals and groups to creatively exploit their own potentials. Your optimistic response to social change inspires others to view the future with greater expectation and hope. You can awaken those around you to an acceptable philosophy for pursuing their destinies. You arouse them to establish constructive motivations that will sustain them through the bitter and the sweet, the highs and the lows, the successes and the failures in their lives.

You are able to grasp the essential meaning behind many of life's mysteries and to dramatize it effectively enough to convince the most determined skeptic. Your words, often seemingly inspired, carry such an impact that they are seldom questioned. Because you are geared to become intimately involved in the affairs of others, you should choose a profession that will serve the public interest. Education would give you a broad yet intimate scope to demonstrate truths as you understand them and to shatter the illusions that restrict expansion of consciousness. It may be that you are a free soul, whose destiny is to serve others.

Your personal relationships must allow you mobility and creative expression. You have the power to move from a life of apathy and indolence to one in which you offer your insight for the benefit of society. You instinctively know right from wrong and can assist others to recognize the difference. The young are especially responsive to you, for you understand the drama of their lives. Even elderly and mature people gain inspiration from your fresh and invigorating life-force. You can stimulate lives that could have become stagnant and without purpose.

You can restore your own life-force by contemplating your experiences and by meditating on the universal energy sources that grant you vision to know the truth. These precious moments will give you guidelines for applying the knowledge you gain.

Jupiter Trine Ascendant

Jupiter trine the Ascendant means that you always expect to succeed. You find it possible to make grandiose plans for the future, because you know how to capitalize on your creative abilities as tools with which to seek your goals in life. Knowing how is not the same as actually doing something, however, and your success may be delayed by the delusion that you can succeed without a lot of hard work. You like the good life and all its comforts, which can be yours if you are willing to make an enormous investment of personal effort.

Although you have high expectations, you secretly fear you won't succeed in winning over your competitors. You overestimate other people's skills and underestimate your own, which can lead you to have a defeatist attitude. Concentrate your efforts on gaining excellence in what you do, so that you can dismiss these anxieties.

The people you work for regard you more highly than you think. Hoping to gain their respect, you attempt to do more than your share in the tasks assigned to you. You admire those who achieve distinction and realize that you must be fully informed if you hope to win similar honors. However, you tend to dawdle when you should discipline yourself in working toward your goals. By indulging in personal pleasures to excess, you waste energy and time that could be used more constructively. Because you are careless about managing your financial affairs, you sometimes can't avail yourself of opportunities when they arise.

Your talents are needed in many fields, but unless you learn to extablish your priorities, you will waste your gifts in nonproductive enterprises. You are too generous in sharing your ideas with others when you should develop them for your own benefit. Avoid borrowing money if you can; because of your self-indulgent nature, it may be painful to repay unless you learn to have greater self-control.

Saturn Trine Uranus

The trine between Saturn and Uranus shows that you have learned from your experiences and acquired discipline. As you project yourself toward future accomplishments, you are excited by the prospects of all the tomorrows. You have earned the freedom you enjoy. Although you have a healthy respect for material things, you are fascinated by your increasing detachment from them. In the future you will be enriched by letting others share the benefits of your knowledge and experience.

You have the talent to mobilize and exploit your resources. You are intuitively aware that success depends on taking measured risks rather than on speculating. Consequently you can teach others how to effectively capitalize on their potentials. You are well qualified for executive positions because of your keen judgment and uncanny insight. Your understanding of people and their motivations enables you to organize their talents to accomplish seemingly impossible tasks.

You are particularly good at handling young people, because they can identify with you and the authority you present to them. They admire you for "getting it all together" and being able to assert yourself without arrogance. They also respect you for expecting them to define and seek their own goals.

You can successfully apply your potentials in many occupations. Suitable fields include mathematics, science, research, and astrology, as well as many industrial positions requiring leadership and organization.

Your ideals are based on solid experience with the tried and true. As you strive to gain your objectives, you uphold the highest values of behavior. You are optimistic about the future for yourself and for those who share your ethical standards.

Saturn Trine Neptune

With Saturn trine Neptune you have the ability to take on enormous responsibilities. You are motivated by a powerful spiritual compulsion to bring about positive changes in the negative social conditions you observe. Early parental training established your high ethical and moral standards. You are sympathetic and understanding toward anyone whose circumstances are more burdensome than yours, and you strive to find ways to demonstrate your concern for your fellow man. When a helping hand is required, you are ready and willing to give it.

To your professional interests you bring wisdom and sincerity. You can express your gifted imagination in many ways that seem inspired. You are intolerant of deception and collusion and will not compromise your ethics for personal gain. Occupations related to the film industry, photography, law, social services, the stock market, or the entertainment field in general would provide you with much personal satisfaction.

Your environment can benefit from your talents. You are keen in appraising conditions that must be changed and in determining the causes. You know how to enlist the services of the proper authorities, and you are familiar with the legal mechanisms that will help restore order out of chaos.

These are the resources available to you. What you do with them is up to you. You can remain a spectator, detached from active participation, if you choose, but it would certainly be a waste of your talents. At the very least you may decide to alert others to the problems of their environment and offer some plans for achieving their objectives.

You have the necessary faculties to succeed as a writer. Your inspiration and talent for observation can give form to the ideas you have. You derive many benefits from every experience. With your vast resources of knowledge, you have the ability to solve any problem.

Saturn Trine Pluto

The trine from Saturn to Pluto gives you the power of concentration. Instinctively you know how to manage your affairs for the most benefit. Your thinking is organized, your purposes are realistic, and your attention to duty guarantees success. You recognize that social changes are inevitable. You accept your responsibilities, knowing you can make an effective contribution and can participate in making productive changes in society.

You have the determination and persistence to succeed in any field in which management skills are essential. Because you consider carefully other people's values and feelings, you are better able to make decisions based on all the available facts. You can effectively manipulate individuals to achieve broad social changes, but you are impatient with those who without trying say they "can't do this," or "can't do that." You are especially capable of handling the resources of a large industrial or social enterprise. In promoting and establishing programs for the benefit of everyone, you try to use public resources. You can stimulate government agencies to assist people in financial difficulties or those who are unable to help themselves.

You may seek a government position to better serve those who rely on your talents and persuasive abilities. Your efficiency may even stir your colleagues to assist you in reducing governmental waste. Because you are aware of what is useful and what is not, you might also serve the public by reducing expenditures and thus lowering taxes.

You have the power to transform the apathy of youth to excited participation in the affairs of their environment. You can dramatize to adults how their lethargy and indolence has resulted in depletion of public resources. You have much to offer, and you should make it available, for you know what's right and what's wrong with society.

Saturn Trine Ascendant

Saturn trine the Ascendant means that you feel a great responsibility for developing your creative talents to derive the greatest benefit from them. You understand that success does not always come easily and that only hard work will produce the results you want. Although your parents may not have been able to give you any financial advantages, you appreciate them for teaching you to rely on yourself. Not a trailblazer, you depend on traditional means of expression for your ideas. You prefer to assert yourself in fields that hold a reasonable promise of security, because you don't like to gamble or take unnecessary chances.

Your priorities are directed to achieving material success and distinction. You measure people by the depth of their conversation, whether they are intellectual or superficial. You like to compare your net worth with that of your contemporaries. You want to be thought of as a person who came up the hard way and succeeded in spite of the odds.

You are loyal to those you care for. Although you may not have a wide circle of friends, you keep the friends you have. You are not especially preoccupied with physical pleasures, primarily because you would rather go without, if you can't have exactly what you want. Actually, you are not easily "turned on" by just anybody. Before you allow yourself to indulge in a romantic escapade, you try to learn what credentials a person has. Your indifference to exclusively physical relationships tends to keep people at a distance. Because you don't really like yourself enough, you think you deserve no more than the minimal pleasures you now have.

Since you are such an isolationist, you deprive yourself of the companionship of people who really appreciate you. You have to show you are warmer than you appear and learn to lower the barriers that keep people from warming up to you. Others respect you for your stoicism, but they may also criticize you for your inability to relate.

Uranus Trine Neptune

The trine of Uranus and Neptune indicates that you resent being told what to believe. You prefer to decide for yourself whether you will accept or reject the ideas that have satisfied previous generations of believers. Your intellectual awareness requires that you logically evaluate all ideologies, dogmas, or theories, whether they are political, philosophical, or religious. You feel that you cannot support a particular belief until you understand thoroughly how and why it was established. Seeking truth rather than illusions, you are suspicious of ideas that may seriously alter your life and destiny. You observe how masses of humanity in the past have been dominated by individuals who forced their ideologies on their subjects, mesmerizing them to accept those ideas blindly and obediently.

To illustrate how these planets produced mass hysteria, we must examine the period between 1938 and 1944, when they occupied this relationship. Adolf Hitler, Joseph Stalin, Benito Mussolini, and Emperor Hirohito hypnotically dominated millions of people and produced an awesome machine that destroyed even more millions and altered forever the destinies of countless others. This planetary combination indicates the indolence and apathy present among people throughout the world, which allowed this destruction to take place.

You and many others who were born during these years can help prevent a repetition of history by refusing to support any individual in power until you know everything possible about him or her. Because you have the ability to see through illusion and dishonesty, it is your responsibility to communicate what you know for the benefit of humanity. You must arouse the public to challenge any public official who will not keep open the lines of communication to the people he represents.

Uranus Trine Pluto

The trine from Uranus to Pluto shows that you are willing to accept the changes that progress necessitates. You not only adapt yourself to current developments but you support new ones if you feel they will prove beneficial in the long run. You understand that reform is needed when existing social conditions no longer allow sufficient room for people to grow or to expand in awareness. When you observe how political, religious, and social structures inhibit individual creativity, you are especially disturbed. You resent being told that you should accept tradition because it is custom that stabilizes society. Knowing that progress requires continual adjustment, you rightly object to this philosophy. Traditions are only valid when viewed in their proper time reference.

You were born at a time when man was thrashing about in a state of utter madness—the Roaring Twenties. The world was caught in the grip of illusion and euphoria, totally unaware that the economy rested on a crumbling foundation. However, the seeds of a whole new dimension of human awareness were also being sown, but it would be many years before they would ripen and be harvested. During this time Carl Jung presented his findings on the individual and collective unconscious, which later provided increased understanding of human motivation. Darwin's theory of evolution was spotlighted by the Scopes trial in Tennessee.

As a product of the new awareness that was sown during the Twenties, you have greater dimension than the people of the preceding generation. You want greater meaning in your life than that provided by a materialistic philosophy. The occult world interests you, and you are fascinated by the enormous capabilities of the mind when it is freed from old attitudes and concepts. You are not afraid to venture into the spiritual world for the resources that may be found there, and you are willing to share your discoveries for everyone's benefit.

Uranus Trine Ascendant

Uranus trine the Ascendant means that you will always be able to express your creativity when you want, mainly because you let everyone know that you will not be denied this privilege. Your creative potentials are considerable, and you only need self-discipline to develop them. But it is useless for anyone to pressure you to do so, because you resent interference in this matter and consider it an invasion of your privacy.

Nothing seems to bother you, and your bright, optimistic outlook shows that you are not troubled by personal problems you can't take care of. You live each day as it comes and are not unduly worried about all the tomorrows, for you know you will take care of them in due time. Generally you are not bothered by subconscious problems because you refuse to dwell on anything negative. Not a clock-watcher, you are freed from being dependent on time. You enjoy a variety of pleasures, some rather ordinary but others perhaps bordering on the ridiculous or bizarre. You are a rebel and in many ways a loner. You don't really care whether others have freedom; that is their problem. You only know that you must be free.

You have an adventurous mind filled with ingenious ideas that you can exploit if you want to. All that restricts you is the money needed for developing them. Since you are not interested in public admiration, you don't feel any obligation to gain status. Your love relationships must be based partly on intellectual rapport, or you easily become bored. You like to believe that you are important in the lives of those you touch; chances are that anyone who forms a close friendship with you is affected by your concern. You understand people better than they understand themselves. You are pleased that the trend among young people is toward greater individuality and that they are more determined to seek their own destinies free from the confinement of tradition.

Neptune Trine Ascendant

Neptune trine the Ascendant gives you such deep sensitivity that it is extremely difficult for you to be satisfied in personal relations. Your expectations can rarely be fulfilled, for you seek the ideal human relationship. A romanticist at heart, you attribute to people qualities they don't possess and then you are disappointed when they let you down. Instead of dwelling on this, you should concentrate on developing your creative ideas. With your imagination and flair for translating your thoughts into inspired action, this should not be difficult. You can easily compensate for the dissatisfaction of personal relationships by channeling your talents into artistic endeavors, where you can be fully appreciated. In the beginning you may have to settle for meager returns from your efforts, until you acquire the skill of a true and dedicated artist. There are also many other ways to use your talents besides in artistic pursuits. It might be a source of great joy for you to work with young people and children and see them develop under your influence.

You tend to dwell on your character faults, especially if others have pointed them out to you. Forget them and go on to develop your abundant positive qualities. You are inclined to feel that you must do more than others in order to get the recognition you deserve. But take care that you don't become a victim of friends who try to take advantage of your indulgent nature. You are not afraid to work hard if your efforts are appreciated. Knowing that you can make a contribution to society in some way, you must persist in finding out what it is, in spite of reversals. You should bring your creative gifts before the public and give your interpretation of what is needed to improve the quality of life for everyone. You can demonstrate your spiritual concern for man by actively helping to arouse every individual to use his or her highest values to make the world a better place to live.

Pluto Trine Ascendant

Pluto trine the Ascendant shows that you have an enormous source of energy to draw on in using your creative abilities. There is literally nothing you can't do if you set your mind to it. You have the strength and self-confidence to project your ideas and win the full support you need. Tolerating the past only for the lessons it teaches, you look eagerly to a future made more secure from the lessons you have learned. You are eager to communicate what you know to others, but you will not force it on them, preferring to wait for an indication that your suggestions are welcome. Lack of funds is no excuse for inaction in your view, for you feel that there is always a way if one wants something desperately enough. You are clever in converting all your resources into the tangible assets you need to implement your projects.

Knowing your failings, you work hard to transform your negative qualities so they do not limit you. Even more important, you understand your capabilities and emphasize them in seeking your goals. The task of making the future secure challenges you to use every resource you have. You know what you're worth, and you expect to be fully rewarded for the contributions you make in your career. You admire people who seek an education, if they are motivated by a desire to be the best in what they do. Ignorance is no defense for lack of accomplishment, you believe, because you know that being well-informed is as accessible as the nearest library.

You know how to get along both with competitors and with associates, and you strive especially to be worthy of the people you deal with. You want to know that you have made an important contribution in stimulating them to reach their goals. But don't assume that without you these people would not be able to succeed. You must realize that many people are quite capable of transforming their own lives and may not need your self-righteous assistance. Be available when they need you, but don't be a nuisance when they don't.

Chapter Five

Inconjuncts

The inconjunct aspect is formed when two planets are separated by an angle of one hundred fifty degrees. It links planetary influences between signs that have no sympathy for each other by element or quality and are therefore functioning under great strain. The inconjunct has the dynamics of Mars, Mercury, and Pluto; the qualities of Aries, Virgo, and Scorpio; and the circumstances associated with the first, sixth, and eighth houses. This aspect relates to the effects produced by aggression; it spills either into the sixth house, where social obligations are fulfilled for personal satisfaction, or into the eighth house, where obligations are fulfilled for the benefit of others.

All signs and their aspectual correspondences react specifically from their opposites. From this we determine that the inconjunct is a product of Pisces and Taurus and of subtle prompting from the twelfth and second houses. Our experience has indicated that the inconjunct shows an attempt to become free from social obligations by performing services for others. It relieves the burden of subconscious psychological guilt for past inaction or transgression. The inconjunct is the opportunity to prevent additional liabilities from accumulating by sacrificing personal desires and offering all available resources for the benefit of others. All inconjuncts have this distinguishing feature, regardless of the signs involved.

The pressure and strain produced by the inconjunct can be relieved only by understanding and compromise, the essential nature of Libra, which opposes Aries. Sharing and giving seem to be the only solutions to the dilemma posed by the inconjunct. Through the inconjunct, one wins approval for what can be accomplished when one is motivated to serve rather than be served. The only alternatives are the negative and sometimes tragic results of poor health and death.

Sun Inconjunct Moon

The Sun inconjunct the Moon indicates that your ties to the past and to emotional security are misaligned with the ways in which you consciously express your will and desire. The resulting stress is usually seen in your relationships. In your desire to hold on to old friends and associates, you make enormous concessions that interfere with your own development. You create situations that bind you with obligations to people and that are difficult to free yourself from. You so complicate your life this way that one would suspect you enjoy suffering at the hands of others. Your eagerness to be of service to people would be better utilized by getting a job with that aim in mind.

There is constant danger of abusing your health when you yield to the demands people make on your time and energy. You must overcome the feeling that you owe it to them. Furthermore, you don't have the right to interfere with other people's lives by taking their responsibilities on yourself. What are you trying to prove? Are you trying to win their approval because you really feel you don't deserve it? Be assured that you are probably far more competent than those you serve, only you don't know it. You should spend more time with your own affairs and capitalize on your own talents and creative abilities. Let your contribution be to develop your potentials and gain recognition for excellence in everything you do.

You are painfully sympathetic to anyone who comes to you with a tale of woe. Channel that sympathy into activities that can bring you some benefits. Many occupations require your depth of understanding, such as medicine, physical therapy, and work with young people and children. In these fields there is a genuine need for your kind of unselfish dedication to others. In a more objective application of your talents, you could be happy working with welfare programs or with fund-raising organizations that serve those who are unable to help themselves.

Relaxation is essential if you want to maintain your general good health. Get away as often as you can to unwind from the pressure of your daily concerns. Avoid visiting relatives if you are expected to "chip in" and help while you're there.

Your romantic interests can be disappointing because you assign undeserved attributes to the person you love. Being rejected is especially painful to you, and you might say, "I've been so good to that person, and I don't deserve to be treated this way." Stop feeling sorry for yourself and learn to accept people the way they are. If you can't accept them as they are, don't try to reshape them to your design, for that always fails.

You can offer your prospective mate many advantages, and you are willing to work side by side to get the things you both want. When you know that you are loved, you are inspired, and the best in you is brought to the surface.

Sun Inconjunct Mars

The inconjunct from the Sun to Mars indicates that there is an element of strain in everything you try to do. You are enthusiastic, energetic, and eager to demonstrate your skills, but you seem to offer your services to the wrong persons. Disappointment is likely when you find out that your efforts are unappreciated. You seem to be on the prowl for problems to contaminate your life, and you don't lack for them. You want to win the approval of everybody you meet and be remembered for all the favors you have done for them. Although you are more than competent by anyone's standards, you are not personally sure of it. The only way you can be convinced is by enduring the abuses of those who are less competent. You specialize in using all your physical resources well, so that you can be regarded as someone of obvious worth. When people bargain for your skills and are willing to pay for your expert abilities, you are finally convinced of your worth. Then you can afford to be selective.

Your talents can be applied in many diverse fields. You could be a diagnostician, medical researcher, industrial researcher, physical therapist, or have a trade, such as a carpenter, mason, or plumber. You would be well paid for your work, because you would do it as though it were for yourself. You don't put your name on any product that doesn't meet with your full approval. Although you may not gain the recognition you deserve, except in your immediate environment, it doesn't matter to you because you are more interested in doing a good job.

You have to be on the lookout for people who will exploit you and try to cash in on your ideas. You are vulnerable to such people because you are so generous in displaying your talents. On the other hand, be mindful of your tendency to use people's ignorance as a device for selling services to them that they may not need.

You underestimate your ability to win the affection of the person you are attracted to. Anyone who is realistic would know that you don't carelessly or insincerely toss your feelings toward someone. You are more than dependable and can fully justify yourself, even to the most demanding critic.

Sun Inconjunct Jupiter

The Sun inconjunct Jupiter indicates that you lack the self-assurance to be completely independent. As a result, you strive to show people how competent you are by trying to do things for them. Through their praise you hope you will gain the self-confidence you need. You overreact to anything that hints of criticism and offer your services in hopes of reversing the negative opinion (which the person may never have had in the first place). Being unsure of your capabilities, you underestimate them and need physical proof of their existence. You are a tireless worker, eager to be recognized as an authority in whatever you do, but even more concerned about developing your talents.

Education is very important to you, and a work-study program would be an excellent idea. You will have to apply yourself with great determination to acquire the expertise you desire, but you do have the necessary ingredients with which to build and become a specialist. You can apply your efforts in such endeavors as education, craftwork, physical therapy, veterinary medicine, or any other occupation in which success means performing an important service. You must always be careful in your relationships with co-workers, however; you are inclined to take on others' duties and responsibilities at the slightest suggestion that you should. Be wary of opportunists who may try to use your ideas for their personal gain. Be cautious about sharing confidences unless you know you can do so safely.

You probably feel that your talents are not adequately rewarded, and you can suffer much discontent because you are not appreciated. In general, you are worth more than you are being paid, if only because of the effort you bring to your job. Seek advice in order to set a proper value on your skills, obtain a suitable contract, and demand that it be observed. This is the only way you can protect yourself.

Your emotional relationships are not easily fulfilled because you don't feel you deserve such a reward. You assume that you don't measure up to your lover's expectations, but of course you do. You always offer more than necessary in a mutual relationship, and you probably get less out of it than you deserve.

Moderation in everything you do is advised. You are inclined to worry that you are not doing your best or not doing enough, which can cause digestive problems and much discomfort. Driving yourself beyond sane levels invites physical exhaustion. Liquor is especially troublesome for you, but if you must drink, never do so on an empty stomach. Liver complaints are rather common with this planetary combination. Get a full measure of daily rest — you'll live longer and better if you do.

Sun Inconjunct Saturn

The inconjunct from the Sun to Saturn shows that you are somewhat careless about your health and that you tend to take abuse from others. You seem determined to allow others to take advantage of your inability to say *no* when they ask favors of you. Perhaps in your early years you did more of the household tasks than other members of your family, because you felt it was your duty. You have a subtle fear of others and the power they seem to have over you. Psychologically, this may be referred to as latent masochism, which means you are seeking ways to be punished for what you consider to be past mistakes.

In your work, you might accept an obscure position in which there is little possibility of promotion, and in time your job would become boring and dull. It isn't that you are incapable of rising to better positions, but you may not be aggressive enough to be noticed by your superiors. Your survival instinct is distorted; you believe it is better not to "rock the boat" than take the chance that you cannot compete with others. But you must realize that others can take advantage of you only if you let them.

Your striving for identity and personal significance will be greatly hampered unless you can detach yourself from others and become self-sufficient. Try to define a goal that you want to achieve and then lay the groundwork and plans to do just that. Forget about what you will do beyond that. When the time comes, you will extablish a new goal. If you take one step at a time, success can be yours. Don't compare your achievements with those of others — your greatest priority is yourself!

In your eagerness to be accepted you become tense and apologetic. You must learn to relax, or these reactions can lead to poor circulation and digestion. Be good to yourself and let others take care of themselves — you're worth more to yourself that way.

Sun Inconjunct Uranus

The Sun inconjunct Uranus shows you often deprive yourself by yielding to other people's demands. It isn't easy for you to give in to others, and when you do you become bitter. Perhaps you permit such intrusions because you feel a deep inner guilt about turning people down. You feel severely challenged by others, especially by their authoritative attitude when requesting your services.

You have to be especially alert to the trap that people use when they say, "I've looked everywhere, and you're the only one I can trust with my problem." With this technique, they are pandering to your vanity and thereby inducing you to yield. You will suffer silently if you let yourself be used this way and if you allow it to continue you may become vindictive.

Beware of other traps also. When you reject someone's demands, they may say, "Aren't you humanitarian at all?" If you feel you must answer that, your reply should be only that you are not sacrificial.

In your profession you will be similarly bothered by colleagues trying to impose on you. You should look for an occupation in education, therapy, rehabilitation, institutional services, or any activity in which freedom is in some way the main objective. Freeing the minds of the young by stimulating them intellectually would serve both them and yourself to great advantage. In whatever work you do, you should be able to see the effects of your efforts. If your contribution is not appreciated you may doubt your competence and value, although you should not.

The people with whom you are emotionally involved expect you to prove that you care. Learn to relax when you suspect that your love is not returned. You can be deceived by people who may use you to satisfy their desires. True love is not difficult to demonstrate, so let the other person make the first move to express it.

Sun Inconjunct Neptune

The inconjunct from the Sun to Neptune shows that you consider your responsibilities the most pressing in the world. There is an element of self-sacrifice in the way you allow others to intrude in your life. You really believe people who suggest that only you can solve their problems. Because of this martyr quality, you seek the most demanding jobs or human situations in order to test your commitment to service. You are unsure of yourself and are continually trying to find ways to prove your competence. In serving other people's needs, you deplete your own energies.

Professional success will be difficult to achieve because of your preoccupation with endless trivia. Exaggerating the importance of superficial matters, you tend to get bogged down by them. You should become selfish enough to express your own creative potential. There will always be opportunities to render service to others after you've gained a sense of your own importance. Welfare programs, hospital work, group therapy, medical research, and rehabilitative functions would provide adequate avenues for expression. In your work, be sure to establish the exact extent of your duties and resolve not to do more than is explicitly required. In other words, don't be a "patsy."

You tend to form alliances with individuals who always seem to need you. They do need you, much more than you need them. Be wary of people who will exploit you, for they may successfully hide their negative ambitions from you. Always be suspicious of the motivation underlying someone's interest in you. Don't fall into the trap of thinking that it's your spiritual responsibility to be of service to others. Your emotional nature is such that you grant others the benefit of the doubt, and later find you have been rejected.

Try not to let everyone treat you as a dumping ground for their negative qualities. If someone needs a confessor, let him seek and pay for professional help. Such people will never pay you for the burdens they unload on you.

Sun Inconjunct Pluto

The Sun inconjunct Pluto indicates that you take on duties that others reject even though you may be bitterly resentful of these duties. You overreact to the expectations of others and usually do more than you need to or should. A guilt factor in your personality makes you continually strive to prove that you are doing your share.

You make punishing demands on yourself, and unless you exercise moderation, this will bring on negative physical reactions. Moreover, other people will be extremely displeased and resentful if you expect them to copy your efforts. Try not to compare yourself with others who are performing similar tasks.

In searching for the approval of others, you drive yourself very hard. You tend to be obsessed with gaining the admiration of people to whom you feel inferior. You are overly preoccupied with the power and position they may have. Concern yourself with personal goals and objectives and develop your potentials to successfully meet competition. You may have to make sacrifices in order to realize your ambitions, but don't sacrifice your ambitions to satisfy someone else's goals.

As the foregoing suggests, you should become a bit selfish. Learn to understand your limitations and define your goals within them. Confide in someone whom you trust to advise you, and take that person's advice.

Your need to like yourself will probably be satisfied when you can see the results of a well-organized plan for achieving success. You must learn to dispense with nonessentials and to focus your efforts on a particular objective. You should refrain from taking on any adversaries until you are fully trained and have confidence that you can succeed.

Don't wrestle with other people's wills. The less conflict you create in dealing with others, the better. Tension and its accompanying problems will soon disappear when you learn to relax.

Sun Inconjunct Ascendant

The Sun inconjunct the Ascendant shows that you are a tireless worker and don't do anything unless you can give it your full effort. You want the approval of everyone you know for what you accomplish. Secretly you may hope to gain some public recognition too, but you don't really expect it. You are generally willing to work behind the scenes, quietly developing your potentials and mastering the skills you need to meet the struggle to earn a living. You realize that your creative talents are useless unless you develop them and make them your greatest assets. You respect people who seek a formal education, although you yourself can do very well merely by developing your latent talents. Always striving for excellence, you are impatient with people who are inefficient or lazy.

You learned many valuable lessons from your parents, and you may have followed their suggestions in getting the training they felt you should have. Actually, you are a specialist. But you underestimate your capabilities and will be satisfied with yourself only when you are successful in your work. You know how to convert your talents into revenue and expect to be well paid for your services, for you know what they are worth. Undaunted by competition, you always try to be the best in whatever you do. Your future is secure, as you are well aware.

You drive yourself excessively, which carries the risk of depleting your physical reserves. Detach yourself from responsibility now and then so you can unwind and get needed rest. You feel a deep obligation to prove your abilities to yourself, although you don't mind it when others make flattering remarks about your skills. You are easily put upon by so-called friends, who always want you to do something for them. This is your chance to know who your friends really are. You should be wary of revealing your ideas to associates, who may try to capitalize on them without giving you the full credit you deserve and without paying for them.

Moon Inconjunct Mercury

With the Moon inconjunct Mercury your emotions and intellect interfere with each other so much that you have difficulty in solving your problems. You overreact emotionally to situations and so cannot rationalize them properly. When you inject feeling instead of examining the facts, any reasonable evaluation of the situation becomes impossible. You infer that criticism is directed at you when that is not the case at all; your reaction is all out of proportion to the truth. But you are emotionally aroused and take out your hostility on those dearest to you without realizing it. People can easily learn to resent and avoid you at the same time.

You carry tremendous guilt for the way you behave, but nevertheless you repeat the behavior when similar circumstances occur. A vicious circle is established, which can eventually cause you much mental anxiety. You should resist taking action on any problem that develops until you can seek an objective opinion about it. Your initial reaction is most likely to be faulty and unjustified when the facts are examined carefully.

You have an unconscious desire to be of service to everyone you meet, but you are resented for this. Instead of gaining everyone's approval for your deeds, you arouse their criticism. It seems you are not content just to perform a service, but have to bring attention to yourself for doing it. This touches a raw nerve in people, who then feel obligated to you and resent it. To begin with, you should concern yourself with your own affairs, for they are your highest priority. Forget about other people until you have your own problems in order. Otherwise you will run the risk of being used by those you show an interest in and will be hurt when you realize what they've done.

You can work out your desire to be of service through professional endeavors. In your job, do exactly what is expected of you and nothing more. Never volunteer, or the chances are you'll complain of how exhausted you are because of all the work you have to do! You are too sensitive and easily irritated to complicate your life unnecessarily.

In your romantic associations you try too hard to be desired. You put yourself in difficult situations with the person you are attracted to and are crushed if your efforts are unrewarded. Try instead to give your prospective partner a chance to demonstrate affection before you assert yourself. Otherwise you may encourage someone to abuse your love and take advantage of you. Learn to let a relationship develop without putting pressure on it.

Moon Inconjunct Venus

The Moon inconjunct Venus shows that you have a low opinion of your personal needs and give a greater priority to persons whom you feel obligated to. Your indulgence of them makes it seem that you are buying their approval. You feel you must make every concession possible in order to become free from continued obligation to anyone but yourself. The only problem here is that this process goes on and on. Your reaction to people is unbalanced and illogical. If you can detach yourself from emotional considerations, you will be able to logically decide how far your obligations go and to what extent you should expect others to make concessions to you.

Unless you do this, you will be drained of all your physical resources and will be emotionally impoverished as well. You play into the hands of people who are on the prowl for individuals like yourself who seem determined to be enslaved. You need to develop greater self-respect in order to earn the respect of the people you deal with. No one can take advantage of you unless you give them permission.

Submission is hardly cooperation. You must insist on discussing your obligations and their limits before you take on any responsibility. Your desire to please and to give everyone the benefit of the doubt can obscure your judgment of what is right and wrong in a situation. Ample proof of this will be demonstrated as you function in your job. Watch out for attempts by co-workers to use your kindly nature to give you more work and relieve them of certain duties. If you don't speak up, they may take advantage of you.

The problems cited above concerning employment also apply to your emotional affairs. You seem to attract indivuals who always want you to prove your love. Again, try to evaluate why this should be necessary and suggest instead that the person first demonstrate sincere interest and affection for you.

Don't lend money or anything else to anyone. Your chances of recovering it are slim. Their attitude is that you can afford it, and you won't miss it anyway. In performing services for others, learn to put a price on what you do. This is why you should not volunteer your time. Most people will assume that when you offer to do something for them it is a gift. If you're going to make gifts, do so to satisfy your own desires.

Moon Inconjunct Mars

The inconjunct between the Moon and Mars shows that you lack self-control in expressing your feelings. You tend to misjudge people and to form binding alliances with individuals who take advantage of your indulgence. Even when others abuse and misuse you, you never raise a hand to defend yourself. You feel powerless to oppose the oppressive demands that people make of your talents, and when they exploit you, you are bitter and disappointed. The most disturbing result of this process is that you may become hardened in your dealings with people. Your greatest problem is to resolve the conflict between your desire to be useful to people and their expectations that you will make up for their deficiencies.

There are many occupations you can follow, for this planetary combination does not incline you in a specific direction. It shows that you are more versatile than most people in being able to handle a variety of occupations. You must be alert to the hazard of becoming locked in a job pattern in which you do all the work while others get the recognition you deserve. You might be the victim of collusion by your co-workers and have to account for their incompetence, as if you were responsible for it. Proving that you had nothing to do with it might be difficult, and you would suffer a loss from that injustice.

Resist the temptation to offer yourself to others. Although it might seem to be the only way to get people to like and admire you, you will actually lose their respect by such gestures. Mind your own business and beg off when people try to get you involved in their affairs. Take care of your own responsibilities and develop the skills that will give you the self-confidence you need to feel satisfied with yourself. You may be criticized for being selfish, but you will save yourself a lot of headaches.

You will avoid a lot of nervous irritability and emotional anxiety by keeping your distance from the people who demand your services and devotion. They need you much more than you need them.

Digestive and possibly intestinal discomforts may result when you get really uptight about situations involving people that defy a solution. Better to lose some so-called friends than take that risk. An intellectual appraisal may reveal that compromise will solve the problem. You must carefully evaluate your priorities concerning others; you may find that you should involve yourself only when your own affairs are in order. You need the calming effect of peaceful relationships and a more easy-going attitude in your other affairs.

Moon Inconjunct Jupiter

The Moon inconjunct Jupiter indicates a discrepancy between your emotional responses to stimuli and your understanding of them. You find it difficult to determine the true significance of events in your life. You know you have a lot to learn, but the process seems so utterly painful because you must endure repeated lessons before you can grasp the full meaning.

You underestimate your abilities, assuming that everyone else is more competent than you. As a result, you take the role of the second-class citizen who is willing to serve others, no matter what they ask. You lack the backbone to tell people to get lost when they attempt to take advantage of your generous nature. However, this problem won't always bother you. In time you will establish personal priorities, learning to take care of your own needs before turning to the needs of others. You simply have to learn that you are worth more than you realize. As it stands, you look to others to reassure you of your competence. You feel guilty when you turn people down who ask for your help. Don't! Your guilt is largely an emotional reaction. Be generous to yourself before others.

There are many ways in which you can serve others and serve yourself at the same time. Occupations related to physical therapy, rehabilitation for the handicapped, travel, or public relations are some ways this twofold purpose can be achieved. You would enjoy some, perhaps most of these fields. You need to feel free to thoroughly exploit your creative talents. You are not afraid of hard work, but you often bite off more than you can chew. Determine exactly what your duties are and fulfill them, but do no more than that. If you allow it, you will be given tasks that others should do and those that they refuse to perform.

You desperately need interests outside those of your occupation. Develop an interest, if possible, in a hobby that really stimulates your creative ability. Whatever you do will prove beneficial as long as you are not obligated to it except when you wish. This type of activity would afford priceless relaxation and give you a chance to unwind. You might choose to conduct Sunday school activities, or work in community affairs, but the important thing is that you will decide how much you are willing to do.

Above all, make sure that people demonstrate their credibility before you become involved with them. You'll save yourself a lot of unnecessary anxiety.

Moon Inconjunct Saturn

The inconjunct between your Moon and Saturn indicates an undercurrent of guilt in your emotional reactions to people. You seem uneasy until you can find some way to demonstrate that you sincerely care for them. In a sense this negative reaction is an admission that you don't feel worthy of them. It would seem that in your early conditioning your parents made you feel that others had the right to exploit you and make you feel inferior to them. As an adult, you can change this. What you truly owe is the obligation to yourself to get rid of the burden of submission to others. Don't let others intimidate you by questioning your emotions toward them. At the same time, feel free to question their feelings for you.

Feeling inferior to others will interfere with your goals in life. Establish priorities concerning the matters that relate to others and those that pertain to yourself. Give attention to your own needs before you even think about doing anything for others. You'll find that they will find a way to take care of their problems. Don't be an emotional patsy for persons who will brutalize you emotionally with *their* guilt and incompetence.

Once you gain a proper perspective on the limits of your obligations, you can plan your future. You may find social service attractive, or education, politics, or medicine. Whichever field you choose, you will bring resources and potential growth that will enable you to accomplish your objectives. You are suited to work as a specialist; you have a good memory, you are responsible, and when your efforts are rewarded you try even harder. If you should decide to go into education, consider research sciences as a platform for your talents. Your attention to detail lends itself well to the precision required in such areas.

Your romantic life may get off to a slow start, and its subsequent development depends entirely on whether you can reverse your inclination to let others walk all over you and take you for granted. You should know how capable you are, and if you capitalize on your assets, others will notice you as a private person, secure and proud in your accomplishments.

You will expect your partner to need you in ways that only you can satisfy. It is essential that there be mutual respect for the individual differences between you and a willingness to serve each other when necessary. Under no circumstances should you accept an arrangement that would obscure one partner while furthering the desires of the other. This kind of burden would grow unbearably heavy and eventually undermine the relationship.

Moon Inconjunct Uranus

The inconjunct from the Moon to Uranus show that you must solve your emotional problems before you can feel really free. You may be distressed by the fact that as soon as you solve one problem, then you discover another. However, in this process you become skilled in dealing with recurring crises. In time, they will no longer occur — and you will be free. The difficulties you experience are a direct result of conditioning by your parents. You were emotionally unprepared to accept the burdens you were expected to carry. Because of this you felt guilty and tried to do whatever you could to rid yourself of this guilt.

In serving others you overreact emotionally, always hoping to finally be released from the necessity of serving. You develop many skills to enable you to succeed in your job. Your best field would be one that involves teaching groups to develop their potentials. You could also use your talents for optimum effect in medicine, and receive meaningful rewards. Research and development would give you access to constructive avenues for future expression.

Be careful that you are not abused by people who claim that you alone can satisfy their needs. This is a confidence tactic to gain your submission and willingness to serve, even though others could do equally well.

Your sensitive, emotional nature should warn you not to become trapped in distressing situations. Your resistance is low, and you could suffer from nervous ailments caused by the pressure of your burdens. It is important that you prevent this by refusing to do anything beyond what is absolutely necessary. Rest and relaxation are essential and should be an integral part of your life.

In your romantic attachments, you may find that you often play the servant role. You hope to be relieved of your problems by marrying out of them. If you feel no guilt for what you haven't done, there is no reason why you can't succeed in this.

Moon Inconjunct Neptune

With the Moon inconjunct Neptune you are sympathetic toward others. You demonstrate how much you care by offering service when help seems needed. Because of your deep-feeling nature, it is difficult for you to remain detached. You are like a mother hen seeking to protect her brood when danger threatens. Unconsciously, however, you are constantly seeking situations in which you can persecute yourself. Thus you are able to spiritually fulfill your social obligations and justify your deep response to them. Your imagination works overtime in creating problems to solve.

In your professional affairs, you overextend yourself unnecessarily, which may anger your co-workers. Such fields as medicine, social programs for public welfare, or counseling at youth camps would enable you to make an important contribution to society. You could derive much satisfaction from such service. Your greatest problem is to find a valid outlet for your natural inclinations that will provide realistic benefits both for you *and* for those you serve. In any endeavor you must determine the limits of your responsibilities and avoid volunteering for additonal tasks. Your physical constitution cannot tolerate abuse. Good food, nutritiously prepared under clean conditions, is absolutely necessary.

Your romantic interests may prove disappointing until you can relate to others honestly and realistically. It is not easy for you to see people as they really are. You tend to project on them qualities they can't possibly live up to, and you feel let down when they don't measure up to your expectations. You are also vulnerable to deception by people who misrepresent themselves. You will have many unsatisfactory alliances until you learn to insist that others establish their credentials before you become inextricably involved.

You are a romantic and can find solace through artistic pursuits or any creative expression. Your inspiration can effectively enrich your private moments with serenity.

Moon Inconjunct Pluto

The inconjunct between the Moon and Pluto indicates a personality that is precariously balanced. You must learn to temper your emotional compulsiveness with objectivity. Perhaps in your formative years you were expected to yield to all your parents' demands; if you defied them, they said you didn't love them. From this experience you may have assumed that to gain anyone's love you must submit to them. Thus you overreact to other people's demands. You wrongly believe that those who use you must care for you in some way. But submission to another only earns you contempt.

Now you may have to unlearn old habit systems and develop new ones to avoid being persecuted by those who would take advantage of you in a weak moment. You will be at the mercy of others until you gather the strength to say no.

Even in your occupation you must be wary of co-workers taking advantage of you. When you are asked to take on new duties, examine them carefully. Do one thing at a time and do only what is specifically assigned; don't become a patsy for someone else's incompetence.

You will do well in occupations in which you can work behind the scenes. Stay away from jobs that may require you to do extra work unless you will be paid accordingly.

Be particularly careful about becoming emotionally involved with persons who try to sway you by their charm. They are probably aware of your vulnerable nature. You can be misled by appearances, so get an objective opinion about anyone to whom you are attracted. Your strong desire for a home and family may incline you to lower your standards for a suitable love partner. Examine all potential mates with care and objectivity to avoid disappointment.

Moon Inconjunct Ascendant

The Moon inconjunct the Ascendant shows that you are a glutton for punishment. You are so eager to show that you really care about other people that you allow them to take advantage of your sympathetic nature. You are emotionally vulnerable to other people's problems and want to help them resolve their difficulties if you can. Generous with your time and efforts, you can always be depended upon to volunteer your services. You simply like to do things for others, but in the process you may undermine your own health.

Unfortunately, you don't differentiate between people who deserve your help and those who are undeserving. Those who don't merit assistance from you may secretly laugh at you for all your efforts. If you will set a price on your services, you won't have to waste so much energy on those who don't appreciate them to begin with.

You will always be able to earn a living because you know how to adapt to a variety of employment requirements. You won't refuse an occupation simply because it doesn't give you status among your associates and friends; the needs of the moment are of more concern to you. You are attracted to occupations that serve the public. Your superiors think well of you as a competent employee who isn't afraid of work, although your friends may criticize you for doing more than your share. You may not have been interested in getting a higher education, but you can always compensate in other ways. If you do get an education you will still draw upon your experience to derive the most benefit from it.

You like to feel that you are providing something constructive in the lives of those you deal with. You haven't forgotten the assistance you received when you were younger, and the help you give is in some way a repayment. If you are appreciated, it is reward enough for you.

Mercury Inconjunct Mars

With Mercury inconjunct Mars, what you know is distorted by the way you use it. You are extremely well informed in many matters but lack the judgment to apply this information for the best results. After you take on responsibilities that may not be yours, you complain bitterly that you have no time for yourself. You want to be approved and considered competent by the people you serve, but oftentimes they are unappreciative of your efforts. If would be advisable to make a list of the most important priorities in your life and then strike out each one that does not contribute to your own benefit. The remaining ones are your most important priorities, which you should apply yourself to. If any time is left after satisfying these, then you can conservatively add those that benefit others. The reason for this is simple; you persecute yourself by assuming you owe so much to others. It is fine to be of service, but you risk being exploited by those whom you serve. When this happens you naturally feel abused and hurt by their insensitivity.

If you still insist that "they need me," seek employment with an organization that exists to satisfy public needs. In this way you can get your anxieties off your chest and earn your living at the same time. Social work, welfare programs, medicine, rehabilitation, and therapy are some of the fields that would be satisfying to you and helpful to others.

You run the risk of physical exhaustion unless you discipline yourself to slow down. Your nervous system is sensitive and cannot take continued harassment. A moderate schedule is essential for your own protection and well-being. You need to get away from your daily routine and enjoy yourself in recreational activities.

Don't underestimate your own worth when you meet people. You tend to indulge the one you feel affection for, but don't let that person force you to prove your love. Not only will you learn to dislike your partner, you will also hate yourself for it. A hard worker, you need someone who shares your desire to succeed and who is willing to contribute on an equal basis for your mutual benefit.

Mercury Inconjunct Jupiter

The inconjunct between your Mercury and Jupiter indicates that you experience some frustration in expressing your creative abilities. Other more pressing matters always seem to force you to defer your personal interests. Everyone seems to bring their problems to you, hoping for a solution. Being generous at heart, you cannot turn them down in their moment of need, and you grant them a greater priority than they merit. Such a feeling of responsibility to others is an overreaction. You may bitterly complain that you never have a moment to yourself, but you do nothing to stop the practice. When you do put someone off you immediately feel guilty and then revert to your old habits. This can be mentally wearing and cause you to neglect more important personal issues.

You need to isolate yourself from the mainstream of life for a time and get a proper perspective of yourself. Establish priorities in your affairs and take them up in the order of their importance. Don't allow others to make you feel guilty for detaching yourself from them. That would greatly restrict your development. Although you are knowledgeable and well-informed on many subjects, difficulties arise when you try to apply your knowledge. Don't be so willing to listen to people's suggestions "for your benefit." You can do without this kind of help. You don't need to compare your efforts with those others to determine your competence. Your competence is more than adequate, but you must have academic training in order to get a better idea of your potentials. Education alone can give you the assurances you need in order to successfully compete with others in challenging situations. You can become an expert in whatever life direction you choose. Knowing you are skilled will help put your anxieties to rest.

Your talents are suitable for accomplishment in education, travel, or public relations. You can rise to excellence in any of these fields if you apply yourself diligently. You have the necessary temperament for hard work if you know your efforts will prove rewarding.

In your personal and romantic associations you undersell yourself. You insist on proving yourself to your lover long before it is sure that the relationship will continue. Don't make promises you can't keep just to gain the favor of someone you are attracted to. Sincerity and honesty will pay bigger dividends. Anyone to whom you have to sell yourself must not be very sensitive to your better qualities.

Worrying over matters that cannot be altered should be avoided. Intestinal and digestive problems can result from an overactive and sensitive nervous system.

Mercury Inconjunct Saturn

Mercury inconjunct Saturn shows that you are responsible and serious, but you emphasize these qualities too much, which can make things difficult. Overestimating what people really expect from you, you go to great lengths in their service. In your desire to gain approval from others, you indulge them to the point that they may become annoyed with you. Your willingness to be the "patsy" for their failings encourages people to lose respect for you. Stop being the willing victim of those who will take all you can give, even if you become mentally exhausted in the process. You seem to have all the symptoms of a confirmed masochist, and this brings out latent sadistic qualities in others.

You will make progress as soon as you stop crucifying yourself for people who are too incompetent to help themselves. Turn your talents to such endeavors as architecture, drafting, engineering, research, science, welfare programs in the service of government, education, teaching, or physical therapy. In these fields you will be able to see rewarding evidence of your efforts. You will still be doing something for others, but you will be free from the harassment that sometimes occurs in personal contact.

Try to establish priorities in your life. Do those things that you know *must* be done before doing anything that other people suggest. Learn to say no when asked to donate your time and efforts; you can say that your current obligations don't permit it. In other words, get people off your back, or it will be bowed under the burden. For the most part such efforts are a useless investment anyway.

Don't look back, because you may be disappointed that you have not yet achieved your objectives. Make a firm resolve to indulge yourself more than you have, but don't indulge in self-pity. Learn from the past and turn over a new leaf.

You should take a good, hard, honest look at yourself. You may not realize that you are talented. Try to detach yourself from the opinions of others and concern yourself with developing your potentials. In the privacy of your own home, try your hand at some craft activity; you will find out how skilled you are. You should also realize that you don't have to be in the shadow of others. At the same time, avoid criticizing people for hurting you; they couldn't have done it without your permission. If you've been hurt, it was probably necessary. This may dramatize the fact that you don't have to win anyone's approval, but you certainly need to confirm your own competence.

Mercury Inconjunct Uranus

The inconjunct between Mercury and Uranus shows that you endure severe punishment in attempting to serve the world at large. You are an intellectual workhouse, and your serenity is constantly disturbed by the problems of others. You work in hesitant spurts of enthusiasm followed by periods of mental anguish for not completing what you start.

You can effectively channel your self-imposed obligations to your immediate environment and humanity in general by choosing an occupation that deals specifically with these matters. Local social welfare programs, fund-raising for medical research, active medical research, and rehabilitation programs for the mentally deficient are some of the ways this can be done. You have projected yourself toward the abstract future, and your future seems secure, if you can look back without regrets for what you didn't do years ago. You may bear a burden of guilt for not doing what you could for others.

Your attitude is admirable, and you cannot be faulted for the contributions you've made. However, in offering yourself in such dedicated service, you are shortchanging yourself. You owe yourself something too. Until you establish your priorities, you will be at the mercy of people who will find things for you to do, to the point of abusing your generosity.

You will find yourself attracted emotionally to people who serve in similar capacities to your own. Selfish people are quickly assigned to the junkpile in your estimation. But don't be too quick to judge — they may be exercising the restraints that you have failed to exercise.

Your biggest problem is to know when you are extending yourself so far that your health will suffer. Have periodic check-ups to determine whether you are taking more out of yourself than you are replacing. If so, you may be heading for a nervous disorder that could be serious.

Mercury Inconjunct Neptune

With Mercury inconjunct Neptune, you feel guilty if you don't respond to outside interests. You make promises you can't keep and console yourself by saying, "Well, at least I tried." However, your reasoning is not in keeping with the facts. You create for yourself painful responsibilities that are usually unnecessary. As if determined to persecute yourself, you worry over problems that may never develop and overreact to those that do. You exaggerate the seriousness of your failures and may even become ill by dwelling on tasks you think others expect you to do.

You are imaginative, inspired, and creative but find difficulty in expressing these qualities to your complete satisfaction. Your work should give you the opportunity to express your talents. It may be difficult for you to work at the kind of job in which you must meet a schedule. You would probably work best alone, so that you would not have to compare yourself with co-workers. Also, you could set your own pace. Working close to others could produce uncomfortable misunderstandings and make your job very unpleasant. You would gain greater satisfaction from working away from exposure to possible criticism.

You must learn to establish your priorities in order to achieve your goals with as little wasted effort as possible. In your desire to gain approval for your accomplishments, you tend to take on extra tasks. This is where your efficiency suffers. Determine your precise responsibilities and never offer to do more than those. You cannot spread yourself so thin and expect to accomplish much. Your nervous energy will not tolerate that kind of abuse.

In your personal relationships, too, you can expect others to take advantage of your willingness to do things for them. Your disappointment can be crushing when you discover you've been used. Wait for others to establish their credentials and prove their sincerity toward you. Take frequent rests and try to unwind. The pressure you labor under may be imagined, but the resulting physical exhaustion is not.

Mercury Inconjunct Pluto

Your Mercury inconjunct Pluto denotes an overwhelming sense of responsibility. You have been conditioned to accept all duties that are assigned to you as important tasks for your total development. In your early years, you might have been bitter at times when it seemed you were always selected to perform the tasks others would not do. This established a pattern of reaction, and now you unconsciously respond to duties with an obsessive determination to get them finished and out of the way. You may also take on duties assigned to others because you can't differentiate between their responsibilities and your own.

Although you are qualified to work well in many occupations, you must avoid becoming involved in your co-workers' tasks and learn to mind your own business. With this planetary combination, you are likely to get into disputes if you attempt to interfere with the way others perform their jobs. You have a genius for implicating yourself without realizing it.

Your intellectual capabilities could successfully be used in such endeavors as medicine, research, analysis, chemistry, or crime detection. You have the persistence and determination to stay with a task until every detail has been examined and evaluated, a quality these professions require. Your deductive ability is uncanny, and it is certain that you derive many answers through your psychic sensitivity.

You relate well to other dedicated people, especially if they serve the needs of society. When someone does you a favor, you are appreciative and never fail to return it. You are sincere in your dealings and expect honesty from others. But you are callous and critical to anyone who fails you, and vindictive if your efforts are not appreciated. You are difficult to work for, since you expect nothing less than perfection on the job.

In your ambition to succeed, you should avoid driving yourself too hard. You disregard safe levels of physical effort, which results in nervous irritability. If would be wise to get away periodically from your professional interests to restore the physical resources drained by job demands. You need vitality in order to function efficiently and cooperatively with fellow workers.

To help you unwind, it is advised that you take up an avocation such as a craft, social programs, or working with young people. Direct your abundant energy where it will serve worthwhile goals and be most appreciated. Regardless of what you do, it is essential to have at least one hobby that captures your imagination and uses your enormous creative potential. The important thing is to "get away," at least in spirit, from your daily routine.

Mercury Inconjunct Ascendant

Mercury inconjunct the Ascendant shows that you try hard to understand the people with whom you are involved. If you have to confront them in a challenging situation, you make a supreme effort to give them the benefit of the doubt. You tend to submit without resistance, assuming that others know more about themselves than you do. More often than not, however, your evaluation and conclusions about people are right, which may make them uncomfortable.

Wanting to win approbation as a sensible person with good reasoning ability, you are crushed when people don't take you seriously and dismiss you with a wave of the hand. You are serious about your continued development and growth. A "jack-of-all-trades" and master of most of them, you are a good learner and an equally good teacher. You never stop learning, and you strive for excellence in everything you do. Although you work efficiently, you may talk too much on the job and annoy those working closest to you. You despise being constantly asked what you are doing and why. But you love it when someone needs your help in learning how to do something.

You don't know yourself as well as you know others. You worry over matters that can't be changed, and if someone tries to draw you into a discussion of your shortcomings, you quickly divert the conversation to other topics. Your friends admire you for your talents, and your superiors realize that you have a sharp intellect. There are few questions you can't answer, even though you may not have received a higher education. You like to indulge in nostalgic memories of days past, remembering them with good feelings. Keenly aware of the power of money, you have planned carefully for security in your later years. Pension plans and regular savings are as important to you as earning a living now.

You should take frequent restful vacations to slow down and relax. You are easily keyed up by the pressure of your daily concerns, so you should get away from them periodically.

Venus Inconjunct Mars

With Venus inconjunct Mars you have powerful desires, but you have difficulty in satisfying them. In your eagerness to gain the approval of the people you deal with, you make enormous concessions to them. You fail to ask yourself, "Why must I win their approval?" Sometimes you do favors for others simply because you want to, but eventually you find that they expect it from you. Then you become resentful toward them and may even hate yourself for it. You do not have a high enough opinion of yourself, for of course you deserve better treatment than that.

It seems as if you have to work hard for any benefits, when other people gain with little effort. You should immediately stop making comparisons between yourself and others. It is better to focus your attention on your own affairs. Overreacting to what you think people expect, you go so far as to rearrange your life to fulfill their expectations.

Your professional achievements will suffer unless you can understand that you are as important to yourself as your competitors are to themselves. Spend some time examining how your co-workers or business associates operate. When was the last time someone did you a favor you didn't have to ask for? You probably can't remember, and it isn't surprising. You alone are to blame if in your job you work in an obscure corner where you are either ignored or not included in the mainstream of activity.

This negative attitude you have about yourself can lead to problems in personal emotional relationships. You give the impression that you will do anything to get attention, which some individuals will use to take advantage of you. You bring out the worst qualities in people, and you may be defenseless to protect yourself against them. As an example, you may volunteer (which you should never do) to help a co-worker catch up with a backlog of work; later you will discover that you have been given that work as part of your regular assignment. When you volunteered to help you probably indicated that you had more than enough time to do it. Thus you fall victim to the negative influences that some people will use. The same kind of situation can occur in your romantic associations; you can be easily victimized by dishonest persons who entrap you and make you submit. Believe only those who can amply demonstrate how they feel by their deeds, not their words.

Venus Inconjunct Jupiter

The inconjunct of Venus to Jupiter shows that you overreact in making adjustments to other people's expectations. Because you are insufficiently aware of your own needs, you generously offer to serve the needs of others. But people are inclined to take advantage of your generosity to the point of abusing it. You aren't at all selective in choosing those whom you submit to, which invites all kinds of problems. Evidently, you were trained in the early years to take an inferior position to others. Perhaps you were told, "Honest work never hurt anyone," even if the people you were helping could take care of themselves. This could make you bitter for all your efforts, which brings so little benefit to yourself. It's one thing to be accommodating, but being a doormat is something else.

There are many occupational functions you can do well. This planetary combination does not of itself give a specific talent, but it does enable you to take on enormous responsibilites and succeed in carrying them out. You adapt to job demands easily, adjusting your personal circumstances as necessary. You are not likely to gain full recognition for all the work you either do yourself or assign to others. Because you underestimate your capabilities, you may be victimized by fellow employees who could take your ideas and use them for their own benefit.

You tend to exaggerate the expectatons of your boss or co-workers and quickly rise to prove your worth in their estimation. You labor under assumed challenges that may never materialize and fear competitors who never existed. You respond to the goals you've extablished for yourself in a particular way, and it is difficult to persuade you to think otherwise. By taking yourself too seriously, you impede your progress. You create projects that are destined to fail because of your impossible expectations.

In general, you are defensive in your relationships with people, even those for whom you feel affection. You tend to project a meek and inadequate image in hopes of gaining their indulgence. You are often victimized and exploited in your romantic affairs and may do all kinds of favors for someone who has no genuine affection for you. You so want approval that you submit to gross indignities, only to realize later that you've been taken.

Most of your physical problems have their origin in your mental attitude. Your weariness may be mental exhaustion from trying so hard to be desired by others. You need to take a more optimistic attitude in order to protect yourself in your relationships with others. Your greatest priority should be to maintain your self-respect by refusing to be used by others.

Venus Inconjunct Saturn

The inconjunct between Venus and Saturn indicates that you feel burdened by excessive responsibilities. You feel that other people always want you to do something for them, and you resent it. Actually, you overreact, assuming they want more from you than they do. It would be unfair to criticize them for this. You really want everyone to approve of you, so you try to buy approval by offering yourself.

You must carefully evaluate your priorities for yourself and for others. Your greatest problem is that you don't like yourself enough, so you feel that you really deserve to be used by others. If you think about it, all you owe anybody else is tolerance and respect. You owe yourself much more than this — for instance, to be free from intimidation, to know your own worth, and to be burdened only by matters that serve your interests. When you have achieved some satisfaction of your own needs, it will be time enough to do for others.

If you improve your opinion of yourself, you can accomplish many things in your career. The same intensity you directed toward others can be used to develop your natural talents. You have enormous potentials for success. You are serious and responsible about doing your work well; in fact, you probably work harder than your co-workers or competitors. There are many fields in which you could find satisfaction and reasonable success, including public relations, interior design, horticulture, real estate, and sales. You are sufficiently flexible to fit into many categories of occupational interests.

Your love interests may be burdensome unless you stand firm and refuse to let your lover consider you as anything less than an equal. You should be suspicious if you are constantly kept waiting, or if your partner always strays over to others at a gathering, leaving you alone. These are signs that interest is waning or that you are considered an object that can be put aside when something more interesting comes along.

If you occasionally find yourself alone, try not to grow depressed and conclude that no one wants you. Use the opportunity to learn new skills or develop those you already have. You have every chance of being greatly admired if you will simply mobilize your efforts toward specific goals. Depression is your worst enemy, for it interferes with good digestion and assimilation.

Venus Inconjunct Uranus

You have Venus inconjunct Uranus, indicating that you often neglect your own desires to satisfy others. When you do something to please yourself, you know you've earned it because of the sacrifices involved. Others seem to feel that you have an obligation to indulge their needs. You comply, but not without bitterness. By overreacting with sympathy and understanding, you burden yourself with their problems. If you don't immediately respond with help, you punish yourself by feeling guilty. You must stop asking people if you can do anything for them in their crises. In other words, learn to mind your own business.

You have a strong desire to communicate with others, but this should not be confused with "buying" their friendship by doing favors for them. If you do this, you will later hate yourself for being "used," even though you will have only yourself to blame. Meet others only halfway until you know they are sincere. You can test the genuineness of their interest by making demands of them.

You are extremely bright and understanding and show honest concern for others. At the same time, you implicate yourself in difficult situations that cause you much mental anxiety. To succeed in your profession, you must be alert. Your competitors will try to win by capitalizing on your weaknesses. Be wary of co-workers who suggest that you perform certain tasks they have rejected. Don't be a dumping ground for everyone else's cast-offs.

Your best fields of endeavor are those that involve people and artistic pursuits in general. Take a hard, close look at your capabilities and realize just how competent you really are. Don't ask for the opinions of your associates, but seek the advice of an impartial observer.

In your personal relationships be particularly cautious if you are asked to give of yourself in a physical way. You tend to be impulsive and excitable, so you may be sorry later for the service you've rendered.

Venus Inconjunct Neptune

The inconjunct from Venus to Neptune shows that you are sensitive, imaginative, and inspired. However, you experience great stress in using these abilities. You attempt to use your talents all at once, as if you had a deadline to meet and were afraid of failing. Don't be in such a hurry; what can't be done today will get done tomorrow. After all, you've set the schedule. Establish your priorities and take care of them in their proper time. It is unrealistic to try to accomplish more than you are constitutionally able to. Learn to make compromises with your desires to avoid physical exhaustion. Your sensitive nature does not permit this kind of abuse.

Your professional life can be oppressive if you allow others to take advantage of your desire to gain approval and praise. You are eager to volunteer your services "beyond the call of duty," but in so doing you deprive yourself of personal needs. Don't try to be liked by everyone. Being well thought of does not relieve your burdens and can frustrate your need to express your creative potentials.

Artistic fields are best suited to your temperament and creative expression. The familiarity of this environment can soften the harshness you often encounter in relationships with co-workers.

Your romantic nature is so yielding and vulnerable that you are sure to have disappointments that are shattering to your sensibilities. Accept a romantic alliance or a lover's claim of affection with reservation. You can be victimized by what you don't know. Ignorance may be bliss, but not for long.

Venus Inconjunct Pluto

With Venus inconjunct Pluto, you may overburden yourself by giving to excess in your emotional relationships. You need to be more moderate in your contacts with others. There is always an element of stress associated with your feelings for the opposite sex. You tend to fall for the sob-story and find yourself making commitments to people who don't mean that much to you. It is your desire for acceptance and approval that makes you overextend your efforts for others.

In your personal, romantic pursuits, you may be misled in believing in the profuse affection shown by your current love interest. You are likely to be disappointed in the end. Be particularly wary of anyone who asks you to prove your love by demonstrating it physically. You are susceptible to such alliances, and you can suffer enormous problems unless you are aware of it and try to protect yourself. Physical problems involving the generative organs are a distinct possibility and may result in permanent damage to the reproductive system.

You can derive much benefit from working for enterprises of a social nature, such as medical research, nutrition and diet, and welfare programs. In any job it is best if you are assigned a specific task to perform.

Seek professional advice before you make an agreement with *anyone.* Your decisions are often made under emotional stress when you cannot reason logically, and these are the times when you need help. Realize that people will try to take advantage of you, which can sometimes be costly.

All kinds of negative elements seem to creep into your affairs. In your job, for instance, you might be involved in the preparations for a social function for fellow employees. In the confusion of the proceedings, you may find yourself paying for things out of your own pocket because someone insists his contribution was paid, and you are left holding the bag. This is not terribly important by itself, to be sure, but the constant repetition of such incidents becomes irritating. So the first thing to remember is: *don't volunteer* either your time or your money. It is enough for you to simply make your contribution.

Venus Inconjunct Ascendant

Venus inconjunct the Ascendant shows that you are more compromising than necessary toward those you are in close contact with. You do favors for people so that they will appreciate you, and you make concessions to them in order to keep peace. But you may secretly hate yourself for this when you think about it later, for you realize that by conceding you've given them your consent to treat you as they wish. You may not have the opportunity to develop all your creative potentials, but you will be satisfied if some of them are developed. You know how to compensate for what is lacking in your life and can get by with a lot less than most people would be happy with. You don't measure your happiness by what you get but by the degree of fulfillment you derive from what you are doing.

You try to communicate with other members of the family and make whatever compromises are necessary to maintain harmony in your home. You are willing to work to get what you want, and you hope that those close to you will appreciate your efforts. Sometimes you feel that you are being taken advantage of, but you make a point of trying to serve in any way you can. You have a fair number of friends, but you question the friendship of someone who asks for a loan.

In your work you adapt yourself to the demands of each job. Overreacting to what you think is expected, you extend yourself too far in complying with these demands. However, you win the good fellowship of your co-workers and superiors alike.

Security is very important to you, but it may seem that you will never have it. Perhaps you will marry for financial advantage, although that would mean making a substantial compromise, which you might not be able to live with. On the other hand, you might justify your decision by looking back at all the concessions you had to make that only served to benefit others.

Mars Inconjunct Jupiter

The inconjunct between Mars and Jupiter represents difficulty in establishing priorities in your affairs, especially in dealing with people. Through your generosity to others you try to buy their permission to indulge yourself whenever you choose. You willingly offer your services to people, assuming that they cannot take care of themselves. In the process you deprive yourself of your resources, and you deprive them of the opportunity to become self-sufficient. If something that must be done isn't done immediately, you feel guilty. You can be a carping critic who is never satisfied unless something is done your way. You often interfere where you are not wanted, which encourages people to resent you. Learn to mind your own business, and don't take your own guilt out on other people; they may have their own guilt to concern themselves with.

There is much you can do if you plan carefully and use your talents where they will be appreciated. Law, government, medical services, welfare programs, research enterprises, physical therapy, rehabilitation of the handicapped, and religious organizations are some of the areas in which you can constructively apply yourself. You need to see the results of your labors, and any of these fields would demonstrate your effectiveness in using your creative resources. You would be especially competent as a teacher because you can stimulate students to manifest their individual potentials.

In your persistent need to be useful you are sometimes victimized by people who will take advantage of you and exploit your ideas for their personal benefit. Learn to withhold information about any project you are developing until you can capitalize on it yourself.

You must protect yourself against connivers who will try to undermine your self-confidence. You are inclined to go along with people who suggest that you are incompetent and to accept a subservient position to them. But this raises serious questions in your own mind, because you consider yourself more than competent. If you stop constantly seeking approval you will never have to submit to interrogations about your capabilities. Develop your talents and test them in competition, and you will gain the self-assurance you need.

In the same way, in your romantic relationships, don't humble yourself as though you don't deserve the best. It's fine to be generous toward the one you love, but be critical in deciding whether the individual is sincere and deserving.

Mars Inconjunct Saturn

The inconjunct between Mars and Saturn shows problems in fulfilling yourself without being destroyed in the process. You have difficulty in exactly determining your responsibilities, both to yourself and to others. Lacking this determination, you often trap yourself by indulging the whims of other people who take advantage of your willingness. Perhaps you feel guilty because in the past you were rather indifferent to others, and you are trying desperately to prove to yourself that you really care about people. You are hoping to win approval and atone for past misdeeds in order to be finally free of liability. The pain of submitting to others is in proportion to the anxiety and guilt you feel when you don't.

Once you can psychologically get off the hook in this regard, there is much you can accomplish for your own benefit. Military service, sports, conservation, and physical therapy are some of the fields to which you could constructively apply your talents. You might work in union activities or public welfare programs, for which you are qualified. If you are not careful, you may become involved in disputes between co-workers, because you can be easily intimidated. Try to control your temper when such incidents develop, or you may spoil future opportunities for advancement. Concern yourself with personal matters and avoid getting involved in the affairs of others.

In relating to others, whether they are competitors or associates, you tend to consider them more gifted or competent than you, and you therefore assign yourself a position of relative unimportance. Learn to be an expert in your chosen profession so that you don't have to seek confirmation of your expertise from others. You must know you're good at what you do in order to succeed.

Unless you are firm in your convictions, you may experience some irritating problems in your personal and romantic relationships. Some partners may try to take advantage of you until you demonstrate strength of character and thereby gain their respect. Don't allow anyone to use your feelings against you in a kind of emotional blackmail to gain your submission. You don't need the kind of person who would resort to such leverage. Also, the physical expression of love should be in keeping with your self-respect.

You may experience some physical problems, such as accidents that result in fractures or somewhat immobilizing conditions such as arthritis or bursitis. As you get older you will tend to eliminate physical activity and exercise, but you should guard against becoming too inactive.

Mars Inconjunct Uranus

With the inconjunct from Mars to Uranus, you function with great drive and originality, but you always seem to be under some pressure. Perhaps you are trying to prove something to yourself or to others. Why are you killing yourself? Is it so important to convince others of your talent that you will risk physical exhaustion in the process? You sometimes act as though you were expected to do more than everyone else. Learn to distinguish responsibility from abuse. It may be that your deep concern for your future drives you to do everything immediately. There is more time than you know, so first establish your priorities, and then you *can* accomplish all you want.

There is an element of guilt underlying your intense preoccupation with doing more than your share. This is extremely important in your occupation. Make sure that others don't make demands of you that are physically impossible or perhaps unnecessary. It is easy for others to impose on you, but only if you permit it. Don't be a patsy for other people's incompetence. You admire those who seem successful and try to emulate them, but this can lead to even greater frustration. Try to exploit your own creativity and uniqueness, for they are your individual contributions, through which you will gain independence.

Learn to be independent of people who challenge the way you do things. If you don't, you're merely an extension of them. You don't take criticism easily and to avoid it, you yield. If you fight for the freedom to "do your own thing," in time you will gain the respect of others, and they will back off.

Even in your romantic interests you show signs of latent insecurity about your competence. You lean toward those who seem totally in command of themselves, even if they make demands on you. You must be admired, though, for the assistance you give others who truly need it.

Mars Inconjunct Neptune

With Mars inconjunct Neptune, you strive to assert yourself positively and constructively, and yet the results of your efforts always seem disappointing. You are overanxious, and in your impatience you fail to notice important factors that hamper your efforts. The resulting strain increases your anxiety, so you pour additional energy into your objective. Thus a circular pattern becomes established. It is absolutely essential that you plan and double-check every move you make. Learn to postpone any hastily made plans, or you will certainly encourage trouble.

Avoid any occupation that involves using machinery or potentially dangerous substances. Your work should not be so physically demanding that it exhausts you. You cannot stand that kind of abuse for any extended time. Find an occupation in which you can set your own pace, one that doesn't require you to meet schedules. Any field related to the arts is suggested.

You tend to become involved in personal relationships that make enormous demands on you. When you overstate your importance to others, it gives them an opportunity to take advantage of you. Your actions seem to benefit others more than you are benefited by them. You have strong physical desires, and to satisfy them you associate with questionable kinds of people. It is difficult for you to see through another's insincerity. There is sure to be some deception in your sexual experiences, either by you or by your lover.

You are extremely vulnerable to infection because of carelessness and an inability to see beyond your own nose. You are especially susceptible to social diseases. However, depending on other elements of your chart, your early training may have so conditioned you with guilt about sexual freedom that you can't experience any sexual activities. In this case, your psychological maladjustment will produce physical problems that are difficult to detect and treat. Such problems are often called psychosomatic.

Mars Inconjunct Pluto

The inconjunct from Mars to Pluto shows you are overly responsive to demands by your environment or by the people in your daily life. You may wonder whether others think of you as a workhorse to be driven at their pleasure. Your compulsiveness in taking on more tasks than you can safely handle results in depleted energy. You are driven by the ever-present thought that there is so much to do and so little time in which to do it. In fact, you are persecuting yourself.

Although your sexual needs are considerable, you may encounter problems in satisfying them. Sex depletes your energy to an unusual extent, so moderation is advised. Make sure you get proper nutrition to help conserve your energy and give you a necessary sense of well-being.

When events don't proceed as you had expected, you tend to feel guilty and to punish yourself unnecessarily. You may become arrogant and bad-tempered because you seem to carry a greater burden then others do. Financial stress can cause you to become overly anxious, especially when others involved seem so casual about it.

It is important that you establish priorities in the matters that require your attention. Learn to manage your time more efficiently and to put aside matters that can be safely postponed. Learn how to just waste time occasionally, and give yourself a chance to simply relax. In time you will realize that you're an important person too. If you will become a bit more selfish about giving of yourself, your friends will be amazed at the change in you. They will also secretly admire you for your newfound courage to say no!

Mars Inconjunct Ascendant

Mars inconjunct the Ascendant means that you tend to deplete your energy by trying to do more than you are physically able to do. You never want anyone to say that you didn't try hard to accomplish everything you set out to. But you are somewhat careless about taking safety precautions because you want to feel that you are fearless in any task you perform. When someone doubts you can do what you say, you feel personally challenged and proceed to prove that you can. Sometimes you regret your impulsiveness, for you tend to bite off more than you can chew. But you will never admit it when the going gets rough.

With all your energy, you are impatient for results and anxious to develop your talents as soon as possible. Your parents probably trained you to respond to challenging situations without taking too much time to think before accepting the competition. You are not a reflective person, which is one of your weaknesses. Learn to consider whether you can succeed before accepting a challenge. Although you are resourceful in capitalizing on your talents, there is still a limit to what you can do.

Your superiors admire your courage, but they deplore your foolhardiness when caution is required. Your refusal to believe that you have any weaknesses can get you into a lot of hot water. Your friends may dare you to do things they wouldn't try themselves, so why should you take the risk?

You like contact with people, especially when they disagree with you, because you enjoy arguments, even if you don't win them. You know how to gain the confidence of those you deal with, because you can do things they are unable to do for themselves. A whirlwind when you set your mind to accomplish something, you drive yourself to exhaustion. Being so restless and energetic, you would enjoy participating in sports, and it would be a good outlet for your energy.

Jupiter Inconjunct Saturn

With the inconjunct of Jupiter to Saturn, you feel painfully burdened by your responsibilities, but you find it difficult to justify these feelings. You carry a burden of guilt from some past incidents in which you avoided duty whenever possible. Now you don't have this freedom to choose, and you are disturbed at not knowing how long this situation must be endured. You need not assume that you must always serve sacrificially to be rid of this burden. You need the advice of someone you trust, who can help you evaluate your priorities and determine the extent to which you must serve others. More important is to know when you must serve yourself.

In many ways your attempts to exploit your potentials are useless because you try to use them to satisfy your obligations to others. In this way you put yourself under binding restraints and will always be at the mercy of those who will take advantage of you. If this continues for a prolonged period of time, you may become resentful and bitter of the people you serve, even though you chose them yourself. This bitterness is really self-disgust for letting yourself be abused.

You must stand way back to get a proper perspective of yourself, honestly and objectively. You are talented, and you certainly know right from wrong, but you seem destined to make life difficult for yourself. Spend some time and effort to develop your creative potentials and become an expert in your chosen field. In order to escape from obscurity you need to have a higher estimation of your own worth.

There are many fields in which to creatively express yourself, such as physical therapy, medicine, education, and construction trades. In any of these, you will have to avoid becoming the victim of less capable co-workers who will try to use your knowledge for their own benefit. Beware of being a "patsy" for another employee's incompetence. It is probably better for you to either be self-employed or to work with a small number of people. There is no limit to how far you can go once you recognize your true capabilities. You are potentially an expert in whatever field you choose, and you can command a high salary for your ingenuity and inventiveness. Know your own worth so you can put a price on your services. Don't undersell yourself — you're probably worth more than you can imagine.

Eat moderately, and never eat when you are suffering from any anxiety. You are inclined to have problems in digestion and assimilation. You must learn to relax in order to stay healthy. Get away frequently from your daily occupation and see unfamiliar faces and places. A brisk walk or physical exercise is especially beneficial for you.

Jupiter Inconjunct Uranus

With Jupiter inconjunct Uranus your dreams for the future undergo reversals that are difficult to control. The problem is mainly that you expect too much, since your dreams are probably unrealistic and far-fetched. Self-discipline and careful management are the only solutions. You tend to listen to people who encourage you to extend yourself beyond safe limits. In your eagerness for instant results, you sometimes fail to plan your moves sufficiently. You overreact to suggestion and condition yourself to submit to others, which undermines your own needs and desires.

You are capable of working well in many occupations. In any job, however, you must be wary of associates who try to trap you into performing their tasks. The problem is mainly that your easy-going nature gives others opportunities to take advantage of you. You must learn to understand what motivates such people to abuse you, and to anticipate it. Be adamant in refusing even their most persistent demands.

You can succeed in medicine, law, research, or education. You must, however, establish your priorities, which are essential to success. You need to manage your time and effort more efficiently in order to derive the full benefit from your talents. Be careful you don't "spill" of yourself to benefit others, unless you are gaining results too.

Your inability to coordinate your skills and efforts with your desire to succeed indicates the importance of gaining the services of an advisor/counselor. A close friend you trust is probably the best bet. But if you don't listen to advice, it will do you little good.

Beware of romantic interests that find you doing all kinds of favors to "prove" your love. Also be cautious of declaring your love unless there is tangible evidence that it is returned sincerely.

Sufficient rest is essential for you to maintain good health and general well-being. Avoid excess in all things.

Jupiter Inconjunct Neptune

The inconjunct from Jupiter to Neptune indicates some distortion between your intellect and your emotions. Your reasoning tells you not to overextend yourself for others, but your emotions make it difficult to refuse. You are inclined to persecute yourself by creating impossible problems, that are so painful to solve that you wind up in an emotional bind. It is sometimes difficult to know which is greater, other people's dependence on you or your need for their dependence. You are constantly struggling to expiate an undefined guilt concerning service to others.

By imagining social obligations that are not your responsibility, you push yourself to extremes. You might even seek out the most painful and demanding profession just to work out your addiction for pain. At the same time you may complain bitterly about your work, without doing anything to find a less demanding situation. You are particularly awed and fascinated by work involving institutions such as prisons and other places of detention for unruly elements of society.

Your positive attitude could be beneficial because you have a warm, sincere understanding of socially afflicted members of your environment. However, even this is dangerous, because you tend to absorb the ills of those you care for. You are unconsciously seeking to take the burden and guilt of humanity on your own shoulders.

You are susceptible to physical problems that are obscure in origin and difficult to diagnose. Oftentimes, the causes may be psychosomatic in origin, caused by your misunderstanding of your responsibilities and by the guilt associated with them.

You need the advice of someone you trust and admire to help you determine when and if you should burden yourself with duties toward others. You must learn to say no, even to those who can't seem to get along without your help.

Jupiter Inconjunct Pluto

With the inconjunct from Jupiter to Pluto, you will have to make significant adjustments in your life to justify the knowledge that you have. The line of least resistance is to complain about your fate and challenge the need to submit to it. This may lead you to become an opportunist, taking from others what you consider rightfully yours. You are missing the message completely if you don't yield to your real task, which is to become fully acquainted with changing social conditions and use your talent to do something constructive about them. You tend to feel overwhelmed by social responsibility as if you must serve in a greater capacity than others. Therefore you may reject your responsibilities. On the other hand, you may give up your desire for personal and social benefits and exhaustively demonstrate your willingness to serve others. Beware of people who may victimize you to satisfy their own objectives. Try to understand the motives of those who enlist you in their cause.

You need to become fully informed about your surroundings to protect yourself from intimidation. Education will give you skills to fairly examine your talents and the contribution you can make in serving others. When you accept an opportunity, it is your spiritual responsibility to distinguish right from wrong. "What's in it for me?" isn't sufficient justification for everything you do.

In seeking your goals, either you will assert your desires on others and cleverly derive benefits for your exaggerated self-importance, or you will bitterly submit and resent others using your efforts for their own benefit.

Both attitudes need adjustment. If you follow a middle course, you may safely express your potentials in moderation and derive satisfaction by contributing substantially to individual and public causes.

Jupiter Inconjunct Ascendant

Jupiter inconjunct the Ascendant shows that you are generous in offering yourself in service to others. Although you really want to be helpful to anyone who needs your assistance, you lack the self-discipline to regulate your affairs so that you can help. You think nothing of making promises without the slightest idea whether or not you can fulfill them. You want to do so much that it is nearly impossible for you to remember what you promise to do and for whom. You insist on being allowed to indulge in your whims when you feel the urge. Remember, however, that when you offer your services, you are reminding people that they are unable to serve themselves. Don't wear out your welcome, trying to do for others what they are quite capable of doing for themselves.

An enormously talented person, you can do more than three other people together. You have good intentions in seeking your goals, but the recognition you get may come from making many starts and few finishes. Feeling guilty for being blessed with so many creative potentials, you want to feel that you are using them as fully as possible. You will probably waste a lot of effort in unrewarding enterprises until you learn to direct your skills and efforts toward a specific objective, and acquire the determination to stay in one spot long enough to realize your ambitions.

Tenderhearted and genuinely concerned about less fortunate people, you are never too busy to listen to someone with a sob story. But you must take care that you aren't made the scapegoat when others are looking for someone to blame for things going wrong. You have a host of "fair weather" friends who may suddenly disappear when you need them. This kind of experience should teach you to conserve your resources. You tend to shy away from examining your weaknesses realistically.

Saturn Inconjunct Uranus

Saturn inconjunct Uranus indicates that you have difficulty establishing priorities in the obligations that you undertake. You may not admit it, but you let yourself be intimidated by others because you want their approval. You deceive yourself in believing that you can do any task as well as it needs to be done. The truth is that while you may do it well, you resent having to adopt new methods or innovations.

In a sense, you are locked up in the past, trying desperately to hold on to old concepts. You resist change because it threatens your security. Since you can't prevent progress, isn't it logical to accept it and adapt yourself to it? The only insecurity you need fear is being out of step with what is generally accepted. Once you adopt the new, it will become part of your arsenal of experience and will sustain you.

Until you react more positively to change, your accomplishments will be limited. When you become more flexible, you can successfully compete with anyone. Although the past seems secure, it is only the experiences you have gained that make it so. Life goes on, and tomorrow, next month, and next year will also become the past. Don't deprive yourself of the wisdom available through experiences that are still to come.

Be prepared for some stress between you and your mate. Your partner will recognize your tremendous potential and want you to develop it. Try to reach a compromise if this becomes an issue in the relationship. Others see your talents more clearly than you, so take advantage of their perspective.

Your life will be enriched if you strive to refine your talents and adopt new techniques that are more productive. Pessimism and a defeatist attitude can cause serious physical problems, such as arthritis or hardening of the arteries. If you are lucky, it will only result in a cantankerous disposition.

Saturn Inconjunct Neptune

The inconjunct between Saturn and Neptune shows that you feel a need to somehow justify your resources and talent. You seek ways to use these resources to relieve the suffering and social injustices you observe. Others may not realize it, but you feel a particular responsibility because you are part of the social strucure that permits these conditions to exist. There is something of the martyr in you when you assume responsibility for more than your share of social obligations.

You may be compelled by a strong spiritual motivation to bring social order to situations in which chaotic conditions exist. Be careful you do not become aligned with programs whose goals are unclear. You may be asked to fulfill a responsibility *that isn't yours,* or you could become the victim of people who would use and abuse you. Hoping to gain spiritual benefits by unselfishly giving service, you may fail to protect yourself. The truth is, you may be using others to relieve your own guilt feelings, saying, "You need me!"

As an important side effect you may develop physical problems that are difficult to detect or diagnose. The true causes may be psychosomatic in origin and are therefore deeply buried in your subconscious. The observed effects rarely reveal the real problem. It is important for you to seek professional help if your problems do not respond to self-treatment. Avoid contamination by anyone who is ill. You should have regular physical check-ups to guarantee your sense of well-being.

You generally know how far you can extend yourself before becoming overexhausted. Take care, however, that you are not so stimulated by spiritual motives as to neglect reasonable safeguards. Your fear of negative results of tests (though they could prove positive as well) may incline you to take unnecessary risks that could be your undoing.

Saturn Inconjunct Pluto

The inconjunct from Saturn to Pluto indicates that you seriously try to do what you can to fulfill your obligations. You are impressed with your personal responsibility to help change unacceptable social conditions. Your greatest problem is that you take on more duties than you can handle and overtax yourself physically. You are afraid of being singled out as one who has avoided responding to the general public's needs. You might even remind others when they are unwilling to make their contribution, thus creating a combined effort, which is essential to success.

Because you fear that your personal efforts are inadequate, you sometimes become depressed about the results you achieve. You consider your co-workers better qualified and certain to move up the ladder first. You therefore tend to discount yourself as a valid candidate for promotions. Your preoccupation with endless details and with perfection is a strong factor in your superior's decision. You labor over trifles, complain about unfair competition, and generally overestimate what others expect of you.

Learn to get a larger perspective of your professional function and focus on providing that service. If you can stop contesting what others are doing, you will become more effective in getting results.

You may feel that people tend to use you for their own ends or that they expect you to cater to their incompetence. It is possible that in your personal relationships, others keep trying to dominate you. Your judgment needs refining, but you must stand firm when others attempt to force their attitudes and opinions on you. Your values are as valid as theirs, and you must communicate that fact with determination. You can only be used if you let yourself be used.

Be wary of contracts unless they specifically state your position and responsibility. Avoid the gray area of "we have an understanding." Live up to the contract, but volunteer nothing additional, or it could prove costly in the long run.

Saturn Inconjunct Ascendant

Saturn inconjunct the Ascendant means that you take yourself too seriously for your own good. You are so dedicated to your responsibilities that they take a big toll on your physical reserves. In fulfilling obligations, however, you are skillful at not going to extremes if you can avoid it. You plan your moves with tactical strategy to derive the most benefit from your efforts, wasting little time and energy on nonessentials. Cautious and reserved, you appear detached and unapproachable to the people you deal with. You offer your services only after carefully evaluating those you will serve to determine if they deserve your assistance. You are sometimes overly preoccupied with the affairs of other people. Although you rarely offer advice unless asked, when you do, your suggestions are often too painful to accept or too demanding. Because of this, others may resent your help.

You generally tell the truth because this is the only way you can live with yourself. You are determined to get the most out of your potentials, so developing your talents is high on your list of priorities. Experience has taught you to be self-reliant, and although you may be a slow learner, you never forget what you've learned. You want to be recognized for excellence in everything you do, and you secretly fear you may not succeed. Your superiors respect you for your honesty and integrity.

You utilize every resource at your disposal to gain financial security. Your friends probably consider you a bit close with your money, but you know that you would never turn to them if you needed help, preferring to get along on your own until fortune is on the upswing. You invest only in enterprises that have a reasonable chance of success, and you seek a comfortable status that you can hold onto. Not easily induced to seek the limelight, you prefer to bask in your accomplishments.

Uranus Inconjunct Neptune

The inconjunct of Uranus to Neptune shows that you are deeply disturbed by social, racial, religious, and political injustice. You feel guilty because these cancerous conditions exist and because you are powerless by yourself to do anything about them. But you know that if enough people can be aroused to honestly deal with these problems, they can be overcome. You are equally concerned about the vast numbers of people who live in poverty because of circumstances beyond their control or who are extremely handicapped, making it very difficult to earn a living. Whatever the cause of their suffering, you know that something can be done to compensate for their disadvantages. For this reason you may decide to work with social welfare, religious, or political organizations. You can easily identify with their purposes and indicate that you care about your fellow man. Perhaps you are also caught up in the very conditions mentioned, so that your concern is more critical than that of the casual observer.

A glance at the years 1922 through 1928 will give some idea of the social effects of this planetary combination. Talking films were introduced in 1923, which heralded the change from domestic to public gatherings. Television was demonstrated in England in 1926, and the first volume of Hitler's *Mein Kampf* appeared. The author of that book altered the lives of untold millions and introduced social, religious, and political injustice on an unheard-of scale, as documented in history books.

It is in response to the reverberations of that era that you will distinguish yourself. You and many others who were born during those years can establish the kind of world that honors the right of all people to be free to choose their destinies. The contribution you make will help provide opportunities for everyone who wants to succeed.

Uranus Inconjunct Pluto

The inconjunct from Uranus to Pluto indicates that you feel powerless to do anything about the sociological, religious, or political conditions under which you live. You feel that your individuality is never fully expressed because the overpowering circumstances of your life do not permit it. It is likely that you have been swept along by the tide of events, with no chance to object. When you look back at the conditions under which you have lived you may become bitter. But be thankful that nothing is ever permanent. When economic conditions deteriorate either nationally or locally, you are probably one of those who is seriously affected. You always have to make compromises in your living conditions until the economy is restored to a growth state. Perhaps, lacking the vision to anticipate declines in the economy, you tend to overburden yourself with excessive credit buying.

The foregoing applies especially to people born between 1909 and 1913. Major developments in science and industry tantalized people then, and the automobile became the symbol of increased freedom for every individual who could afford one. But the appearance of so many new products on the market put a severe strain on personal resources as people struggled to obtain them.

You are somewhat fearful of the awesome power held by political leaders and industrial giants, on whom you depend for employment. You are among those who sought protection from economic disaster by joining powerful unions that would represent you at the bargaining table. But you must continue to struggle to preserve the economic security you've worked all your life to acquire. You must try to increase your present fixed income so that your buying power will remain the same.

Uranus Inconjunct Ascendant

Uranus inconjunct the Ascendant shows that you are inventive and clever in capitalizing on your creative abilities. Always on the lookout for novel ways to use your talents, you generally succeed in finding them. You want to be admired for finding new and better ways to gain your objectives. Being progressive and eager to develop, you are not satisfied with traditional methods unless they can be improved upon. People who prefer tried and true ways of doing things may not accept your ideas easily, so you may have to develop them privately until you are sure they will work. You are especially concerned with finding labor-saving techniques that will give you greater freedom to indulge in personal interests. Although your outlandish suggestions may be criticized, you will not fail to arouse the interest of people who can visualize their financial advantages. You should guard your ideas and not share them with anyone until you have legal protection.

With your ingenuity at finding new sources of revenue when you have to, you will always be able to earn a living. Your retirement security is reasonably assured if you realize that you must have a program for that purpose alone.

You are admired by friends who are more aware of your gifts than you are; they may make proposals you could take advantage of. You are effective in your job, and your superiors know it, even if they don't say so. You are strongly motivated by a desire to use your talents for the benefit of many people.

In partnerships you may have difficulty because you are preoccupied with your own interests, which take up a lot of your time. Because you are so enthusiastic about any current interest, you tend to get lost in your work.

Neptune Inconjunct Ascendant

Neptune inconjunct the Ascendant means that you try hard and truly want to win the approval and cooperation of the people you deal with, but it often doesn't work out that way. You tend to contaminate your good intentions with self-seeking suggestions that make people suspicious of you. When you assert yourself, you act so uncertain that people question your competence. You have trouble finding ways to capitalize on your creativity and tend to dawdle in trying to accomplish your tasks. The result is a number of jobs started that may never get finished. Your failures result from insufficient planning and lack of mental organization. Try to obtain the services of an advisor who can guide you in your plans.

Unrealistic about financial matters, you tend to be disappointed in the results of your efforts. You are easily misled by suggestions from well-meaning friends, which may leave you high and dry financially if you follow them. You are generous in offering assistance to others, for you are sympathetic to their needs and feel an obligation to help if you can. But in so doing you neglect personal matters that need your attention, and the favors you do for others may never be appreciated. You have your priorities mixed up. In your desire to win people's approval you persecute yourself by serving their needs.

If you want to gain the respect of those you work for, you must learn to discipline yourself. You give the impression that you are easily distracted and therefore undependable. Don't be so impressed by your colleagues' credentials, for this tends to deflate your hopes of emulating their success. You are best suited to work alone, where your mistakes and missed schedules can only disturb yourself.

Pluto Inconjunct Ascendant

Pluto inconjunct the Ascendant means that you are too serious about your responsibilities to others. You act as though people have some hold over you and can force you to submit to their desires. Concerned about negative conditions in your environment, you volunteer your services to do something about them. This puts you in the mainstream of social activities, which may divert your attention from private affairs. Employment conditions are particularly important to you, and you feel the need to improve them if you can.

You know how to use your talents for earning a living. But you need to have some insurance against financial stress and may be interested in investment funds or retirement programs as a cushion against that possibility. An opinionated person, you are easily upset when the evidence forces you to admit you are wrong. Your ideas are sound, but they lose their effectiveness when you try to force them on others. Wanting to be admired and recognized as a person of strong character, you smolder inside if your actions show otherwise or if someone succeeds in disclosing your weaknesses for all to see.

You are not always kind in your remarks about people you consider unqualified to hold important positions over you. You tend to the opinion that they must have acquired their authority dishonestly.

You enjoy competition and secretly hope that some day you will have the opportunity to show what you can accomplish if given the authority.

Chapter Six

Oppositions

The opposition aspect is formed when two planets are separated by one hundred eighty degrees and are therefore in opposite signs of the Zodiac. The natures of the planets are affected by the dynamics of Mars and Venus, the qualities of Aries and Libra, and the circumstantial affairs of the first and seventh houses. The opposition resolves the psychological misalignment produced by the two planets involved. Initially the aspect causes alienation in relationships, because one is unable to resolve the raging conflict and controversy set up by the planets. But the pressure of the opposition can be relieved by understanding and love. A planet that is sixty or one hundred twenty degrees from either of the planets in the opposition is the arbitrator that can resolve the conflict. A planet so situated will also favorably aspect the other planet in the opposition by establishing a line of communication that brings the planets to a position of compromise. When there is no planet in the arbitrating position, the quality it would have produced must be adopted anyway.

Cancer and Capricorn, the Moon and Saturn, and the fourth and tenth houses represent the forces that make it difficult to resolve the opposition. They show how one builds barriers to protect the vulnerable and insecure emotions. Withdrawal does not allow love and understanding to develop. Without these qualities the similarities that unite cannot replace the differences that divide and alienate.

Ordinarily, the conflict and uneasiness of the opposition aspect is projected to other people. It's qualities and attitudes induce discomfort in others because the individual is embarrassed at having these qualities. But the opposition is the easiest aspect and conflict to resolve. The problems it represents are freely projected, and there is ample opportunity to work them out.

Sun Opposition Moon

The Sun opposition the Moon shows that there are difficulties between you and the people you deal with. You have a natural conflict between your emotions and your ego, and you unconsciously communicate this psychological hang-up to your associates, family, friends, and even your romantic partners. You often act in a hesitant spurt of enthusiasm, which is followed by anguish that your action may have been ill-advised. When you try to assert your own individuality, you are often torn by loyalty to those closest to you. You would prefer to have their full support so you could avoid the painful explanations and guilt that seem to accompany anything you want to do.

Relationships mean a great deal to you, and you long for someone whom you can totally identify with. Although you enjoy casual contacts, they never sufficiently satisfy your need to belong. You want a person who will fulfill your every need: love, friendship, sustaining you in your goals, sharing in your setbacks, fortifying you in your weakness, inspiring you in exploiting your creative talents, and sharing the full benefits of your combined efforts. A tall order, to be sure, and you will have to make concessions to obtain that kind of partner. You will have to be more giving than receiving, more compromising than obstinate, and more humble than arrogant. This too may be a tall order, but you can do it, or at least give it a good try. Any progress will prove beneficial.

Your greatest handicap is your unwillingness to let go of the past. Don't be afraid that people will consider you indifferent and unfeeling—you could never be unemotional. Make a realistic appraisal of what you want from your life and file a plan with yourself to achieve it. Don't wait for people to open doors for you. Some things you must do for yourself, even if it means you have to indulge in yourself.

You will experience some problems with partnerships until you know where you stand and can state your position honestly. You might feel sorry for yourself or become bitter when matters don't progress exactly the way you want them to, but that's life. The hard knocks are what make the success that follows so precious. Try to maintain a moderate physical pace, for you can't get away with burning the candle at both ends.

Sun Opposition Mars

The opposition from the Sun to Mars indicates that you are a fighter who will not back off from a challenge; you eagerly seek competition. But by responding to every challenge as though your very life depended on it, you probably cause dissension. You aggravate people with your arrogance, making them feel they must defend themselves against your abuse. You enjoy the battlefield of encounter because this is where your superiority can be established, once and for all. To need that kind of confirmation you must be terribly insecure. Winning the battle is not necessarily winning the war, so you will continue to pursue adversaries until you realize that your victories are hollow. You demonstrate incredible lack of sensitivity and an inability to look at yourself realistically when you perform this way. You have to prove your worth to yourself, not to other people. If your training is adequate and you've learned from experience, what more do you want? Your competence should be evident from your effectiveness in dealing with people, doing your work, and deriving satisfaction from your orderly affairs. Tend to your own business and let others tend to theirs.

When you come to grips with the problems discussed above, it will be a sure sign of your developing maturity. Once past that hurdle you can proceed to achieve your personal life goals and gain recognition for a satisfactory performance. You might find it rewarding to work as a police officer, legal adviser, or arbitrator in union disputes. Or you might participate in sports, exploration, or other demanding physical enterprise in which your abundant energy can be exploited to fullest advantage. Whatever field you choose, it must hold sufficient challenges to allow you to prove what you can do even under pressure. You can win the admiration of the public for distinguishing yourself this way. The greatest benefit will be your inner sense of accomplishment in fully realizing your potential.

Your desires are strong and not easily quieted. When you see what you want, you go after it. If you fail, you will accept what is available. Your responses are very physical, and visual effects alone are enough to arouse your interest. But you also want companionship, and this will be your ultimate aim. You may have to compromise considerably in your expectations if you want to be sure of securing a mate. With the vast experiences you have behind you, that should not be difficult.

Sun Oppositon Jupiter

The Sun opposition Jupiter shows that you are energetic, enthusiastic, and well-informed in using your creative talents. You know how to put your best foot forward in achieving your ambitions, but you take great chances when you should plan carefully. You assume that people will make way for you as you climb to your goals; when they challenge you instead, you can't help but be disappointed. You make glowing promises, but you are irresponsible and negligent about keeping them. Your associates call you a fair-weather friend who can't be found when the going gets tough.

You know how to turn on the charm to gain the approval of those you deal with in your daily affairs. It may be, however, that you are not totally honest with yourself and others, for you bend the truth to gain your objectives. You are inclined to make a grand display, playing the successful role, but in fact you are constantly fearful of the competition that may one day topple you from your throne. You need to become totally aware of reality in your striving so that you only take on exactly what you can cope with. Stop playing the confidence game with those around you. They know you better than to fall for it. You cannot afford to lose precious allies for the momentary pleasure of victory.

You are enormously talented and creative. These qualities should be directed to such fields as education, the media, business management, travel, or public relations. You must have self-control in order to obtain the best results in any of these endeavors, as well as a willingness to accept the full responsibility of your position. You must know your limits and delegate others to perform the tasks that go beyond those limits. You are ambitious for recognition, but as you climb to the heights of achievement, you should seek counsel. Try not to lose contact with those who may have made your success possible — they will support you if you remember them for their efforts.

In your romantic contacts you are demanding and expect to be given just about everything you ask for. Lacking continuity of feelings, you may indulge yourself for a long time before taking a partner. Even then, you will grant yourself privileges that you won't allow your partner. You need to be constantly on the move, and you enjoy traveling. New places mean new people and new distractions. You must be discreet at all times, or through unexpected developments you risk losing everything you have gained. It is hard for you to believe that such things could happen to you.

Slow down, for you have a lifetime to live. Pay attention to your diet and don't overindulge in food or drink. Plan to take vacations from your daily routine as often as possible to restore yourself to the vigorous health necessary to sustain you in your ambitions.

Sun Opposition Saturn

The opposition of your Sun to Saturn indicates that you are undergoing a crisis in consciousness, trying to discover who and what you are. You see challenges where they may not exist, and you need to be constantly reassured of your self-worth. You are trying to resolve your personal insecurity so that you can get on with the business of making a place for yourself. Most of your lessons will be learned through personal dealings, in which many crises will be resolved. Others feel as threatened by you as you feel threatened by them. Eventually you will achieve a proper perspective, and your self-confidence will be restored to normal.

Once you have confidence in yourself, you can go on to success in such endeavors as teaching, contracting, conservation, law, mathematics, architecture, political organization, or any function in which you must express your talents and resources efficiently and with authority.

Your partner in life will probably be your greatest source of advice and sound guidance. Discuss with your mate any pending decisions. Try not to become so hardened by experience that you are unmoved by emotional considerations. You should be concerned with the feelings of others as you assert yourself in the world. Temper your judgment with tenderness.

Your lack of self-love is your greatest deterrent to success. If others won't give you room to expand, take it anyway. Don't wait for accolades from your competitors — you may wait a long time. But be careful that you don't restrict others when they try to express themselves. You must observe the same rules of behavior you expect others to abide by.

As for your health, keep your salt intake at a minimum, and avoid remaining sedentary for long periods. This can have an important effect on your circulation.

Sun Opposition Uranus

The opposition of the Sun to Uranus represents a high-strung, irritable, and nervous disposition, indicating that you often need to relax. You fear competition, and yet you seek out people who will challenge you. Because you are insecure and doubtful of your competence, your self-esteem constantly needs to be reaffirmed. Dealing successfully with others is the best way to prove yourself, you feel. You must surely realize that you are exceptionally talented and can succeed if you really want to. You can meet people at the highest level of authority and easily match them in performance.

Until you learn to compromise with others, you will find it difficult to achieve your objectives. There *are* other points of view, and many are as valid as yours. It isn't easy, but *try* to listen well to what others say. It is to your advantage to realize that you don't yet know it all, that there are still many lessons to learn. If you accept this, you can go far in many professions. Science, social service, and education are some of the many meaningful fields in which you could excel.

The same competitive factor spills over into your social world. Your erratic behavior can alienate you from those who may mean the most to you. You have highs and lows of temperament, which make you unwelcome in many circles. Because of your impatience with anyone who seems dull and unexciting, you may lose friends and associates who will not tolerate your outbursts. The fact is, you wouldn't tolerate such behavior in someone else.

You make enormous demands on those with whom you are emotionally involved. Your lifestyle is exciting, but you expect others to match your interests. You are promiscuous by temperament, if not by physical makeup, and this is an important part of your personality. You don't want to be confined, yet you try to confine others.

Relaxation is extremely important for you. Your state of nervous irritability will improve with periodic withdrawal and rest. Your health depends on getting moments of emotional tranquility.

Sun Opposition Neptune

The Sun in opposition to Neptune indicates that you will be challenged by problems that you will find difficult to understand and diagnose. Early in your life you misunderstood authority and assumed that you were singled out for discipline. You responded defiantly, unwilling to submit to anyone's domination. It has thus been difficult for you to gain a proper perspective of reality. You create imaginary problems where none exist and cannot perceive the genuine and obvious obstacles.

This attitude has produced strains in your relationships with others, and it is difficult to know who is right or wrong. In your insecurity you eventually seek contact only with people to whom you have no commitment. Your reasoning is that if the relationship fails, you won't feel any guilt. However, in time you will overcome this attitude. With maturity you will learn to rely on your inner resources to protect and guide you in future relationships.

You are afraid of challenges because you doubt your own capabilities. When threatened, you tend to back off and allow others to benefit from opportunities that you saw as obstacles. Being self-employed will allow you to become independent and gain full awareness of your creative potential. As you improve and become increasingly successful in your work, you will welcome competition and will then be able to take employment involving others.

Your suspicious nature tends to alienate you from individual romantic relationships. Because you are afraid of becoming entrapped you shy away from emotional involvement. You tend to bring out either the very best or the very worst in others. Only you can determine which of these extremes you will tolerate. In your desire to endure suffering as punishment for your subconscious desires, you may submit to many indignities before you realize that you have brought it upon yourself.

Learn to face reality, and don't let your emotions color it to satisfy your feelings at the moment. Direct your goals toward fulfilling some important social responsibility.

Sun Opposition Pluto

The Sun in opposition to Pluto shows that you are defensive when challenged by others. In competition you resort to extreme measures to guarantee winning. You generally assume that your opponent has more power than you and that your own position is insecure. If it becomes obvious that you cannot win, you may turn your back on the threat and pretend it doesn't exist.

Nothing bothers you as much as being unsure of a situation. At times you will strike first, hoping to protect yourself, only to regret your imprudent action. At other times, you will encourage others to act while you conserve your energies.

Your extremist temperament may alienate you from those whose cooperation you need to shore up your own defenses. You assert your will with such defiance and aggression that only the stout-hearted can put up with it. You need to use logic and temper your attitude with greater compromise. You may be preoccupied with sex and its power as a lever against others. Be careful that you don't destroy yourself in the process.

The most persistent challenge you face is to recognize the right of others to assert themselves. Unless you allow this, you will be constantly harassed by people who will refuse to support you. You might also experience difficulty in regaining debts owed you. These problems will be only temporary if you learn to cooperate with those whom you feel threatened by. Stop suspecting everyone whose opinions differ from yours.

In time you will gain enough confidence to make your own decisions. You will feel sure of your own worth, and the security of your professional or domestic situation will no longer bother you.

At some point in you life you will undergo great changes and psychological realignment. At that time you will be able to stand alone, fully self-assured. If you tolerate others rather than resent them for threatening you, you will realize that you have the authority to accomplish your objectives independently.

Sun Opposition Ascendant

The Sun opposition the Ascendant shows that you are easily impressed by people you meet and hope that they will be similarly impressed with you. You attract powerful individuals with strong egos who always try to gain dominance over you. Without realizing it, you are showing that you doubt your own significance, in the hope that others will reassure you. Somewhat unsure of yourself, you fear you will be rejected in your relationships. You become affiliated with successful persons whom you can admire because you need to know you are genuinely appreciated, not merely tolerated. In other words, you are always looking for backhanded compliments. You enjoy having people fawn over you because it bolsters your sagging opinion of yourself.

In personal relationships you try too hard to do everything you think is expected of you, as if to make doubly sure that your friends think well of you. You must become independent of the security you had in your parents' home and transfer your need to belong to someone you can relate to personally.

Before asserting your own opinion you always try to put yourself in the other person's place. This can be a definite asset if you decide to go into business or a profession, because you would give your clients the impression that they are the most important people in the world. Flattered, they would happily pay for your services. Those who are the recipients of your services know your worth better than you do.

You have no difficulty in communicating with people, perhaps because you really enjoy having people around you. But you have to work hard to convince associates that you are as capable as they are, and if they don't accept this, you prefer to work alone. You need to assert yourself more aggressively when competing for job opportunities, or you will be left out.

Moon Opposition Mercury

The Moon opposition Mercury shows that you have difficulty bringing your emotions into balance with your reasoning; there is distortion between your feelings and your intellectual processes. You react to personal and social situations in a confused way, which produces problems in your relationships. Your responses are sometimes so emotional that it is impossible for people to make adequate compromises with you. At other times you evaluate a situation involving others with such cold logic that they doubt you have any feeling for them at all. You offend without knowing it and then wonder why people seem to be alienated from you. This lack of integration between feeling and thinking can be corrected if you will make it a point not to make any decisions until the other persons involved can express their opinions. If you truly care, you will examine the facts they present and try to meet them halfway. This is a more tactful way to act and will result in more mature judgment. You tend to jump to conclusions impulsively, but if you can make concessions when this urge erupts, you will like yourself more. Also, the people you deal with will be far more comfortable in your company.

You can see from the foregoing that it is extremely important for you to work out this imbalance. If you can learn to be more compromising, your professional endeavors will be much more pleasant, whether you work with individuals or with the public at large. By admitting it when you are wrong, you will earn the close fellowship of those you work with. Try not to take criticism too personally. When people challenge you or question your opinion, take it as an opportunity to correct any misunderstanding of what you mean. As Alexander Pope said, "To err is human; to forgive, divine."

Differences of opinion with your mate may cause you some distress in your domestic affairs. You are easily irritated and argue at the slightest provocation. Perhaps you are an impulse buyer who runs up bills for useless items. You worry excessively about family matters that don't deserve so much attention. Stifle the inclination to tell others the details of your private and domestic affairs. Most people have an adequate share of their own troubles. If you want to report the news, get a job with your local newspaper. Don't jeopardize your standing in the neighborhood by circulating stories, even if they are true.

Moon Opposition Venus

The Moon opposition to Venus shows that you are challenged by other people no matter what you try to do. They especially try to take issue with you when you want to show appreciation for favors they have done. You are generous in praising those you deal with but somehow you try too hard to convince them of your sincerity. In your desire to be loved, you don't want to risk anyone's displeasure. You really want to cooperate with others, but they don't react as though you do. The people you love most misunderstand you, so you are often at odds with them. Others tend to be defensive and suspicious of you when you show an interest in them, because you give the impression that you want something from them.

Try not to expect too much from those you are attracted to. It would be beneficial for you to get involved in enterprises or social endeavors with the people you are fond of. Learn to relate to them on an intellectual level, to understand them and their problems, and to be generous and helpful when they indicate a need for assistance. Let them get to know you and understand that you don't want anything from them except friendship. As you adjust your desires to be more cooperative with others, you will find that they will make concessions to you.

You have a taste for expensive things and could easily spend more than you earn to satisfy your longing for comforts. The real reason you seek these physical comforts is to compensate for the difficulties you have in achieving emotional satisfaction. You could find that there are always strings attached to the possessions you acquire. You may try to use sex as a device to attract the physical security you want. But this tactic can introduce unhealthy complications in your relationships and could eventually lead to legal problems. You may not like to hear the truth, but your current and future happiness depend on it.

You can be successful in activities that bring you before the public. It might be better not to work at all closely with the affairs of the people you would serve, at least until you can become more detached in your attitude. You tend to personalize incidents in the affairs of others, and your judgment is colored by emotional considerations as if these matters were your personal concern. Learn to mind your own business.

Important emotional crises can occur in your life, which would indicate that maladjustments continue to exist between you and the people with whom you are closely involved.

Moon Opposition Mars

The Moon opposition Mars indicates that you are constantly involved in crises in the relationships in your life. This will continue to be true unless you can learn to compromise. Even as a young person you got into disputes over the most insignificant matters. Intense in your feelings, you are quick to strike back at criticism, no matter how innocently intended. You have a sparkling personality and are outgoing and aggressive when you meet people. But in your eagerness, you sometimes choose to befriend individuals who are temperamentally unsuitable. You seek physical or material relationships and usually pay little attention to a person's other qualities. Because you don't have the patience to nourish a permanent relationship, you "love them and leave them." Those closest to you are alienated by your overbearing attitude. You tend to be emotionally pushy and intolerant of anyone who refuses to submit to your demands. Men with this aspect lack tenderness, while women tend to assert themselves with unusual arrogance.

Your argumentative nature may cause you some problems in your occupation, for you deeply resent criticism. You don't respond too well to authority and act very stubborn when required to follow rules. If you can learn to understand that everyone must follow the rules and that not everyone can be a leader, you may succeed very well. Your aggressiveness can be an asset in meeting competition. But you should tone down your frequent emotional outbursts, which are generally out of order in a business enterprise. You must make a special effort not to indulge yourself this way, or you will find that your fellow employees will avoid you, and your superiors will not be happy about the overall effect you create. People may be uncomfortable in your company because they know that you tend to fly off the handle at the slightest provocation.

You must learn to exercise greater self-discipline in your relationships. If you do not, you will permanently alienate many people who will not tolerate your kind of abuse. Given a chance, most people are willing to meet you halfway. You can get far better results if you assert yourself in a more moderate way and try to compromise in reaching mutual understanding.

Digestive upsets are common with this planetary combination, mostly because you don't know how to relax.

Moon-Mars in opposition shows a conflict between your emotions and your assertive faculties, which can be modified with even a small amount of effort. You can become more serene about your life circumstances and bring them into some degree of order. You will find that the results are much better than the results you get when you are antagonistic.

Moon Opposition Jupiter

The Moon opposition Jupiter shows that you are a highly developed individual with much creative ability and a generous appreciation for the talents of others. You may sometimes question the importance of your own abilities, and for this reason you seek out people who are talented. You hope they will reassure you of your own competence. Lacking the discrimination to make a personal evaluation of your worth, you feel the need for expert advice. But be careful that you aren't misled; casual acquaintances may take advantage of your emotional vulnerability.

There is a discrepancy between your emotional reactions to stimuli and your comprehension of what these experiences really mean. You tend to believe what is least painful to your sensitive feelings, but you can make serious mistakes this way. Generous to a fault, you can be deceived when you bestow your generosity on those who don't deserve it.

You are benevolent toward people who seem to lack the advantages you have. It would seem appropriate to select an occupation in which you could help such people, perhaps through welfare programs, rehabilitation of the handicapped, public relations, physical therapy, or through foundations that serve those in need. You would derive an enormous sense of well-being in these endeavors, knowing you are making an important contribution to their objectives. Don't be afraid to develop new techniques for improving your talents.

Your free time could be devoted to church activities or to civic and community affairs. Avoid direct competition with strong character types. They will only depress you by their overwhelming strength in gaining your submission. Accept only those challenges that you feel fairly certain you can succeed in.

You give every potential companion the benefit of the doubt, overindulging their whims in order to win their affection. You are worth a lot more than that, and you should not make a commitment to anyone until his or her credibility is established. Don't make gestures of love until the individaul you care for shows sincerity and honesty in caring for you.

Be moderate in eating and drinking, for you react to rich foods as though they were poison. You may be inclined to put on weight and disinclined to strenuous physical exercise, so caution is advised.

Moon Opposition Saturn

Your Moon opposition Saturn confers depth of understanding, but it also indicates periods of considerable pessimism and depression. These periods develop because of your emotional reactions — you are inclined to be apprehensive and fearful about people and events. You take life seriously, and no event or relationship is ever casual or superficial. In your early formative years you were strongly conditioned to accept duty and responsibility as an essential part of growing up. However, you found it difficult to accept such pressure, and your emotional sensitivity made you assume that perhaps you were not loved or were being rejected.

You relate better to older people, and even in youth you associated more easily with adults than with those your own age. This may have caused you some loneliness, especially if older groups would not accept you because of your age. It would not be surprising if you had become a loner.

Your professional opportunities may be limited unless you can become more optimistic. Although you accept duty, it is never without some bitter reminder of the parental influences of your childhood. You tend to project this bitterness in your relations with superiors, so that getting along with them may be a problem. You will function better if you can be self-employed or can at least exercise self-determination in performing tasks. It is important that you establish your own goals and construct a plan of action to realize them.

You could find expression in medicine (especially geriatrics), human research, welfare programs, education, law, hotel and restaurant management, or government service. Learn your craft well, and don't belittle those who can teach you what you need to know. Keep your feelings anchored in professional activities.

If you are still influenced by your early conditioning, you will choose a mate who is an extension of one of your parents. You will probably seek a person who is strong in character, self-disciplined, and demanding. But you would derive more emotional satisfaction from a relationship with someone who can compensate for the austerity of your parents. If you have successfully modified your attitude toward people so that you aren't on the defensive, you would enjoy having a liberal-minded mate who could help you exploit your potentials to their fullest.

Whichever sort of mate you choose, it is unlikely that your own family environment will be a replay of your childhood. You will want greater flexibility for your children to enable them to become secure, independent adults.

Avoid eating cold lunches, if you can, and use salt in moderation. Frequent rest is advised, and try to get away occasionally from the pressure of everyday routine. Digestion may be a problem if you allow tension to build up, especially from emotional stress.

Moon Opposition Uranus

The Moon in opposition to Uranus indicates mental and emotional stress. You are trying to integrate your feelings with logic to achieve a better balance between your inner and outer lives. You constantly feel the need to make decisions involving others, and these decisions cause you much emotional turmoil. If your feelings dominate, you alienate yourself from others, but if logic prevails, you feel crushed. Only experience can teach you to compromise so that both impulses are satisfied. The whole process *will* succeed if you are patient; this conflict can be resolved.

The crisis lies in your insecurity about projecting yourself in relationships that seem threatening. You are eager to make contact with others who will respond warmly to you. The important thing is to be yourself, realizing that others may have the same apprehensions you have. People will warm up to you and become friends if you give them the chance.

Your occupation should involve you in the personal affairs of others. In helping others to acquire self-confidence you will increase your own. Teaching is especially recommended because it will force you to project your creative abilities. The constructive results you achieve will make you more totally aware of your potential development.

You may become involved in the most unusual romantic alliances. You tend to innocently form attachments with individuals who are either already attached or who are at least spoken for. You have a fascination for bizarre or complicated relationships. Perhaps this is your way of avoiding responsibility, which can never develop in such situations. You are emotionally promiscuous even if you never actually indulge in physical promiscuity. Others will insist that you put up or shut up.

Try to get as much rest as you can. Your keyed-up nervous system can seriously affect your digestion. A serene outlook will do wonders to help you avert physical distress.

Moon Opposition Neptune

With the Moon opposition Neptune you are extremely talented and creative. Because you respond so deeply to stimuli, you may have difficulty in separating truth from fiction. The illusions you create about yourself and others make your relationships disorderly or confused. You become deeply involved with and even entrapped by the conditions of your environment. You closely identify with other people, places, and things and in the process sometimes lose your own identity. An escapist, you are trying to avoid finding a solution to your own emotional insecurity and instability.

Although you are creative and have much artistic appreciation, you may find it difficult to express this in a useful way. Others sometimes use you as a means for their own self-expression, which makes you feel abused. You should develop your talents through training. In this way you can define your objectives without relying on people who may not have your best interests at heart. It is important not to compare yourself with others. You need self-confidence to assure yourself that you can succeed without outside help. People will climb over you, if you allow them to.

In your professional skills, you underestimate your potentials and tend to assume that others are more qualified. Because you are extremely sensitive and exquisitely aware of other people's problems, you could be a fine doctor, analyst, counselor, or researcher. You work best alone and can accomplish a great deal when not distracted by others who may be parasites.

Your personal relationships suffer from the same illusions as your other interests. Satisfying romantic alliances require your realistic attention and willingness to make necessary adjustments. The love between you and your mate must include acceptance of domestic responsibilities and human frailties, and the understanding that compromise can avert estrangement. Remember that the ideal is an illusion that rarely exists and that would not be recognized even if it did.

Moon Opposition Pluto

Your Moon opposition Pluto shows you are very demonstrative in your affections and easily hurt if your love is not returned. You may try to get even by using daring methods to dramatize your pain. Your tolerance for emotional pain is very low, and you never seem to get what you want without much hardship. Perhaps you have a memory of some punishment associated with your parents that has left unhealed scars. This could produce bitterness and resentment toward anyone who attempts to control you. You are suspicious of anyone who tries to get too close to you and resent intrusion into your private life.

You are naturally defiant of authority and may have difficulty in dealing with the general public, although your job may require such contact. Try to have consideration for the feelings of those you serve. If you aren't careful you may become cranky and hard to get along with, although you won't realize it.

Because of your strong physical needs you tend to be somewhat careless in seeking satisfaction. Examine every lover's credentials carefully, or you may find yourself involved with dubious characters who could cause serious trouble and embarrassment to your job, your home, and your reputation. It isn't easy for you to accept advice, but at least try.

In a romantic partnership you tend to be argumentative over money, joint resources, and positions of authority in the home. You are aggressive in love and can alienate a partner whose identity you have challenged. You must learn to be more passive.

You demand a great deal of life and the permanent relationship you seek. It is imperative that you compromise in your expectations, or you will search far and wide to no avail. Don't assume that others only want to use you; you attract all kinds of individuals — good, bad, and indifferent. It is up to you to choose wisely.

Moon Opposition Ascendant

The Moon opposition the Ascendant shows that you try to become personally involved in the affairs of the people you know. Not content with casual encounters or impersonal communication, you seek to be absorbed by others so they will turn to you for sympathetic understanding. Subconsciously, you need someone to need you at all times. You are trying to transfer the parental loyalty of your childhood to people with whom you can become intimately identified. This seems to be the only way you can conserve the emotional security you are accustomed to.

You have a wide circle of friends who think highly of you because of your generous and kindly disposition. Nevertheless, you find it difficult to form individual, binding relationships, because you are never really sure you can fulfill the responsibilities they entail. To avoid this problem, you circulate freely among a number of people you feel comfortable with, who appreciate the favors you do for them. You want to be loved, and you constantly dwell on this fact. Although you adapt fairly well to changes in a relationship between yourself and another person, you secretly worry that you've failed to make a sufficient contribution to sustain the relationship.

Because you function well in a social environment, public relations would be a comfortable field for you. You hate being alone, so any professional interest should involve personal contact with the public. You may have some difficulty in achieving your material goals, however. Your sometimes fickle behavior gives your superiors the impression that you are unstable and therefore unreliable. It is important that you learn to stand alone and secure in your independence. You persist in the hope that everything you desire will someday be realized.

Mercury Opposition Mars

The opposition between Mercury and Mars shows that you have an active mind with limitless resources of intellectual ability. You are restless and impatient to demonstrate your competence whenever you can. But people who feel threatened by your mental superiority will oppose you, and you seem to attract such individuals. You have to resist the tendency to argue when compromise and mutual understanding can achieve more positive results. Unless you make a sincere effort to compromise, you will make matters worse. Refuse to argue when provoked by someone, and then you will be forced to discuss your differences and hopefully resolve them. Until you can reach out to people this way, you run the risk of being unpopular. It isn't that you are unable to relate to people, but that you strike them at first as hostile, which makes them defensive. You find fault with everything, as though you were sure of your own perfection. The sign that reads "STOP, LOOK, AND LISTEN" was probably meant to protect people of your temperament from accidents. Try looking at things from another person's point of view; you might learn a lot. Don't draw any conclusions until you really hear what other people have to say. Your ability to judge will improve remarkably at once.

You have the opportunity to be successful in anything you choose, although you may miss it by assuming that you know all the answers. Start with the premise that you know nothing and then begin to learn from every source available. You will endear yourself to persons in authority who may be very helpful to you. Play dumb if necessary and become really informed where it counts. You can never know too much.

You may be attracted to such occupations as public relations, law, counseling, education, or even acting. You don't lack any talent in communicating freely; you simply have to learn to voice your opinions more moderately and discard the brutal technique. Don't speak up in your own defense unless you are truly being challenged. To do so is a waste of time and effort that could be used more constructively.

Be diplomatic at all times in your contacts and dealings. You cannot afford to allow enmity to develop between you and people who may prove useful to you later. Above all be very careful about your language. Profanity only cuts off the lines of communication between you and others; resorting to it shows you are fighting a losing battle.

Mercury Opposition Jupiter

The opposition of Mercury and Jupiter shows that you are inclined to go to extremes in your expectations. You have a fertile imagination and much inspiration, but you may lack the practical sense to use them constructively. You don't like to take on responsibility, assuming you can achieve without diligent application and hard work. Although you are well informed on many subjects, your opinions are based on shabby evidence. You alienate people because you strike them as being a "know-it-all." You are inattentive to details when making judgments, which forces you to revise your position later. Your sometimes irresponsible statements are inconsistent with your mature mental development. You would do well to become a better listener and thereby gain some wisdom. In your case silence would surely be golden. If you listen to both sides before jumping to conclusions, you will reap great dividends and win many friends.

You have an insatiable appetite for knowledge and are intensely curious about everything. You must be careful, however, for you may not follow up your initial curiosity, and fragments of information are never a good substitute for the whole story. You need to discipline yourself and resist the tendency to hop from one subject to another, becoming a jack-of-all-trades and a master of none. Once you focus on a specific objective and determine to persist, there is much you can accomplish.

Law, education, writing, and public relations are some of the fields in which you can apply your creative talents and become successful. Aim for objectives that are within the realm of probability. As you reach your goals, redefine and clarify your next ones. In this way you won't be disappointed at not reaching the moon. You should also plan to continue your education as your level of accomplishment increases. You need to stay abreast of current developments if you want to remain competitive.

Be careful to avoid legal entanglements; you tend to pass over the small print and suffer losses as a result. Get a good and trustworthy attorney to take care of matters that you may not fully understand. You can't afford *not* to afford his services.

Your personal and romantic relationships are inclined to be a bit untidy. You tend to assume that a friend is seriously interested in you, failing to realize that he or she may be using you only to satisfy selfish desires. Insist on deferring your declaration of love until you can determine your lover's credentials. Unless you are honest with yourself, you will be the victim of insincerity by your associates.

Mercury Opposition Saturn

The opposition from Mercury to Saturn shows that you are strongly opinionated and defensive. You have considerable intellectual ability and can accomplish any goal you set for yourself. You may be inclined to bend the truth in order to get your way with people, but people are more discerning than you realize and often are aware of your deceptions. In this way you will lose friends, which can make you depressed when you are alone. An isolationist to begin with, you alienate your few associates with your criticism and scheming. All this adds up to the fact that you must learn to mind your own business and have respect for the privacy of others. Don't assume that other people think a certain way and then complain because they don't think that way.

Your professional life will be strained unless you can become engrossed in your own affairs and forget what the competition is doing. Becoming skilled and competent in your job will give you the security you need. Some professions to which you can certainly make a significant contribution are: architecture, drafting, science, research, education, politics, government service, conservation of natural resources, and accounting. Many of these are challenging occupations that should command all of your attention and make sufficient demands on your talents. If you apply yourself, you will gain the recognition you deserve as a specialist and expert in your field. Then you will have no fear that anyone can upstage you or exploit your knowledge for their benefit. Don't isolate yourself so much that you don't see other opportunities that may come your way. Stop looking for recognition from your colleagues — your effectiveness should be all the proof you need of your own worth.

If you can occupy yourself with your own affairs, you will not be angered when associates are promoted. You must understand that when you've proved yourself, you too will be considered for promotion.

You should maintain high moral and ethical standards to eliminate possible attacks on your reputation, which could seriously damage your prospects for growth and prosperity. This kind of recognition you can do without.

Always read contracts carefully, or better still, get the advice of counsel. You can easily miss an important detail that may have serious repercussions later. Don't say yes when you mean no just because your schemes will be more successful if you agree. In general, if you keep all your affairs in order, you will reduce the chances of having troublesome complications that only divert you from your objectives.

Mercury Opposition Uranus

The opposition from Mercury to Uranus shows that you have enormous intellectual vitality as well as a genius for incurring the wrath of others. You assume that your opinions are the only valid ones, and you resent it when others challenge them. You have been so accustomed to having your own way that you refuse to compromise, even though peace may be assured if you do. You freely accuse others of error even when the evidence supports them. Unless you can modify this "know-it-all" attitude, you will alienate yourself from many of your closest associates.

The startling thing is that you should know better than to challenge others, because you see the truth so clearly. No one can ever really deceive you, so what are you worried about? In fact, you aren't really sure of your competence and need to reassure yourself through conflict with others. But if you don't concede when you are wrong, you may never know where you are failing.

Compromise is your key to success. Science, education, social service, philosophy, and psychology are fields in which you can discover who you really are. The contributions you make in these fields will convince you that meeting others halfway guarantees success and establishes your credentials as a true friend to everyone.

You must control your extremely emotional nature and your rejection of facts before you can successfully enter a romantic partnership. You insist that your lover tell you the truth, but then you complain bitterly about it. Strangely, you can be extremely tactless when you "tell it like it is."

Your nervous system is probably frayed from the endless abuse of anxiety and irritability. Learn to control your temper and stop while you are ahead. When your nerves are shortcircuited, you are the loser.

Mercury Opposition Neptune

With Mercury opposition Neptune you are imaginative and creative and have high aspirations. However, you are easily distracted by people who challenge your efforts to express yourself. In competition, you may even begin to doubt your own abilities. You are naive in many instances and fall victim to the subversive tactics of competitors. Your dreams are unrealistic, and you are unable to accept the abrasions of your experiences with dignity. Defeat may cause you to become paranoid, imagining conspiracies against you. Let others justify themselves to you, and learn to distinguish fact from fiction.

Your professional interests should be accomplished through self-employment. It is too risky for you to work or compete professionally with others. As a creative individual, you can find gainful employment in writing, art, music, or dancing, which do not necessarily involve working with others. Medical research is particularly appropriate for your talents. Also it would give you isolation from the destructive qualities you bring out in others.

With your appreciation of the finer things in life, you need to be free of artificiality in your way of life. You sometimes recoil from challenges because they would disturb the serenity you desire and find so difficult to achieve. You are easily threatened, and your self-confidence is undermined.

Your personal relationships are sure to be unusual because of the variety of individuals who interest you. A constant disbeliever, you are suspicious when anyone claims to love you. You alienate many possible romantic associations because you fear someone *may* be trying to take advantage of your weaknesses. You could deprive yourself of much happiness if you interpret innocent and sincere gestures as attempts to exploit you.

Make an honest effort to understand human nature and be willing to make a sincere contribution in serving others.

Mercury Opposition Pluto

With your Mercury opposition Pluto, mental and emotional anxiety prevails. You are extremely sensitive to any social problems you observe and cannot rest until you've made some effort to resolve them. Everything is in a state of crisis, you feel, until you can gather your forces to solve a problem that you sincerely believe is your responsibility. You are impatient with yourself and others to get things done immediately. You are certainly competent, but you need to be constantly reassured of this, so you project crises in your own life and with the people around you. Moderation and compromise are necessary if you wish to prevent others from breaking off with you.

When challenged, you are emotionally and intellectually arrogant, because you fear that your credibility is being questioned. You tend to draw premature conclusions based only on the obvious aspects of a situation. A more penetrating examination might reveal details that would force you to modify your judgment. You will have to cope with this problem before you can successfully handle your professional interests. Many difficulties will persist with your co-workers, who will not tolerate you unless you change your attitude.

You are suited for such fields as medicine, research, analysis, union activities, chemistry, and teaching. However, you must come to grips with the qualities that make it difficult for others to get along with you. You are extremely argumentative when provoked, and this can interfere with realizing your goals. Learn to mind your own business, and learn to respect the feelings of others. This can help greatly in gaining their cooperation and support when you need it, as everyone does on occasion. Others will appreciate your efforts if you compromise a little.

Finding a suitable mate may not be difficult for you, but you are more likely to keep the mate you find if you will meet your partner halfway in compromise. Your strong ambition and desire for financial security may drive a wedge of dissent between you. If you disagree about important matters it would be wise to seek guidance from someone who is an authority in such things. Resist the desire to project your ideas onto your partner or to make unacceptable demands. This will alienate your mate as surely as it does your associates.

Ideally, your partner's objectives should be consistent with yours; then you could undertake a cooperative program in which you would support each other.

You can enjoy continuing good health if you will try to do everything in moderation. Unwind by getting away from the pressure of competition. Your savings are very important, for they will allow you to be less anxious when unexpected expenses occur. But remember, in your relationships with others, what you are is more important than what you have.

Mercury Opposition Ascendant

Mercury opposition the Ascendant means that whenever possible, you try to share the opinions of the people you associate with. Fearing you will be rejected, you wait until you have heard what your associates say before you express your views. Although you do this cleverly, you still don't succeed in convincing people that you have a mind of your own. Because of this, you are not taken seriously. You want everyone to think you are the most agreeable person they ever met. People feel comfortable with you, because you never threaten them by saying they are wrong, even when they are. Actually, you are trying too hard to be liked; you would be more respected if you were more sincere and less conniving.

You try to say the right thing at the right time so that people will admire you. Most times you succeed in this, but when you don't, it can be awful.

Actually, you are a masterful conversationalist and can hold an audience in the palm of your hand. So there is no need for pretending to be other than what you are — a delightful person to have around.

Sometimes you bend the truth about your family background or heritage in order to make a good impression. Or you alter the facts to make them fit your objectives. With your gift of effective communication, you would be most successful in an occupation that requires close, intimate contact with people. You are very adept at social activities, public relations, and communications, where you have every opportunity to show your skill in handling people.

Though you really like and need people, you don't want to feel obligated to them. You are independent and resent having your freedom restricted, even temporarily. You try to form friendships with persons who can help you in reaching your objectives; in return, you are willing to serve them when they need help. It will be difficult for you to rise to the position you seek unless others intercede on your behalf. Don't forget them when you succeed.

Venus Opposition Mars

The opposition of Venus to Mars shows that you are a glutton for punishment. You have a strong desire nature, and you are lively, aggressive, and even sparkling at times. But you are not a very compromising person, which makes for some problems in relationships with others. You tend to be argumentative when people object to the demands you make of them, for you cannot understand why they should object. You exude much animal magnetism, which may be offensive to some people, especially those of the same sex. Relying heavily on this quality, you have no feeling of emotional responsibility for people who are attracted to you and to whom you are drawn. You are extremely sensitive, and when people behave harshly toward you, you become fighting mad. Still, you seem to be very insensitive to the feelings of others and can be abusive without realizing it. You alienate yourself from your closest friends this way, and when it is all over you wonder exactly what went wrong.

Until you learn to compromise, you will experience many ups and downs in your professional affairs. You must accept the responsibility for any alienation between yourself and others because you are so totally preoccupied with yourself and indifferent to the feelings of others. Don't let a personal habit be a major deterrent to success. In dealing with people, avoid jumping to conclusions and defer judgment until you can examine all the facts. To get these facts, you can talk intelligently with those who know more about the problem than you do. If you will give people the opportunity to present their opinions, you will win their respect and admiration forever. First make them comfortable by implying that they are superior to you (even if that is debatable); then you can reveal your opinion and the reason for it. They will not fail to be impressed by your maturity and congeniality.

You are forward in expressing your feelings for people but are hurt when the feeling is not returned. You need to give others the right to make up their own minds. If they care for you, they will let you know. If they don't, would you want them to lie and say they do? Of course not!

Try to develop an interest in abstract subjects such as art, literature, theater, dancing, etc. These interests can convey that there is more to you than one would surmise from your animal magnetism. Only those you encounter casually can be content with a purely physical relationship. If you want to attract someone in an enduring contact, you must make a greater contribution.

Venus Opposition Jupiter

The opposition from Venus to Jupiter indicates that you don't trust your competence in dealing with people and circumstances; you are never really sure you can adequately cope with relationships. You are indulgent to others in the hope that they will confirm that you are indeed capable. The challenge of constant competition reassures you of your skill in handling even the most demanding problems in your situation. You seek social approval for everything you do and are upset when it is not forthcoming. Presumptuous in your expectations of others and somewhat conceited, you alienate even your closest friends by boring them with endless trivia about yourself and your affairs. It is a sign of immaturity if your self-regard depends on the approval you extract from your associates.

You are conniving in your dealings with people, and you tend to use them to satisfy your objectives. When you find that you have been used also, you become bitter. You associate with those who approve of you and detach yourself from those who don't. You will go along with any prevailing opinion if it suits your purposes. The only time you compromise is when it costs you little or nothing. Your inconsistency in applying justice is remarkable. And yet, with all these negative tendencies, you can be generous to your benefactors and sympathetic with the problems of your associates.

Business is probably the area of your greatest creative self-expression. You are essentially a wheeler-dealer who enjoys direct combat with adversaries, for competing successfully confirms your competence. Argument, or what you call discussion, is the skill you use most effectively. You know how to charm people and get them to lower their defenses while you prepare their defeat. Not altogether honest in your dealings, you "bend" the truth when it suits your purposes. You can be hypocritical when it serves your ends.

Your romantic relationships are touch and go — you make sincere-seeming gestures until your lover suggests a more contractual arrangement, when you suddenly lose interest. "Always a bridesmaid or best man, never a bride or groom," seems particularly appropriate for you. Whether you will be married depends on your willingness to accept the responsibility of such a contract; it isn't that you lack the opportunity.

Venus Opposition Saturn

With Venus opposition to Saturn, you are inclined to regard your experiences as being almost useless. With this aspect you will always be challenged by competitors until you realize how important you really are. You must stop underestimating your self-worth. Remind yourself continually that you can match your competitors, and don't give others more credit than they deserve. If you will examine your good qualities carefully, you will see that they compare very favorably to those of others. Stop hiding the truth from yourself. Perhaps when you were very young, you were led to believe that you were less talented than others in every way, and you still act on that belief. You need competition to prove how capable you are; if you reject competition you will never truly know your capabilities.

Throughout your life you will have to make concessions to others without knowing whether or not they are worth the effort. In time, however, you will be able to judge people without having to endure the painful experience of submission. As your judgment becomes sharper, you will become very skilled in solving problems for yourself and others.

You may suffer emotional frustrations during the early years, but as you become more mature you will understand that no one gets everything when he or she wants it. You may compensate for privations that you experience in your personal life by becoming successful in your profession. Real estate, law, insurance, designing, sales, and buying are suitable fields. All of them require responsibility, attention to detail, integrity, and honesty if you are to be proud of your accomplishments. It is advised that you work alone or at least be able to set your own pace. Working with others in an intimate atmosphere would not be advisable because you would arouse their criticism. You have talent, but your employer may refuse to recognize it in order to avoid paying you more.

Don't anticipate an early marriage unless you are prepared to make enormous concessions to keep it together. Better to postpone a binding partnership until you can be more selective in choosing a mate. If you marry for security it may last, but it will be little more than a corporate merger with little emotional satisfaction. If your upbringing was austere and you saw privation and financial difficulties in your parents' lives, there is even more reason to wait for financial independence before taking a mate.

Venus Opposition Uranus

With Venus opposition Uranus you are somewhat emotionally unstable. You have strong desires and don't care who knows it. Your intensity in expressing yourself often leads to uncomfortable and even dangerous relationships. You seem intent on exploring every kind of human contact, totally disregarding the dangers involved. You are a rebel who insists that experience is the best teacher. Perhaps, but it is also the most painful way to learn, since the residues linger and may even haunt you later in life. You are impulsive and even reckless in handling money, probably overspending on clothing or on pleasures to indulge in.

You depend on your bright and witty charm to carry you to success in your job. It is possible for you to enjoy warm personal and social contacts with your superiors. Any profession in which you must deal with the public could provide you with much satisfaction.

You don't submit to authority without challenge, which can be a deterrent to realizing your goals. You enjoy competition, because you have enormous assets to help you succeed. But if there is no excitement accompanying the competition, you lose interest. You are willful, determined, and persistent, and you take on responsibilities with ease. You may alienate your closest friends or associates as you climb to success, because you will detach yourself from them if it is expedient.

Your romantic affairs will always remain just affairs unless you can learn to compromise and meet others halfway. You tend to want fulfillment without making a contribution to sustain a permanent relationship. If your attitude does not change, you will enjoy a succession of full and satisfying romantic alliances. But you will have no assurances of truly "belonging" to someone in the latter years of your life, and loneliness is very uncomfortable for you.

Venus Opposition Neptune

With Venus opposition Neptune you have a boundless and sometimes dangerous imagination. In your desire to achieve the highest human experiences, you may take unnecessary risks. Your idealism is linked with clouded vision, and when the cloud lifts, you may suffer disappointment. Your dreams are easily shattered because they are unrealistic. You imagine qualities in others that they can't possible come up to. Once someone deceives you, your trust will be difficult to regain.

You have artistic leanings and should try to become involved in artistic pursuits. Be honest with yourself in evaluating your talents. If you will accept less challenging tasks your self-confidence will not be destroyed by competition. You can express your creative potentials and derive much satisfaction from your contribution, but don't compare yourself with others. You are only responsible for exercising your own capabilities, so forget about how others function.

Because of your deeply sensitive nature, you would probably work best with someone you sincerely trust. In your profession, don't expose yourself; let someone else be your spokesman. If you speak for yourself, you'll only antagonize others in an undefinable way, and you will wonder just what went wrong.

Your suspicious nature is strongly evident in your personal and romantic attachments. Here you are your own worst enemy. In close dealings with others, you often suspect dishonesty, which causes them to erect protective defenses. You are never quite sure whether your feelings are love or fascination, and you fear negative results. This is not a realistic framework for developing true love. You must "come clean" in discussing problems that arise between you and you partner. Much damage can result if you don't.

Venus Opposition Pluto

With Venus opposition Pluto, your intense emotional nature may create many problems for you, as you strive to force your demands on others. On the other hand, you may avoid involvement with others, fearing the responsibility of an emotional attachment. In either case, you will alienate yourself from those who may be dearest to you.

In any permanent relationship, money is often seen as the cause of disharmony. The real problem, however, is usually the excessive demands you make of your partner, or your partner's possessive attitude toward you. You must appraise your feelings realistically to see if the two of you have simply grown apart, or if you have tried to remake your partner to fit your ideal image.

Before making any contractual commitment to someone, you should try to examine your prospective mate's potentials carefully. This means realistically evaluating his or her capacity to fulfill your needs, both as a partner and as a parent of your children. The best physical mate does not necessarily make a good parent. There may be an inability to accept the responsiblility of a family and the restraints to personal freedom and mobility.

Any problems you may have, however, can be resolved if you are willing to compromise. The freedom you can enjoy together may be greater than any freedom you could have separately.

Early in your professional career, as you are trying to become established, you will encounter certain difficulties. Some individuals may try to take advantage of your naivete to create trouble between you and your superiors. You are sure to encounter severe competition from your co-workers, who will feel threatened by you.

Avoid forming a close alliance with anyone until you are sure that person can be trusted with your confidences. This is especially true of your boss.

Being friendly with him may give you job security, but it will certainly disrupt comfortable working conditions with your fellow employees, and these are the people you have to live with each day.

To be truly effective, try to maintain a purely social attitude in your professional endeavors. Any emotional involvement will unnecessarily complicate your goals. It is easy to be victimized by a person for whom you feel an emotional attachment because it is so difficult to say no, even to excessive demands. If you allow yourself to be used, you will increase the chances of being abused.

Venus Opposition Ascendant

Venus opposition the Ascendant indicates that you are drawn to refined and sophisticated people. You are well-mannered, and generally people have a good opinion of you. You make concessions if it seems necessary to maintain harmonious relations, and you refuse to judge someone whose conduct does not come up to your expectations. Too frequently you give people the benefit of the doubt and see in them qualities they don't possess. Wanting to believe that you choose to associate only with persons of the highest character, you are disappointed if they don't really measure up.

Although you appear self-confident and assured, the fact is that you are not comfortable unless you have someone around to give you the support you need. It is difficult for you to stand alone. There is no deception in your claim that you are happy to meet people, because you truly enjoy their company and conversation. You work hard, although subtly, to make sure that people are warmly disposed toward you, and you try to emphasize your better qualities to prove you are worthy of their friendship. To put others at ease, you play the innocent role and make it clear that you won't threaten them. You hope no one perceives your negative qualities and discovers how insecure you really are.

Your best publicity agents are your friends, who freely extol your virtues when anyone asks them. In the company of your superiors or anyone you admire, you tend to be shy.

Always on the lookout for ways to improve your social status, you prefer the company of successful people or those who are obviously on their way up. You have no qualms about forming close relationships with people who are financially secure if this will increase your chances of a permanent association. On the surface you are docile, gentle, and charming, but underneath you conspire and connive to make a better life for yourself through the people you deal with.

Mars Opposition Jupiter

The opposition from Mars to Jupiter shows that you enjoy challenges and eagerly seek them out. You are physically competent to take on any adversary to prove to yourself that you can succeed, and you do need to prove it. You use competition to reassure yourself of your capabilities. You might fail, but you are willing to take that chance. However, you sometimes bite off more than you can chew, which you regret later when you are thinking it over in private. You operate on the premise that the one who strikes first has the advantage over his opponent, but that is true only when one has first made careful plans. Being both imprudent and ostentatious, when you succeed you make grandstand plays to call attention to yourself.

You resent people who demonstrate their superiority over you, and you may resort to unfair tactics to discredit them. This tendency alienates your associates and friends, who view you with suspicion and give you a wide berth. They may also try to destroy your credibility because of their resentment. You must be careful not to cut off all sources of support, for it can be lonely to be cast off by your peers.

Your best opportunities to gain recognition and express your creative potentials would be in law, government, sports, communications media, acting, teaching, or public relations. Once you learn to temper your combative tendencies with moderation, you can achieve great heights. Even your competitors will admire you for a job well done. Your only problem is your fear of inadequacy in the face of responsibility. Careful planning and application should relieve you of any anxiety in this respect. You've got to know you are qualified to meet challenges without feeling threatened by competitors.

Your physical desires are as powerful as your ambitions. You are not satisfied unless you can express your sexual appetite when aroused. This can cause problems, unless you are lucky enough to have someone available at all times. This will not be an important matter if Saturn makes a contact to Mars, giving you a built-in factor of self-control. Your mate must match your physical prowess in this respect, or complications will develop that can seriously endanger the relationship.

Moderation is advised in everything you do. Indecision will be an irritant until you recognize your self-worth and can take a firm stand without waiting for approval.

Mars Opposition Saturn

The opposition between Mars and Saturn indicates some conflict between your desires and your sense of responsibility. You alternate between moments of intense activity and periods when you cannot seem to gather the energy to accomplish anything. Your temperament is either aggressive or completely apathetic. You find it difficult to maintain a moderate position that would allow you to achieve your goals without "highs" and "lows." You are the only obstacle in your path to achievement. You need to become self-disciplined in using your energy constructively, and you must establish goals within your reach. Resolve firmly that you will not let feelings of futility keep you from reaching them.

You tend to be awed by the accomplishments of your associates or competitors, probably because you give them greater credit than they deserve. You desperately need competition so you can evaluate your own worth; ignorance of your capabilities is your greatest liability. The chances are that others will always have a higher opinion of your potential than you, and you will need to be reassured that your talents are genuine.

Once you get over the idea of your own unworthiness, you can go far. You must like yourself enough to feel that you deserve the success you can achieve, but you will have to assert yourself. You could find some expression in law enforcement, industrial engineering, military service, conservation, or physical therapy. Initially, you would probably work best alone, until you can convince yourself that you could make a significant contribution in your field. Later, you could work satisfactorily with others without feeling threatened by their competence. You tend to establish goals somewhat out of reach, which makes you unhappy with your accomplishments. It would be better for you to grow into higher levels of responsibility by taking one step at a time. In that way your current security is never jeopardized.

Your personal and romantic relationships never measure up to your expectations. Your desires always seem to be frustrated or to encounter great difficulties. The phrase, "After you get what you want, you don't want it," is descriptive of your feelings in these relationships. In any case, it is doubtful that your desires will be fulfilled to your satisfaction, and some denial is to be expected.

Moderation is necessary in all your affairs, or physical depletion can result. Rest is very important in order to maintain physical well-being. Accidents resulting in fractures are common with this planetary combination, as are problems affecting the joints, such as arthritis and bursitis. Moderate exercise is helpful if you get sufficient rest.

Mars Opposition Uranus

With Mars opposition Uranus you have a genius for arousing others to challenge you. You enjoy competition and have a flair for gaining dominance over others. The simple fact is, you are arrogant, demanding, and authoritative in your dealings, which tends to disarm people. You seem to thrive on bickering and argument, even if you aren't serious about it. This is just another way to provide continuing excitement.

Your behavior has little to do with your competence, although your forwardness often convinces others that you know what you are doing. With your flair for expression, you should seek occupations such as selling, politics, group interests, or science, that depend on this quality. You could become interested in hazardous occupations like flying, racing, exploring, or mountain climbing, but you must be extremely careful and take all safety precautions. Because you are accident-prone, these endeavors are not recommended. You tend to throw caution to the winds, especially when someone is watching. Your desire for approval is so strong that you will even risk danger to gain it.

You don't tolerate any restrictions on your freedom and mobility and need to be constantly on the move. Is this because you are afraid others will discover how insecure you really are? Perhaps your life-style is a defense against admitting that you are mainly a "physical" person.

You aren't the easiest person to get along with. Your outbursts of temper and cantankerous attitude really rub people the wrong way. A revolutionary, you are basically against tradition with all its limits to individuality. You are critical of anyone who wields authority and want your own way so much that you become violent when anyone tries to deny it. Your unpredictable nature may cause you to lose dear friends who will not tolerate your arrogance.

Mars Opposition Neptune

You have Mars in opposition to Neptune which shows that often you do not benefit from your aggressiveness. You are eager to please, but when you do favors for people, they are often suspicious of your motives. In turn, you are disappointed that they doubt your sincerity. After repeated incidents of this type, you determine not to become involved in the affairs of others. The real problem may be *your* motivation in asserting yourself. Perhaps you aren't completely honest in what you do and how you do it, and this arouses suspicion. It's what you *don't* say that later incriminates you. Your desires sometimes border on being uncontrollable, and others feel endangered or threatened by you.

You will have to develop two important qualities before you can be successful. First, you must be willing to accept reality, no matter how painful; and second, you must learn to relate emotionally to others. You already have a strong physical mechanism, and these qualities will encourage others to respond to you more completely.

Be careful in selecting a profession, and avoid any occupation that has even the slightest hint of illegality. An established firm would be best suited to your talents and your fertile imagination. Learn everything you can about your job and your immediate associates, for if anyone can be made the "patsy" it is you. Don't get involved in any activity in which there is any likelihood of physical danger. Learn to reason with your intellect and not be led by your fascination for thrills and the unknown.

Avoid drugs, alcohol, and the occult. They are not for you, because you are too susceptible to them. You are easily mesmerized by illusions and those who create them. If you want to indulge in artificiality, work in the theater. Your faculties will serve you well in acting or related enterprises. Above all, be a realist in your goals. Ask those who are more knowledgeable to help you plan realizable objectives.

Mars Opposition Pluto

With Mars in opposition to Pluto you have a defiant attitude toward the effects of your aggression. Lacking sufficient control of your energy, you are surprised at the response you stimulate in others. You challenge people to be on the defensive in their dealings with you. You tend to overdramatize your competitors' motives and may even raise unnecessary barriers to protect your own interests. Your actions often cannot be logically justified.

Your intense sexual nature may lead you to form strong alliances, but it may just as easily cause severe rifts in your relationships. If you use your magnetism to gain control over others, you may later find yourself the victim of another's obsession with power. The problem is to determine whether you are motivated by a lust for power and control or whether you should use your energy as a force for social responsibility. You could be spiritually dedicated to make necessary changes in your environment. However, you may encounter powerful forces with the economic advantage to frustrate you in your objectives.

Above all, it is important that you evaluate the positive and negative aspects of any proposition. Consider the values of compromise before taking action. You must carefully judge the effects you hope to achieve and be reasonably certain that you will not deny other people's rights. You will still alienate some persons as you assert yourself. Only you will know if the achievement of your goals justifies this.

You are sure to encounter problems in your personal affairs. It is almost certain there will be problems affecting your marital status if you are too demanding of your mate. Domestic turmoil could result from mismanagement of income, disputes over authority, or extreme jealousy expressed by either of you. You may have some problems concerning an inheritance or credit responsibilities.

Mars Opposition Ascendant

Mars opposition the Ascendant shows that you attract people who threaten you, as though you had a chip on your shoulder and dared everyone to knock it off. You don't really have that much self-confidence; your aggressive actions are an attempt to convince yourself that you do. You need constant encounters to improve your skill in dealing with people who would otherwise take advantage of you. Meeting others in competition is how you learn how to assert yourself constructively, with greater self-control and discipline. Naturally argumentative, you are not the easiest person to get along with. You must learn to be more compromising if you want peace and harmony. Making concessions shows strength of character, not weakness, and if you realize this, you will be respected for your maturity.

In personal relationships, your offensive tactics force you to raise your defenses when the going gets rough. While it is necessary to fight for your independence, you must show some restraint so you don't incur everyone's displeasure. You want to be recognized for your ability to succeed in spite of challenging competition. But an attitude of superiority often masks feelings of inferiority or inadequacy.

You have a lot of creative energy you should express. Remember, it's what you do rather than what you say you can do that is important. Knowing that your future success and happiness depend on you alone, you must realize that you will have to make some contribution to ensure them. Take advantage of your closest friends, who can offer worthwhile suggestions, and when their ideas help you, show your appreciation.

You may have some difficulty in getting your superiors to give you a more important position, because of your inclination to flare up under pressure. You tend to speak out of turn, which arouses suspicion that you cannot handle the authority delegated to you. Develop more self-control, or you will run into many troublesome situations that could be extremely difficult to resolve.

Jupiter Opposition Saturn

The opposition from Jupiter to Saturn indicates that you fluctuate between knowing what you are worth to having grave doubts of your value. You are never completely sure of yourself and need to be constantly reassured by others that you are as talented as you think. Probably some strained contact with superiors, perhaps your parents, has given you this poor understanding of your capabilities.

This is a push-pull planetary combination. Because you need approval, you seek people who will make demands on you to prove your competence to them and to yourself. If their praise is not forthcoming, you reject them and alienate yourself. You seem to be looking for yes people to give you the approval you require. But how hollow the victory that is forcibly extracted. Wouldn't it be simpler to accept competition from your peer group and make your determination that way? You obviously cannot face the truth, and your progress will be slowed until you can be honest with yourself. You generally reject other people who have qualities like your own.

You are inclined to be irresponsible and look for the easy way out of duty. This attitude needs severe adjustment. First, you must face reality and accept the responsibilities it brings; second, you should learn how your behavior hurts people and try to be less indifferent to them. If you can change in these ways, you can rise to any goals you set for yourself. You might become a lawyer, educator, or physical therapist. However, if you doubt your own competence, your associates may also refuse to attest to it. You have work to do, and it is advised that you begin soon, if you haven't already.

The same problem in evaluating your worth will crop up in personal relationships, both in friendship and in romantic interests. You might well decide to use better judgment in these instances, because it wouldn't do to sever an alliance with someone very special to you. You don't usually make generous overtures to anyone, even to a lover. Even though you casually reject anyone who doesn't voice enthusiastic approval, you are surprisingly shattered when you are rejected and can't believe you deserve such treatment.

Once you know what you are worth, you won't feel threatened by anyone. Then you can proceed to develop your potentials for success.

Jupiter Opposition Uranus

The opposition from Jupiter to Uranus indicates a high degree of enthusiasm and intellectual development. From your earliest years you have encountered many challenges to your incredible gift of knowledge. This has given you the ability to meet competition with assurance and courage. You are afraid of no one, especially in a battle of wits. Your intuitive ability is a decided asset in gaining victory over others, regardless of their degree of education or skill.

The world is yours for the taking, and there is virtually no field of endeavor in which you can't succeed. Your best interests would be served in occupations related to law, politics, education, travel, religion, or the occult. In any of these, you can exploit your potentials to their highest level of development and creative expression. Your fund of information is too precious to keep to yourself, and your dynamic expressive ability should be used to stimulate and benefit others. No one else can more dramatically demonstrate that only education provides freedom. You can take on enormous burdens without weakening under pressure.

You must be conscious, though, of the danger of becoming authoritarian and despotic in using your power. You will alienate many of your closest allies and friends as you pursue your goals in life. You may wonder why they can't *see* the future as clearly as you, and you may hold them in disdain for this. It is your responsibility to understand other people's limitations and to make allowances for them.

Throughout your life you will be severely challenged. Remembering this may guide you when your ego gets inflated with your own self-importance.

Exercise moderation at all times. Face the mirror honestly and accept the truth about yourself. Realize that with your intellectual advantage, you have a greater burden of responsibility than lesser minds.

Jupiter Opposition Neptune

The opposition from Jupiter to Neptune shows that you often make promises you either can't or won't fulfill. At the time your motives may be honorable, but you are quite unable to follow through. Perhaps you feel that others continually expect a lot from you, which you resent. As a result, you will slowly become alienated from anyone who suggests you do this or that as a favor. You are often in disagreement with people who insist they know more than you and who dare you to demonstrate your competence. You must avoid such challenges. Another tactic that may be used to urge you on is praise, such as, "no one knows more about this than you, so you should do it." Avoid responding to this type of appeal, too. It is the same trap under a different name.

In your professional pursuits, be cautious about accepting responsibilities for which you are not paid. You generally bite off more than you can chew.

It is easy to yield to demands and later wonder if that was really your duty after all. You are suspicious of other people's motivations in their relationships with you. These suspicions have grown out of past experiences when people have violated your trust. But be careful that you don't overreact. Don't neglect to do the things you must, although it isn't always clear exactly what you should do. It is better for you to work with others for broad social causes so that you do not feel unilaterally guilty when failure results.

You have the courage to challenge authority when you suspect connivance or collusion. You also take issue with anyone who assigns you a responsibility arbitrarily. If during a fund drive you are told, "This is your fair share," you hit the ceiling. Your response is, "Since you know nothing about my personal financial obligations, you cannot possibly determine what my fair share is, and I resent it!"

In your romantic relationships you are impractical. You believe that your love interest has the qualities you admire, but if you find you are wrong you are very disappointed. You don't endure emotional rejection gracefully and may even become vindictive. Accept others as they are; learn to stress their positive points and minimize the negative.

Jupiter Opposition Pluto

With Jupiter in opposition to Pluto, you need vision to cope with people who resist you in your desire for growth and expansion. You are disposed to question every ideology and to challenge dogma by asserting your own. Therefore your search for answers to life's mysteries will create conflict with others. Your social values are often not in step with those of society, and you alienate the very people who can help you make dramatic changes in social attitudes. You have a "saviour" quality that people will sometimes disdain, if you pompously declare your mission to serve mankind.

On the negative side, you may be inclined to seek positions of power in order to more effectively manage other people's lives. You may try to gain financial advantage over people as an additional pressure on their destinies. In this way you may win a qualified victory over them, but if you use them in your anarchistic rise to power, you will never gain their respect and admiration.

Be careful not to become affiliated with illegal enterprises merely because they offer better returns. The society you manipulate can legally restrict and even confine you — even the wealthy are imprisoned. You must carefully weigh your activities against the risks involved. What may seem right for you may be completely wrong for society.

On the other hand, you may be motivated to correct social injustices and start a crusade against social harassment. You may focus on how you can best serve others through intimate response and spiritual dedication to their problems. Your dramatic flair can arouse the general public both through skillful personal contacts and through the media.

Be specific about your aims to serve as spokesman to help others achieve their objectives. Also, it may be better to be chosen than to immodestly elect yourself on the assumption that without you they will suffer disappointment or defeat. You have a lot to offer people; don't spoil it with arrogance.

Jupiter Opposition Ascendant

Jupiter opposition the Ascendant indicates that you are generous toward your associates and civil with competitors. You are polished and refined, sometimes to the point that others may be suspicious of your motives. You prefer to associate with people who seem sure of themselves and their goals. Unless you see a future in it, you refuse to bind yourself to any obligation. You attract fortunate people to you, and you share their optimistic feeling that you will become successful. Just as an investment broker deals in financial resources, you deal in the resources of people — who they are and what they can accomplish for themselves and for you. You pride yourself on your good judgment, but you ignore the fact that you are a taker, not a giver, except when it suits your long-range purposes.

It isn't easy for you to establish roots, partly because you feel that without them you are more free to take advantage of opportunities. An "idea" person, you know how to exploit your creative potentials to derive the most benefit from them. You are a good conversationalist and can liven up any discussion with tales that may be tall stories but are never dull or boring.

Your desire to achieve was probably stimulated by your early home life, which may not have been totally satisfying. Because of that fact, you resolved to better yourself and your circumstances whenever possible. You try to convince yourself that given the chance you would show people how capable you are. But you do this because you don't want to be reminded of your material and emotional responsibilities. You know you should settle down and admit that you need to relate to others in order to succeed.

Your greatest problem is that you use people to serve your personal objectives. You must learn that being generous is as beneficial to you as accepting the generosity of others.

Saturn Opposition Uranus

The opposition from Saturn to Uranus indicates that you have a problem in relating to others. You relate, but in a competitive way for no particular reason. There are times when you are right and should maintain your position, but not so that you jeopardize the cooperation of those closest to you. You do need others to help stabilize you when you disregard the most basic logic in handling your affairs. Learn to respect and value those who are genuinely concerned about you. First, you must learn the lesson of compromise. Later, when you've acquired the wisdom of experience, you may have earned the freedom you seek.

There are a number of professions for which you are qualified. Among them are science, research, logistics, statistics, mathematics, and industrial management. When you gain a position of authority, be careful not to subvert it by being officious. You tend to arouse the resentment of your subordinates, who will do their best to "sandbag" you, and you will be defenseless against this. But you will also feel aggressive toward your superiors, who will prey on you.

You must make many adjustments if you want your life to function in an orderly way. First, resist the desire to start at the top. There isn't much room there for those who haven't earned it. With this planetary combination you have a terrific opportunity to meet people who will teach you lessons the best schools cannot. But you *must* be willing to learn. Put your "know-it-all" attitude on the shelf until you do know what's what; then you will use your knowledge with humility.

As time goes on, you will become less fascinated with the physical and more interested in human values that can enrich you in the future. You will appreciate those who helped you become successful, and you will share your knowledge and wisdom as others shared theirs with you.

Your partner probably deserves more credit than you know for sustaining you when you have had doubts about your potential.

Saturn Opposition Neptune

The opposition from Saturn to Neptune indicates that you naturally distrust others when you are forced to compete with them. You are given to irrational fears of failure, which cause you to seek refuge from competition. This extreme caution and reserve makes others suspicious of you, and a vicious circle is established.

You may be ambitious for worldly achievements, but you lack the prudent judgment to realize your ambitions. You will continually encounter people who seem deceitful and cunning, so you will feel justified in using similar tactics. Proceed with caution because you may be misinterpreting the behavior of others.

You may attempt to relieve the pressures of a hostile environment on various elements of society. Others may question your motives, but what they don't see is your desire to unburden yourself of guilt for existing conditions. You may be ridiculed for sacrificing yourself to an unappreciative society, but you may still persist. Some people will deny that is your duty, but with these planets in opposition, you can be assured that it is.

You will endure extreme torment in your personal relationships, because you find it increasingly difficult to distinguish the honest from the insincere. Others will try to take advantage of you. You may make a sincere gesture toward the object of your love and find later that you have been victimized. This could represent severe financial and emotional losses. You must accept people at their potential best and worst, for you will certainly attract both types.

In your search for the ideal person to whom you can relate, you may suffer persecution until you can face reality. You may choose to become a loner as the only way to protect yourself. Beware of depressive moods, for they may make you vulnerable to psychosomatic illness.

Saturn Opposition Pluto

The opposition of Saturn to Pluto shows that you can be victimized by others in their quest for power. You may become involved in enterprises that are at best questionable and at worst potentially dangerous. If you get into social situations that have negative or nonproductive objectives, you may find it extremely difficult to safely extricate yourself.

You must examine each of your associates thoroughly to protect your own interests. Accept no promises of financial gain until you see evidence to support those promises. Someone may offer you material benefits that are unrealistic or extreme, so you must be suspicious of anything that seems "too good to be true." The chances are that it is. This goes for personal, emotional relationships also. The investment you make will probably be of more benefit to your partner than to yourself.

Your professional affairs may become unstable because of a power play at the top that will somehow involve you. The results can undermine your position. You are sure to encounter people who will make impossible demands of you, and severe alienation is sure to follow.

Your social conditions may be extremely harsh and may not provide you with constructive avenues of expression. Fear of poverty and loss of social status could drive you to use devious methods for obtaining security and protection.

The serious conditions that often attend your life struggle need careful evaluation and constructive planning. You must learn to either transform your environment or remove yourself from it and make a new start. Plan your objectives and each day lay the foundation on which to painstakingly build your future security and realize your goals. This is the best course if you wish to enjoy a life enriched through your own efforts and free from unnecessary difficulties.

Saturn Opposition Ascendant

Saturn opposition the Ascendant shows that you are defensive in your associations. You have to exert a lot of pressure to get a response from people, and most times you don't think it's worth the effort. You tend to be so preoccupied with your own affairs that you can't be too concerned with anyone else's. But at the same time you accuse people of being indifferent to you. The truth is, you are so reserved about projecting yourself into their lives that you give the impression you think yourself better than they are. So they keep their distance and are not likely to warm up to you.

You assume people will not appreciate your talents, so you don't offer your services. Convinced that others are more competent, you are afraid to accept challenging competition. You need the approval of others to reassure yourself of your skills. You cautiously test people's reactions to what you do and draw their conclusions for them before they have a chance to express an opinion. Probably you had an austere beginning and are not accustomed to being praised for your efforts. Although you have a mind of your own, you are never sure you can exploit your ideas and get a favorable response, which you desperately need. A minor chore like asking for a pay increase is a major event to you, and you have to have a lot of determination to do it.

You prefer people to come to you, because you fear they won't accept you if you go to them. You may be obsessed by the thought that your subconscious fears are obvious to everyone, but of course they are not. The only guilt you should feel is in your failure to assert yourself enough. Because you are more competent than most of your competitors, you will never take on a task you can't handle. Until you try, of course, you won't know this. You secretly fear responsibility, but you are more than able to perform your duties and fulfill your obligations, both to yourself and to others. You need the reassurance of knowing that achievement is well within your grasp.

Uranus Opposition Neptune

With Uranus opposition Neptune, you are sometimes unaware of the freedom you enjoy, so that you may fail to affirm your right to it when some important political or social upheaval threatens it. You are inclined to let someone else take the necessary steps to prevent erosion of individual liberties by these overwhelming changes. Through the years you may have identified so completely with a particular religious, political, or social faction that you have unknowingly abdicated your right to any control over those you blindly follow. You must always be alert to the possibility of being disillusioned by political leaders who engage in secret alliances or who withhold information from the people they represent. You will have to be really shocked by the revelation of truth before you will get angry enough to take an active part in protecting your freedom.

You were born at a time when political unrest, nationalism, strong economic structures, and powerful military machines were being developed. The apathy and indolence of the masses permitted world leaders to undermine the integrity of individual freedoms and then hurl their people into a major world conflict a few years later. These hostilities were a product of the unrest that had grown during the previous dozen or so years.

You intuitively understand the trouble that is brewing in the cauldron of national and international politics. When disturbances occur they only confirm what you suspected would happen. Because of this understanding, you have a responsibility to arouse the people when public opinion can reverse some threatening danger. The same hold true for religious, racial, or social problems, especially when you realize that your economic security and general peace of mind are at stake. Be careful, though, that you don't become affiliated with fanatic organizations whose motives can be questioned.

Uranus Opposition Pluto

The opposition from Uranus to Pluto indicates that you are suspicious of any major sociological, religious, philosophical, or political development. Immediately assuming that your individual rights will somehow be denied or diminished, you feel threatened and jump to conclusions before you have examined the developments fairly. It is not that you are unwilling to undergo change or progress, but you want sufficient time to adjust to it. You want the privilege of thinking for yourself, but in your insecurity you need the approval of someone you admire and respect so that you can feel safe in expressing your opinions. Your opinions are absolute and leave little room for compromise. Attracted to powerful individuals who seem to have your best interests at heart, you will offer them your complete support. In this way you escape from guilt if they fail to live up to your expectations; you can always blame someone else when things go awry.

This planetary configuration occurred between 1900 and 1903, when many changes took place that people had to adjust to. The lighter-than-air ship and the motorcycle offered new modes of travel. The wireless helped to shrink the world, as did the development of heavier-than-air ships.

You can stimulate younger generations to accept change as a necessary factor in progress. You can show how blind obedience to leaders whose powers are too broad and vision too limited can seriously upset the balance of individual freedom. By taking an active part in choosing competent officials and representatives, you can demonstrate how destiny can be altered. You should also emphasize that something as dear as freedom requires everyone's total dedication to preserving it. In this way people can determine their destiny with some assurance that it will remain intact, yet still make necessary concessions to change.

Uranus Opposition Ascendant

Uranus opposition the Ascendant shows that relationships stand in the way of achieving the freedom you want. You attract people who demand their own freedom, even though it means you must curtail yours, and this annoys you. Attracted to people who are defiant of authority, you'd like to share the enthusiasm of their independence. You feel uncomfortable when anyone asks you to make a commitment, for you consider contracts and related obligations as too limiting and frustrating. Marriage in the traditional sense is not for you. You prefer a more liberal association in which the only binding agent is your emotional attraction to your partner. You enjoy a wide circle of friends who share your views and with whom you feel safe and secure.

Your contemporaries admire your ingenuity in using your creative talents. You are drawn to occupations that give you freedom to work in your own way, unconfined by rules and regulations. You don't like to be told when and how you should do something or to receive an ultimatum if you don't submit.

Rebellious by nature, you probably left home at an early age to seek your own goals. Although you have a mind of your own, you probably are not fully prepared to accept responsibility for your actions. You tend to avoid competition on the excuse that it is the trap of a regulated society.

Although you secretly hope to make a substantial contribution to improve society, you may lack the motivation to actually do something to prove your concern. Your resentment of authority may cause problems in reaching your goals. You make your own rules to serve as guidelines, but they are not very demanding. Part of your role in life is to help others gain their freedom by urging them to get an education and to learn about the social and political issues that can affect them.

Neptune Opposition Ascendant

Neptune opposition the Ascendant shows that you are greatly influenced by the people with whom you associate. But it is difficult for you to distinguish between those who are your friends and those who are not. Because of this, some people may take advantage of your emotional sensitivity to make you feel obligated to them. Your opinions of the people you deal with are too idealistic, and you are hurt when they disappoint you.

When you volunteer to help people, you must protect yourself. Offer to help only when you know positively that someone needs your assistance. You tend to love everybody and overburden yourself with concern for their welfare. Actually you are trying to compensate for your inability to stand on your own; you need someone who needs you in order to have a feeling of belonging. Being alone makes you feel helpless, so you seek out obligations to others.

Since you are imaginative and creatively inspired in expressing yourself, you should direct your talents to writing, music, or the arts. Avoid competition until you gain the expertise to meet challenges without being crushed by failure.

You depend on others to provide the opportunities you need to earn a living. Because you feel that you don't deserve to be happy and contented, you overemphasize your negative qualities. But you are more loved than you realize, and your friends are deeply concerned for your welfare. Seek their advice before making a commitment so you won't regret it later. When superiors make a promise to you, get it in writing or have someone present who can back you up when they don't fulfill it.

In a romantic alliance you are easily mesmerized by a stronger personality. You should never agree to a permanent relationship until you know the person well and know that the feelings between you are sincere.

Pluto Opposition Ascendant

Pluto opposition the Ascendant shows that you attract people with powerful egos and strong temperaments. You have a strong desire for close, intimate contact with many of the persons you associate with, and this alone should be a warning to you. When you discover that someone is trying to make you over to satisfy his own desires, make a fast exit. But this is also a sure sign that you try to do the same thing to those you are attracted to. You make extensive demands of the people you deal with, but you resent it when similar demands are made of you. This is essentially the meaning of the old saying, "Birds of a feather flock together." Such problems can ruin otherwise fascinating relationships.

Your talents lie in your ability to mold people, so public relations is a field you should apply yourself to. Political, social, and financial activities are other areas in which you could find a great deal of satisfaction. You express yourself with dramatic flair, and people are impressed with your ability to command attention.

You generally get what you want when you want it, and you don't tolerate refusal of your demands. If you are motivated to change people's attitudes about their social obligations, you can accomplish miracles. You will be able to gain the support of your friends in seeking to improve intolerable social conditions. However, elected officials will try to discredit you and turn public opinion against you. But you aren't afraid of such tactics, because you have information about such officials that could be equally embarrassing to them.

In personal relationships you may have difficulty in achieving the success you enjoy in public conquests. When you relate to people at close range, you can become burdensome and make others feel uncomfortable. You understand how people think, and may even be psychically tuned to them. This ability helps you deal with people.

Index

Sextiles

[*see Saturn sextile Uranus*]
Uranus sextile Neptune, 115
Uranus sextile Pluto, 116
Uranus sextile Ascendant, 117
Neptune sextile Sun
[*see Sun sextile Neptune*]
Neptune sextile Moon
[*see Moon sextile Neptune*]
Neptune sextile Mercury
[*see Mercury sextile Neptune*]
Neptune sextile Venus
[*see Venus sextile Neptune*]
Neptune sextile Mars
[*see Mars sextile Neptune*]
Neptune sextile Jupiter
[*see Jupiter sextile Neptune*]
Neptune sextile Saturn
[*see Saturn sextile Neptune*]
Neptune sextile Uranus
[*see Uranus sextile Neptune*]
Neptune sextile Pluto, 117
Neptune sextile Ascendant, 120

Pluto sextile Sun
[*see Sun sextile Pluto*]
Pluto sextile Moon
[*see Moon sextile Pluto*]
Pluto sextile Mercury
[*see Mercury sextile Pluto*]
Pluto sextile Venus
[*see Venus sextile Pluto*]
Pluto sextile Mars
[*see Mars sextile Pluto*]
Pluto sextile Jupiter
[*see Jupiter sextile Pluto*]
Pluto sextile Saturn
[*see Saturn sextile Pluto*]
Pluto sextile Uranus
[*see Uranus sextile Pluto*]
Pluto sextile Neptune
[*see Neptune sextile Pluto*]
Pluto sextile Ascendant, 121

Squares

Sun square Moon, 126
Sun square Mercury
[*astronomically impossible*]

Sun square Venus
[*astronomically impossible*]
Sun square Mars, 127
Sun square Jupiter, 128
Sun square Saturn, 129
Sun square Uranus, 130
Sun square Neptune, 131
Sun square Pluto, 131
Sun square Ascendant, 132

Moon square Sun
[*see Sun square Moon*]
Moon square Mercury, 133
Moon square Venus, 134
Moon square Mars, 135
Moon square Jupiter, 136
Moon square Saturn, 138
Moon square Uranus, 139
Moon square Neptune, 139
Moon square Pluto, 140
Moon square Ascendant, 141

Mercury square Sun
[*astronomically impossible*]
Mercury square Moon
[*see Moon square Mercury*]
Mercury square Venus
[*astronomically impossible*]
Mercury square Mars, 142
Mercury square Jupiter, 143
Mercury square Saturn, 144
Mercury square Uranus, 145
Mercury square Neptune, 146
Mercury square Pluto, 147
Mercury square Ascendant, 148

Venus square Sun
[*astronomically impossible*]
Venus square Moon
[*see Moon square Venus*]
Venus square Mercury
[*astronomically impossible*]
Venus square Mars, 149
Venus square Jupiter, 150
Venus square Saturn, 151
Venus square Uranus, 153
Venus square Neptune, 153
Venus square Pluto, 154
Venus square Ascendant, 155

Inconjuncts

Oppositions

Mars opposition Sun
[*see Sun opposition Mars*]
Mars opposition Moon
[*see Moon opposition Mars*]
Mars opposition Mercury
[*see Mercury opposition Mars*]
Mars opposition Mercury
[*see Mercury opposition Mars*]
Mars opposition Venus
[*see Venus opposition Mars*]
Mars opposition Jupiter, 308
Mars opposition Saturn, 309
Mars opposition Uranus, 310
Mars opposition Neptune, 311
Mars opposition Pluto, 312
Mars opposition Ascendant, 312

Jupiter opposition Sun
[*see Sun opposition Jupiter*]
Jupiter opposition Moon
[*see Moon opposition Jupiter*]
Jupiter opposition Mercury
[*see Mercury opposition Jupiter*]
Jupiter opposition Venus
[*see Venus opposition Jupiter*]
Jupiter opposition Mars
[*see Mars opposition Jupiter*]
Jupiter opposition Saturn, 313
Jupiter opposition Uranus, 314
Jupiter opposition Neptune, 313
Jupiter opposition Pluto, 316
Jupiter opposition Ascendant, 317

Saturn opposition Sun
[*see Sun opposition Saturn*]
Saturn opposition Moon
[*see Moon opposition Saturn*]
Saturn opposition Mercury
[*see Mercury opposition Saturn*]
Saturn opposition Venus
[*see Venus opposition Saturn*]
Saturn opposition Mars
[*see Mars opposition Saturn*]
Saturn opposition Jupiter
[*see Jupiter opposition Saturn*]
Saturn opposition Uranus, 318
Saturn opposition Neptune, 319
Saturn opposition Pluto, 320
Saturn opposition Ascendant, 320

Uranus opposition Sun
[*see Sun opposition Uranus*]
Uranus opposition Moon
[*see Moon opposition Uranus*]
Uranus opposition Mercury
[*see Mercury opposition Uranus*]
Uranus opposition Venus
[*see Venus opposition Uranus*]
Uranus opposition Mars
[*see Mars opposition Uranus*]
Uranus opposition Jupiter
[*see Jupiter opposition Uranus*]
Uranus opposition Saturn
[*see Saturn opposition Uranus*]
Uranus opposition Neptune, 321
Uranus opposition Pluto, 322
Uranus opposition Ascendant, 323

Neptune opposition Sun
[*see Sun opposition Neptune*]
Neptune opposition Moon
[*see Moon opposition Neptune*]
Neptune opposition Mercury
[*see Mercury opposition Neptune*]
Neptune opposition Venus
[*see Venus opposition Neptune*]
Neptune opposition Mars
[*see Mars opposition Neptune*]
Neptune opposition Jupiter
[*see Jupiter opposition Neptune*]
Neptune opposition Saturn
[*see Saturn opposition Neptune*]
Neptune opposition Uranus
[*see Uranus opposition Neptune*]
Neptune opposition Pluto
[*occurred before 1800, not in this book*]
Neptune opposition Ascendant, 324

Pluto opposition Sun
[*see Sun opposition Pluto*]
Pluto opposition Moon
[*see Moon opposition Pluto*]
Pluto opposition Mercury
[*see Mercury opposition Pluto*]
Pluto opposition Venus
[*see Venus opposition Pluto*]
Pluto opposition Mars
[*see Mars opposition Pluto*]
Pluto opposition Jupiter

Conjunctions

_____

_____

_____

_____

_____

_____

Trines

_____

_____

_____

_____

_____

Sextiles

_____

_____

_____

_____

_____

Inconjuncts

_____

_____

_____

_____

_____

Squares

_____

_____

_____

_____

_____

Oppositions

_____

_____

_____

_____

_____

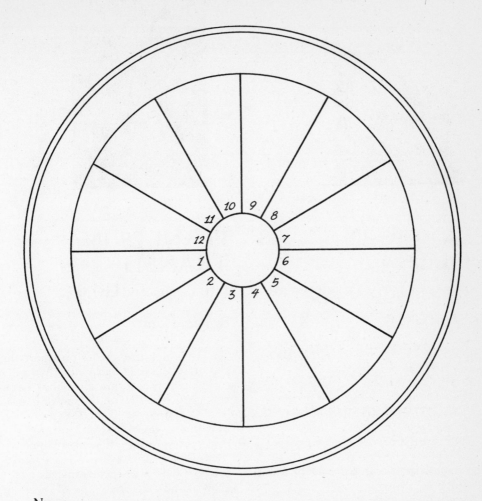

Name _____

Birthdate _____ Fire _____

Standard Time _____ Earth _____

Greenwich Mean Time _____ Air _____

Sidereal Time _____ Water _____

Birthplace _____ Cardinal _____

Longitude _____ Fixed _____

Latitude _____ Mutuable _____

PLANETS IN YOUTH

Patterns of Early Development

Robert Hand

In this book, a major astrologer looks at children and childhood.

As Hand says in his introduction, "...the child as an adult in the process of becoming is the orientation that this book takes."

Not only will parents welcome this book, readers of all ages will use it to understand their own patterns of early development.

The first four chapters discuss parental influences, explain the effects of various planetary energy systems and explore the meanings of all the different factors in a child's chart. There are interpretations of charts of three children, including Judy Garland and Shirley Temple.

The major part of the book consists of 300-word delineations of horoscope factors. Every planet in every sign and house, as well as in every major aspect, is interpreted in language that emphasizes possibilities.

ISBN: 0-914918-26-5
384 pages, 6½" x 9¼", paper $18.95

PLANETS IN TRANSIT

Life Cycles for Living

Robert Hand

This is *the* definitive work on transiting planets. Its psychological insight and completeness as a reference book have brought Robert Hand recognition as a leading astrologer. Hand takes a humanistic, multi-leveled approach to transits: the events that may happen, the feelings you may experience, and the possibilities of each transit for growth and awareness.

This book covers complete delineations of all the major transits—conjunction, sextile, square, trine and opposition—that occur between transiting Sun, Moon and all planets to each planet in the natal chart and the Ascendant and Midheaven, as well as complete delineations of each planet transiting each house of the natal chart. These 720 lucid delineations are full of insight for both the professional astrologer and the beginner.

ISBN: 0-914918-24-9
544 pages, 6½" x 9¼", paper $22.95

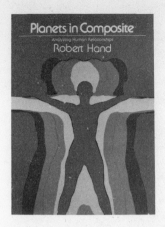

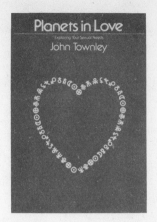

PLANETS IN COMPOSITE

Analyzing Human Relationships

Robert Hand

Robert Hand has written an important reference book that is much needed in the astrological field, a definitive work about human relationships.

After extensive research and professional experience, Hand has concluded that the composite chart technique works more effectively than other techniques as a method of interpreting relationships.

Planets in Composite, contains an introduction to casting and reading the composite chart, five case studies and twelve chapters of delineations. You will find 374 interpretations of composite planetary positions including forty-one delineations of the Moon's nodes.

Planets in Composite is the most authoritative book ever written about the astrology of human relationships.

ISBN: 0-914918-22-2
384 pages, 6½" x 9¼", paper $19.95

PLANETS IN LOVE

Exploring Your Emotional and Sexual Needs

John Townley

This is the first major astrological work to take a direct and detailed look at human sexuality. It explores the variety of relationships people form to satisfy their individual emotional and sexual needs.

An intimate analysis of sex and love, *Planets in Love* is not a collection of chatty commentaries on paired Sun signs but 550 in-depth delineations of all planetary positions by sign, house and aspect.

In addition, the book includes numerous case studies illustrating the use of the natal chart in interpreting an individual's unique expression of love.

This is a mature text that takes a sophisticated approach to love, sex and sexuality.

ISBN: 0-914918-21-4
384 pages, 6½" x 9¼", paper $18.95

PLANETS IN HOUSES
Experiencing Your Environment
Robert Pelletier

This major work brings natal horoscope interpretation to a
new level of accuracy, concreteness and richness of detail.

While the fundamental forces at work in a chart can be
found in the relationships of the planets, signs and aspects, it is
the houses that bring chart-reading down to earth, indicating
how planetary energies will work themselves out in daily life.

Pelletier synthesizes the meaning of each planet in each
house—as derived by counting from each of the houses and in
relation to each of the other houses with which it forms trines,
sextiles, squares, oppositions, inconjuncts and semisextiles.

So if you've been waiting for the definitive work on house
meanings, a book that will both encourage the beginner and
challenge the expert, this is the book for you.

ISBN: 0-914918-27-3
384 pages, 6½" x 9¼", paper $19.95

COMPENDIUM OF ASTROLOGY

by Rose Lineman and Jan Popelka

The more you understand astrology, the more you can do with your life. You can gain insight into human behavior, attain self-understanding and achieve full self-development. The *Compendium of Astrology* is all about astrology—the most comprehensive astrology book ever published. The *Compendium* contains the basic information needed to build a horoscope, provides a step-by-step guide that will lead beginning astrologers to in-depth knowledge of principles, calculations, and encourages them to pursue further study and research.

Part I presents a thorough grounding in the principles and theory of horoscope analysis. It explores familiar topics and detailed subjects like Vertex, East Point and asteroids. It covers the finer points of theory as well as the meanings of signs, planets and houses.

Part II introduces astrologers of all levels to several house systems and presents alternative mathematical methods with easy-to-follow examples.

Part III shows how to assemble and synthesize the astrological factors contained in a horoscope. Numerous examples clarify delineation techniques. Interpretations are given for all major aspects formed by planets. Special techniques help astrologers understand relationships and reveal future trends.

A large two-column format enhances the presentation and allows more material per page than any similar book.

This book belongs on every astrological student's bookshelf and on every astrologer's desk for easy reference. The *Compendium of Astrology* is the most complete astrological book on the market today.

ISBN 0-914918-43-5

304 pages, 8 × 9¼", paper, $14.95

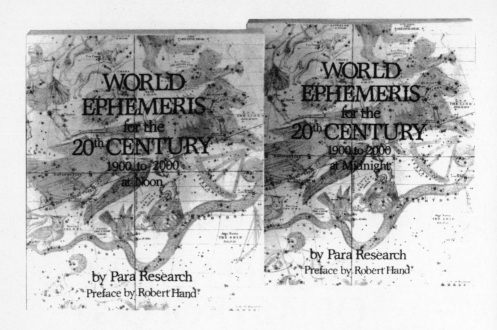

WORLD EPHEMERIS
FOR THE 20TH CENTURY

by Para Research

Preface by Robert Hand

The *World Ephemeris for the 20th Century* is the first computer-calculated and computer-typeset ephemeris with letter quality printing. Now ease and clarity in reading is combined with accuracy and precision of data to provide the most complete and convenient ephemeris available for astrological calculation and analysis.

Available in either Midnight or Noon calculations, the *World Ephemeris* presents the Sun's position accurate to the second of arc; the Moon's mean Node and the nine planetary positions are given to the minute of arc.

Positions are reported for every day of the 20th Century. One hundred and one years in all.

Midnight Edition: ISBN 0-914918-60-5
624 pages, 8 x 9¼", paper $13.95

Noon Edition: ISBN 0-914918-61-3
624 pages, 8 x 9¼", paper $13.95